Praise for

The Question of Empathy

"'What is this wonder,' Carol Jeffers asks, 'that allows us to connect across time and space or to connect at all?' In this erudite and affable exploration of how empathy ignites within us, Carol Jeffers speculates on the future of this pivotal emotion in our digital world. *A Question of Empathy* arrives at a time just when we need it most."

—Brenda Miller, author of *Season of the Body*

"Articulate and scholarly, *The Question of Empathy* is a book for our cynical age. Using examples from art, science, and philosophy, Carol Jeffers addresses the concept of empathy and how we, as connected human beings, can tap into empathy's many forms to relate more fully to one another. Her expressive and metaphorical language reaches beyond familiar tropes to engage the reader in a dynamic discussion about empathy's value and purpose and offers powerful motivations for making empathy a pathway to understanding the other, to embracing our differences and to celebrating our similarities. *The Question of Empathy* is a book you will want to—no, need to—return to time and time again."

—Jeanne Lyet Gassman, author of *Blood of a Stone*

"The first chapter of Carol Jeffers' new book, *The Question of Empathy*, is called, 'In the Rhizome': A beach in California; An old bench; An inscription, 'I shall always love a purple iris.' Empathy is a word too often misunderstood—but not by Jeffers. She understands perfectly that the ability to experience the moment with another person opens all the doors, that those doors are meant to be open, and that it will take work and commitment to the task. Her tone is pitch-perfect, her insights into the simple ingredients of our humanity clear, obvious, and radical. Look up 'rhizome,' and settle in for a fabulous, eye-opening read. Brava, Carol Jeffers!"

> —**Dean Robertson**, author of *Looking for Lydia; Looking for God*, Jessie. *The Adventures and Insights of a Nineteenth-Century Woman*, and *Jessie. The Further Adventures. The Virginia Years*

"Carol Jeffers has written a remarkable exploration of empathy, which is the ability to understand and connect with the feelings of others. As if through a prism, the author offers a spectrum of examples and viewpoints ranging from theories of philosophers to masterpieces by Van Gogh and Cezanne, and from personal encounters in nature to epiphanies experienced by her students. Despite an outside world torn by strife, the field of neuroscience peers inside at mirror neurons associated with empathy and offers potential for greater understanding. In *The Question of Empathy* a recurring and powerful metaphor is the rhizome, buried root structures bridging separate plants. Jeffers likewise gives us hope for nurturing empathy, the heart of our humanity."

> —**Allene Symons**, author of *Aldous Huxley's Hands*

"In *The Question of Empathy*, Carol Jeffers weaves her vast knowledge of visual, tactile and lyrical art in a metaphorical contemplation of the human virtue of empathy. As works of art such as Van Gogh's Irises, and literary works such as Golding's Lord of the Flies are explored, readers will start to wonder how and why empathy is, or is not, stirred within us. Are the characteristics of empathy built in to our biological and/or neurological make-up? Or is this virtue a learned response, modeled for us, and thereby taught to us, by our ancestors?"

—Joan Hicks Boone, author of *The Best Girl*

"Carol Jeffers ornately describes of the compassion that dwells within us, though we may not award conversation to it, though it may thirst and hunger in the chamber and not be satisfied, though it may lay us down to sleep and awaken us at dawn, and though it may seem passive, it breathes and its breath, often an impenetrable fog lying hauntingly over that deep water, slow moving and churning, reflecting the measure of man, and to be found not wanting."

—Keith Deel, author of *FLUIDIS*

The Question of Empathy:

Searching for the
Essence of Humanity

by Carol Jeffers

ISBN 978-1-63393-669-0

Published by

 köehlerbooks ™

210 60th Street
Virginia Beach, VA 23451
800-435-4811
www.koehlerbooks.com

The Question of Empathy

Searching for the Essence of Humanity

Carol Jeffers

VIRGINIA BEACH
CAPE CHARLES

To Marcus, my grandson,

who was born with empathy

and

To Gene, his grandfather

who nurtured it

Table of Contents

"I believe empathy is the most essential quality of civilization."

Roger Ebert

Chapter I

In the Rhizome

Strolling among the dunes and driftwood, and the mock heather and yarrow of Moonstone Beach on California's Central Coast, you are likely to come across a humble wooden bench made remarkable by what it declares, by the empathy it stirs, and by the stories it invites us to share. Rough and weatherworn, the bench is evocative of the salt air and wild daisies, the restless tides reshaping the continent's rocky edge, and the wide sunset views it is meant to afford. But it has become legendary and invokes much more than a simple seascape. From its niche in the coastal ecosystem, this bench triumphs in returning us to the cultural sphere, to the human hands that created and mounted a small plaque to the backrest, and to the soul forever inhabiting the carved letters proclaiming, "I shall always love a purple iris." Like the bench itself, the thought is at once simple and elegant, forthright and mysterious—a paradox, to be sure, but also a metaphor for that innate capacity enabling us to wonder, to imagine, and thus, to empathize.

If the plaque captures your imagination, as it has mine and others, judging by Internet postings, then you may wonder whose words these are. Full of whimsy, or poignancy, or both, they resonate and inscribe themselves upon our hearts. Who is it that we have to thank for this unexpected delight and for the images it inspires, the stories it prompts? What is the meaning, symbolic or otherwise, of the flower we imagine, springing from its rhizomic underground network to be capped off by its distinctive beard, caterpillarlike and golden in the April sun? Or maybe we envision a couple who once shared the bench. Is she gone now, his purple iris? What was her story or his? Theirs? What is *ours*? We might ask that last question as each of us takes a small part in creating this larger narrative, one echoing beyond the beach itself. And where might that narrative take us?

Each time I return to Moonstone, the bench reminds me of the story always unfolding even as it retells itself, an ever-expanding narrative that begins with our shared curiosity and appreciative smiles and builds to the empathic response that connects us all to the spirit of the plaque and the mystery of its maker. I watch as others pause to read the line, then turn from it slowly, thoughtfully, before continuing on to the observation point, where the best views of the otters and seals are to be had. I wonder what images, what stories the bench—our shared touchstone—conjures up in them.

Perhaps there are those weekenders who, like me, envision a loved one—an uncle, in my case—who cherished their iris beds, tended them faithfully through the summer and fall, and patiently awaited the blossoms, lavender and lovely, in the spring. Or perhaps they think of their children who, like my own, found the quivering petals fascinating and delighted in stroking the fuzzy beards. I wonder too if upon their return to the routines of the workweek, these weekenders might Google the bench's poetic proclamation and come across the image of two purple irises, one pinned on each side of the plaque. If they do, perhaps they too will savor the moment and its mystery, even as they wonder about this online tribute and the new connections and stories it encourages.

Like the iris rhizome itself, these connections are bound to crisscross, to entangle and create an unruly latticework of horizontal stems with their all-important nodes sending out new roots and shoots that allow for more connections still. And like those in the botanical sphere, connections of the cultural kind are often random, sometimes serendipitous, and always meant to replenish the rhizome, if not to expand its reach. As a professor of art education, I find that my stories and images of the Moonstone bench are tightly intertwined with Van Gogh's *Irises* (1889), which, in turn, overlap with former students' experiences of the painting. I envision the canvas at the Getty Center in Los Angeles—its stunning blues, violets, electric aqua, a splash of white—leaping from the museum wall. In the perpetual crowd gathered before it, I imagine my students over the years, so many resonating with the artist's work and poignant life story. They read the wall text and learn that Vincent began the painting upon his arrival at the asylum in Saint-Rémy-de-Provence in May of 1889, and they almost always agree with brother Theo's assessment that the composition, bursting with more than two dozen purple irises, a solitary white one among them, is "filled with air and light."

In another instant, I am whisked off to the South of France where I follow Van Gogh's path, hiking the trail that led him and the pain he carried from the center of Saint-Rémy past a mulberry tree still young in his day, past the stone farmhouses, old even then, past the dark-green cypress trees and pale-gold wheat fields rising up to meet the asylum on top of the ridge. I stand in Vincent's meager cubicle of a room—or one very much like his—and look out the window at the garden below. The lavender beckons now, but I imagine the irises that bloomed a month or two earlier and try to get a sense of what he saw, a feel for his world in Provence in what turned out to be the last year of his life.

In still another image, I am back in the classroom, drawn into one of my student's assignments. Christina, a twentysomething prospective elementary teacher, is explaining to the class why she has chosen Van Gogh's *Irises* to serve as her personal metaphor. While growing up, the wistful Christina tells us, she had always felt different from everyone else—a painful, sometimes humiliating and always lonely experience for her. But now that she is older, she sees herself as the white iris: unique, but not alone, a part of the iris garden's beautiful air and light. Holding up her reproduction of the painting, she smiles and says she is proud of her individuality, her identity, just as she is proud to be a contributing member of the group. Her classmates smile back, an affirmation welcoming her into their purple midst, and I am convinced that Christina will always love a white iris.

What is this wonder that allows us to connect across time and space or to connect at all? What allows us—compels us, even—to snatch these existential moments from afar, from across the room and hold them close? They are as random as they are resonant, and somehow these empathic tangles twist within our corporeal and spiritual beings, knotting the two together.

If the answer lies matted in the rhizome, then we must also acknowledge that bamboo and crabgrass are part of this metaphor, their crisscrossing roots and shoots bound to complicate the question of empathy. Are we meant to see ourselves, backs bent, brows sweating, chopping back the bamboo's unruly growth? Must we remember the knuckles bloodied again and again clawing at the stubborn crabgrass, or are there other metaphors to raise us from our knees, free us from the paradox that gives the bench's purple iris its certainty and uncertainty? Perhaps we could tell different stories—tales of wizards and incantations, say—that cast us into a land beyond the rhizome. Or we might share different images of miners digging into the depths, detectives searching for clues, all intent upon unearthing the wonders of human connection.

We might understand our connections as demonstrations of empathy's work, outward manifestations of an inner capacity and will to survive as a group-living species. Connections may be obvious, the critical nodes in the human rhizome that permit us to feel rooted, secure enough in our own situations even as we send out shoots seeking to explore and, finally, to understand the situations of others. But we might also know that empathy can be as elusive as the breeze in a bamboo forest, whispering cryptically, sometimes stirring us but often leaving us to fall silent, exasperated and alone.

Listen with care, the rustling bamboo warns, or we will be caught up in a terrible tension between the obvious and the elusive, the certain and the uncertain. The winds will rise angry and cold, hurtling us and the detritus of humanity around and around with the force of a tornado. We will not hear empathy above our wails nor recognize it in our synapses, feel it in our marrows. No, empathy will not be honored in the tea ceremony or welcomed into the human dance.

Yet, empathy quivers throughout the bamboo forest, rattling the leaves and entangling itself deep in their density. Look closely, the winds murmur, and we might see it in a brain scan, in a pair of well-worn shoes, or a seaside bench. We might recognize its power in images of a slave ship, the falling towers, and that historic 2008 election night in Chicago's Grant Park. Based on what the neuroscientists, psychologists, and philosophers have said, we might even imagine how empathy thrives in the thickets between nature and culture, where it favors neither one nor the other but both.

Empathy might sprout anywhere, rhizomic and undaunted by the rise of a self-obsessive "cultural narcissism," unjust political structures, and corrupted capitalist economies, only to struggle in that contested space between self and other, between thought and feeling. Marked only by misty boundaries, this borderland opens new—if uneasy—spaces that encourage anyone, everyone to reach for the stories that tell us about ourselves and the fragile planet we must share. We must tell them again; this is our imperative. Now, in the face of so much incivility and climate change, on the verge of meltdown and extinction, we are required at last to understand our own entanglement and to know that, like the worldwide bamboo rhizome, our empathy can flourish even as it faces yet another of its mysterious die-offs. And we will hope the irises, purple and white, bloom again.

Empathy is neither easy nor straightforward. Perhaps it closes its eyes to us even as we strain to look into its face. But if we keep our eyes open and study images that shape and reflect us, perhaps we will find it on distant shores or under our noses. Images present the evidence, hold the key to our human odyssey. We live in a visual age; an age of images tumbling, jostling, and so insistent that, in another nanosecond or two, they will surely overtake the planet. Computer generated and hand rendered, still and moving, we cannot hold back what they unleash in a roiling avalanche of pictorial energy and emotion, revelation and distortion. Images fill our pores and take us to the edge of asphyxiation; they are the selfies and snapshots, videos and video games, movies and trailers, TV broadcasts and commercials, comics and cartoons—the semioticians' signifiers—that show us who and what we are but say little about why we are left gasping. They create story worlds but dictate what we see of them and how we picture ourselves within the frenetic chapters.

Because the avalanche is relentless, we cannot help but pay attention, uploading and downloading what will always dazzle our senses. Images have the power to inflame passions, to awaken empathy, but their sparkle can also deceive this biology and lead us into a culture where we cannot recognize ourselves or anyone around us. They are powerful tools that move us, indeed, but we may not be the ones with the skills to use them wisely or well. We are still too dazzled to learn what images might have to teach.

They blanket us, and we are trapped in a snowy air pocket yet safely ensconced within the membrane of a shiny bubble that contains what Susan Sontag calls an "image-world." This means that we can only interpret the exterior, or "real" world, through the "reports given" by the images cascading over us. We take them to be true, these two-dimensional reports of events and objects, attitudes and circumstances—the web of reality—they are meant to represent. But Sontag warns that images have the power to *mis*represent what we see—what we value and would like to have around us.

Still, we covet images, pledge our allegiance to their falsehoods, ultimately using them as "substitutes for firsthand experiences" of a multidimensional world. They become extensions of the things they pretend to represent and may or may not reveal the cause or origin of such things or explain the connections between them. Images, as Sontag points out, are things themselves, yet we treat them as valuable objects to be collected and curated with care. Though they are mere representations, after all, their visual codes and their magic bewitch us, telling us what to look at, how to package our worlds, and where to find our places in a society constantly producing and consuming images.

Images cast their spell, and we are instantly overcome. They dominate our lives, indeed, and according to classicist-archaeologist Nigel Spivey, they tell us how to behave, what to think, and how to feel. Images of death, he argues, captivate us most. Their eerie incantation haunts us, its smoke and crackling sparks putting us on edge. But we need the tension these images spark, Spivey insists, and we rely on them to reassure us, even as they terrify our fragile beings. As he sees it, we use images of death to confront what frightens us most—what we feel so deeply, so viscerally about our own mortality.

Images of death can help us peer through the smoke and imagine what lies beyond this earthly life. In them, we find the proof we need, the comfort we crave, and allow ourselves to believe that the departed can remain among the living after all. Clutching at their likenesses, we keep them close, immortalizing the dead as we hope others will do for us when we are gone. These images are the "reports given," the "substitutes" opening a crack that let in the promise of a radiant light. They become our crystal balls revealing the lie of our physical end. We will not break their spell, and they will continue pushing and pulling us throughout our hazy, if well-illustrated, story.

Images of the body are also busy and work their own wizardry, mesmerizing us in a mirrored world dedicated to personal appearance. We are transfixed by their flash, the spellbinding codes that map movement, contour, and proportion onto our own body images. They are clever, these two-dimensional reports that (mis)represent the fullness of our corporeal existence. Still, the biology they sketch resonates deep in our marrows and speaks loudly of beauty and power, strength and grace, speed and skill—even as its relentless murmuring brings up anxieties about frailty and mortality. Still, images of the body tempt us with their potions, the liquid magic we drink when we want to hear more about our individual identity and stature, our physical gifts and invincibility. Their trick, though, is to turn us into cultural beings who are not so unique after all. Waving their wand, they spirit us away and cast us into another story where we blend together to share a collective experience.

These are manipulative images, indeed, and, as Spivey claims, the ones to take on the work of shaping the beliefs we share and to act as the mirrors reflecting the values that define and homogenize our cultures. Images of the body, he says, have their way of holding societies together. Yet, Sontag has told us they are things, not bonds—commodities whose value lies in (mis) representing our unity. Images of the body are the substitutes we use for firsthand experiences of a cultural life that is so often messy and ambiguous—and always open to interpretation. They become a shorthand, effectively cutting through the noise of diversity. They are the propaganda needed to soothe or incite, but mostly to deflect the doubt and any impertinent questions that would penetrate the facade. The tumult of human communities past and present were not to be revealed, not by these images.

It seems the European hunter-gatherers of long ago could read the shorthand and understand the bewitching propaganda of their fertility figures. In Spivey's view, they clung to the figures—to the likes of the *Venus of Willendorf*—believing these little dolls could ward off the danger of extinction while embedding reproduction as the value that would reassure the terrified tribe. These venuses, with their tiny, rounded bodies, their hugely exaggerated breasts and abdomens, were endowed with the promise of an existential magic and the hopes of a Paleolithic people crouched on the edge of survival. But the Venus of Willendorf also wears a headdress and beads around her breasts. Could she reflect the priestess who celebrated motherhood, lactation, and an abundant food supply—signs of a culture thriving and in balance with the natural world? We cannot know what her powers represent, and she will reveal no more.

The stylized figures of ancient Egypt remain silent as well, and though these images are repeated everywhere—as if keeping up a chant we cannot hear—they will not break the rhythm or reveal their code. Nor will these figures divulge the contents of the report they gave without fail to generation after generation of slaves and scribes, priests and nobles throughout the history of the long-lived civilization. Today, it is difficult to understand the drumbeat that once was so resonant. But we hear its echoes and work hard to see through the pulsing propaganda, hoping to uncover the stories inside these cultural patterns.

Perhaps the stiff, lookalike figures—resolute, unwavering in their stance—illuminated a story about the importance of order and stability, each of its chapters another guarantee of the pharaonic culture's permanence and another rebuke of the mighty Nile's impulsive, havoc-wreaking nature. Or these figures may have narrated an equally unambiguous story, one clearly denying the possibility of famine, failure, and social unrest. This was the story meant to suppress uncertainty and any potential for change, progress, or social mobility. Without taking into account the vagaries, the contradictions of human nature, both stories promised eternal life. We are left to wonder if each version in its own way foreshadowed a future captured in recent images from Cairo's Tahrir Square of thousands of surging bodies, certain of the struggle, all chanting in loud protest and filled with fury and determination, adding still another unambiguous chapter to the story of the Egyptians.

Twenty-first-century images come tumbling across our screens, bits and bytes jostling to reproduce themselves and magically transform their infinite permutations into the pixilated patterns we recognize as Instagrams and Google Maps, Hulu videos and Facebook profiles, Yahoo updates and Ubisoft games. Their electrons excite our neurons and entangle us in the digital rhizome we know and love.

Images crisscrossing on the screen trick us into believing we are the curators of the image-world's unruly jumble. We are the ones to choose which images will accompany us on our dazzling journey through time and space, the requisite smartphone, iPad, and laptop in hand. Only we know which selfies to snap and send, what celebrity or sports figures to track, which maps to pull up and games to play. This image-world is ours to customize and cuddle up with anytime, anywhere—each individual bubble now airily decorated to represent the pampered personality inside.

Drinking the Kool-Aid, we cannot see the trick of it all, the image-world's sleight of hand. In our trance, we do not doubt our private galleries or suspect that what we have tailored is not so unique after all. Ah, how gullible, how reliably susceptible we are. As it turns out, our cozy bubble is rather like the others bobbing around us, just another in the collective fizz. Hidden in the foam is the sorcery of the digital code secretly reproducing itself to create the visual codes that so bewitch us. Its magic wand has much to proclaim about our culture of bubbles—modern day hunter-gatherers teetering on the edge, fattened by an abundant supply of sugary froth and the images that temporarily satisfy our tribal appetites.

Our hunger gnaws, but we will not venture outside the shiny membrane to forage in a jungle hung with risk, burgeoning with the demands of firsthand experiences. We are too restless to sort through all that the real world offers and much prefer the ease and comfort of sweet substitutes—images so convincing and instantly gratifying that we need not ask which is real and which is not.

Just like that, the bubble fills with the sights and sounds of Le Mans, and we are strapped into a Jag E-Type, in control of its screaming engine, coming out of the corner and maneuvering to take the lead on the straightaway. The adrenaline surges, and we are driving at two hundred miles per hour—not playing a game of *Gran Turismo*. Inside our shiny membrane, we can stare down the throbbing life-and-death situations a game like *Street Fighter* throws at us, proving how fierce and unflinching we are while landing kick after breathless kick in its gritty arena. Or we thrill to the excruciating suspense of the spooky *Silent Hill* series and put ourselves in a "gotcha" game so disorienting that we jump, sometimes out of the chair—spooked by our own startle reflex. This bubble is a visceral place, where all doubt is banished along with any sense of real time. The clock may be gone, but the bubble throbs with the rhythm of a pounding heart.

We turn from games to videos and infuse our bubbles with the newest YouTube antics—the kittens and toddlers that make us laugh. There are the memes as well, spoofs of spoofs layering the culture with silly satire—more than a few showing us that Psy is not the only one to prance with Gangnam style. We also stare at the breaking news, the must-see footage beamed around the world that gives us the illusion we are keeping up to date, along with everyone else tuned into the twenty-four-hour news cycle. These are the images that turn us into junkies, insatiable consumers fed by all manner of media outlets bent on bringing us the latest in a never-ending series of tragedies and disastrous events. We sit up, pay attention to what screams with the story of human suffering—pictures that make some cry and others numb.

What the TV journalists know is that we must see the devastation up close; we expect to see them bent by hurricane-force winds on an eerie beach, earning their credentials in real time, an angry ocean slapping at their heels. We watch as foreign correspondents dodge rockets and sniper fire in the pock-marked streets of ancient cities, gripping their microphones ever more tightly. Only the bravest crossed the Ebola River to cover the deadly virus that spread wildly. But pregnant journalists cannot afford to swat away Zika mosquitoes.

There are no alternatives for Sontag's "substitutes," and we have seen them all, the "reports given" by floods and fires, earthquakes and tsunamis, bombings and nuclear meltdowns, massacres and still more massacres. We know them by name—Sandy, Katrina, Irene, Fukushima, Chernobyl, and Three Mile Island. We too have stood in the rubble of Haiti and Syria and felt the sorrow of Boston and Aurora, Sandy Hook and Oklahoma City. Brussels, Paris, Nice, Orlando, Istanbul, Berlin, Baghdad, Istanbul . . .

Safe inside our lookalike bubbles, we share the stories that terrify and reassure, that emphasize the rawness of crumpled buildings and broken bodies, the instinct for survival against all odds, and the spirit unbroken in the face of so much devastation. We are the ones who stare into this hollow-eyed face, recognizing the look that haunts the desperate family members and rescue workers still searching for the missing among the ruins. Searching for our empathy, we gasp when a new face appears; a survivor is found after six days of digging into the darkness. She wears a different look and goes by another name. It is Jeanette, we learn, a Haitian bank teller buried by the 2010 earthquake, who blinks in the stabbing sunlight. "Thirsty," she says in English, even as she lifts her voice to sing in French. "Don't be afraid of death," she translates for us. But just then, the pop-up ads jolt us out of

Port au Prince, and later, out of Christchurch and Santiago, much like the commercial jingles that bounce us back from the Jersey Shore, from the Ninth Ward, or from Aleppo and Benghazi, or from families grieving the loss of loved ones on downed Malaysia Air flights 370 and 17.

Back we bounce to the kittens and toddlers, to an adrenaline-soaked straightaway, and to the horse dance—make that the Harlem Shake or the Dab or . . . We'll have to ask Ellen DeGeneres. Ours is an à *la carte* culture, what prompts us to pick and choose from a blizzard of images—the avalanche of visceral truths based on these things that lie. We do not ask which of them rings true to our twenty-first-century values, whatever they may be, wherever they are found among our curated collections of valued commodities. Yet, we share a single story chanting loudly about order and stability, uncertainty and change—a story soaked in the uncertainty of empathy and the stability of hedonism that will not respond to Jeanette's advice: "Don't be afraid of death."

Sometimes our shared story turns on a single image thrown from the image-world's barrage. Even if we refuse to look at it and TV journalists refuse to broadcast it—beheading after beheading in the desert, for instance—the image explodes in our midst. We are hit by the sting of flying questions that will not be deflected, by the shrapnel that shreds our sense of well-being—our complacency—and challenges the status quo. This time, there is no video, no game to dull its burn or blunt the shockwaves ringing with moral outrage. The crater this image creates will not soon be covered over or filled in with the magic of things that glitter.

Its gouge holds the truths we prefer not to see or the lies we embrace—fake news and disinformation. For a moment, maybe longer, this image angrily confronts a culture sleepwalking through its own moral codes, deluded by the propaganda affirming its self-righteous sense of decency and propriety. One culture is blasted out of its stupor by the image of child-sized coffins, twenty of them delivering tempera-painted dreams to the skies above a blood-soaked nation. An earlier culture screams for the nine-year-old in the jungle, a culture made more frantic and impatient by the photo that captures her run from the fiery napalm that burned her naked body.

A still earlier culture is forced to see the hideous cost of the cotton and tobacco cargoes it imports, but only when confronted by an ink drawing identifying the human cargo lying at the heart of this heartless operation. Depicting the below-deck conditions aboard the English slave ship *Brookes*, this eighteenth-century drawing made its viewers gasp in horror—gasp for breath—as they struggled with the claustrophobia of seeing an airless hold crowded with bodies barely alive, men's and women's, shackled and stacked head to toe during the long Atlantic crossing. For the first time, these conditions were made visible, visceral, and the polite and proper people bore witness to what could not be denied. This was the report given and fleshed out by the questions that would penetrate—and galvanize—an abolitionist movement in England and beyond.

It is widely believed too that Jacques Louis David's *The Death of Marat* (1793), painted during the most wrenching days of the French Revolution, was a catalyst that sharpened the passions and convictions of republican radicals already on the edge, raging in the streets of Paris. The image of journalist Jean-Paul Marat, the so-called voice of the people, lying bleeding, murdered in his own bathtub, captured a pivotal moment that rallied their cause—its simple message slicing through the frenzied chaos of the Reign of Terror and justifying their guillotine's noble work.

Today, we see something more ironic, a haunting image of a martyr forever idealized by the poignant depiction of the once powerful Jacobin lying in a divine light, while the assassin's depraved dagger lies in the shadows below—the glint of its bloodied blade confronting us with the profanity of it all. Sometimes described as a "secular Pieta," the painting and its unholy story are still piercing for the truths and lies they distort, for the decency and depravity they confuse. The painting cuts both ways, between frailty and immortality, rallying us to our cause of invincibility. It is still a grenade in our midst.

Images confuse us, demanding much while we give so little in return. As if to break through the haze, René Magritte offers his iconic painting pointedly titled *The Treachery of Images* (1928-29). The renowned surrealist is unambiguous, presenting a pipe, one like he or any other bowler-hat-wearing Belgian might have clenched between his teeth back in the day. To our eyes, the magic of this hyperrealistic image is still bewitching, and the pipe is still a pipe, even though Magritte tells us otherwise. *"Ceci n'est pas une pipe,"* his script declares (This is not a pipe). We smile, refusing to believe what is perfectly obvious—in effect, agreeing with Michel Foucault's poststructuralist analysis of this "non-affirmation" between text and image—and the spell remains unbroken. As if to reassure us, Banksy, the London-based street artist, offers his recent work, what is clearly a piece of industrial pipe, its metal jutting from the gallery wall next to its own proclamation: *This Is a Pipe* (2010). But we can see that it is not a pipe, it is art. We are confused—and delighted to be so. Images demand so little, and we give them too much. What is the trick of this trick?

Challenged by the magic, academic wizards have thrown themselves into the work of cracking the visual code that casts its spell over us. Shut in their laboratories, they pore over dusty volumes, looking to concoct their potions and distill the truth serum—the purified antidote for the image's clever trickery. In search of the eureka moment, they choose their ingredients methodically from among the bottles of essences and tinctures whose India-inked labels read *text and context, form and meaning, consciousness and preconsciousness, perception and emotion.* They add them to the bubbling brew that began with a hefty measure of theory, the extract of culture or biology, and a dash of conviction. Sometimes, a wizard's work calls for a spark, a pass of the crackling wand before the beaker is ready to spill its highly specialized explanation—the liquid wisdom that will undo the magic of Sontag's image-world. Skeptical, we take a sip but will not drink it all down—and we wonder if the suspicious concoction is potent enough to work its own magic. After all, this truth serum must out-trick the image with a trick of its own.

We sip what the poststructuralists and postmodernists offer and are roused enough to give some attention to the likes of Michel Foucault and to Roland Barthes, who find images to be a kind of language outside the world of words, a nonverbal proposition that may or may not affirm its verbal counterpart but is always filtered through the experience of culture and history. Context, they say, is the key ingredient, what shapes us as cultural beings enjoying the banter of images. But with another sip, we become dubious, wondering about the trick of the filters. How are we to know what culture and history allow in and what they strip out? Where is the integrity of the visual dialogue?

Barthes answers by insisting that visual art should question the world, not explain it. But this truth does not satisfy us, so we turn to another potion that entices us to taste the work of Marcel Danesi, Umberto Eco, and other semioticians who treat images as signs and symbols—representations—to be read as texts. As Danesi sees it, visual art is text constructed in a "visual mode," and like any text, it is also an artifact that can evoke fundamental feelings and sensations. Perhaps we take in his point that the juxtaposition of artifact with feeling creates "a powerful means for making meaning in the world and for extracting meaning from it." But like the filter, this "means" will neither question nor explain which signs are in or out, what meanings the text-bound image permits us to make or take. Without an answer, we are honor bound to put aside the contents of another evasive, if earnestly, labeled bottle.

Still, meaning-making has its allure, its unexplained process a deliciously secret ingredient that draws us all, wizard and nonwizard alike, to the image. Meaning itself may be the magic spark that allows us to mix up our truths and lies. Curious about the possibilities, we search for meaning's promise in the brew offered by the hermeneutical aestheticians who begin their work not with filters but with a highly suggestive fusion. These wizards, Nicholas Davey, Hans-Georg Gadamer, and even the philosopher Martin Heidegger, among them, assure us that this fusion—a careful blending of an image's embodied idea with its form and material presences—is the solution responsible for the trick of interpretive meaning-making.

What's more, this meaning-making works to disclose the truth of the image's being. Uncertain of such a truth, we take another drink and another, but wonder still about the fusion's formula for giving the image its power to stand on honest interpretation and speak in a voice we find direct and clear. This image is also strong enough to transplant us into a magic rhizome of ideas where meanings are rooted in manipulative connections. How can empathy exist under such conditions?

Van Gogh's paintings of a pair of work shoes spoke to Heidegger of earth, imagined clods that took him deep into the truth of a nineteenth-century peasant woman tending the fields. You and I might imagine a man who stood in them—a miller grinding the grain, a carpenter sweeping up sawdust, or even Van Gogh himself. The image suggests, and can be made to untangle, some of its truths, along with its network of matted meanings—but it will not give up the trick of its neatly packaged lies. And our wish is granted: The shoes, like the pipe, or the purple iris and the white one, still weave their magic.

Perhaps the trick of the image lies not in meaning-making, but in some other project buried deeper in the triadic interaction of idea, form, and medium—the project of perception, perhaps, whose process seems as mysterious as it is necessary. Surely, the wise wizards have dug into the mystery and unearthed the essence of a process known to take us in completely, directing the triad to capture our gaze and hold it steady.

In the same moment, this wily process determines how we take in the image's clever allure. Remembering the beaker marked "perception," we turn to the wizards of psychology, willing to swallow a bit of what they concoct—a code-cracking theory to explain the magic giving us special powers to apprehend the whole of an image (including its trick) in a single perceptual act. Unlike the word-by-word, line-by-line approach required by the printed page, the image, they note, allows us to read what is encoded in its spatial patterns and abstract symbols in a nonsequential way—and to decode their cues as quickly and easily as we recode them in our own magical stories. In an instant, the perceptual spark takes us from conscious perceiver to cognitive problem-solver working out the analysis of the parts and the synthesis of the whole.

To Rudolf Arnheim and other Gestaltist wizards, the three-way interaction of idea, form, and medium becomes a twosome of perception and conception that charges one visual code with its power to seduce. This serum, with its strong taste of vision and cognition, its odor of linguistics, seems palatable enough. But in the end, its truth is still hypothetical and focuses on the *what* of perception, not on the *how* or *why*. We are left wanting more. Perhaps another vial, one specifically labeled "physiology of perception," will explain the project at hand—the one to undo the trick of the image.

One sip and physiology's extract greets the tongue with something very different—an unusual but not unpleasant taste challenging the ideas of linguistic filters that flavor the potions of hermeneutics, semiotics, and perceptual psychology. Its color is different too, cleaner, more saturated, and with another swallow, the purity of physiology reveals what Martin Jay calls an "optical unconscious" or "preconscious, unfiltered perception." He is the wizard offering a perception that is "nativistic," more biological, raw, and more direct than any theory focusing on conscious and cognitive apprehension. Jay finds some support for this approach in the neuroscientific research bent on demystifying the workings of the visual cortex in the human brain.

Recent studies seem to crack the code of how we see, breaking the process into several stages and recoding them alphanumerically as V1 through V5. As we might expect, the process begins when light strikes the retina's photoreceptor cells. But neuroscience reveals what the eye is actually seeing, and it is not whole images, inverted or otherwise—not even patterns or symbols.

In fact, we pick up only the merest of edges and contrasts, angles and shadows in V1 seeing—what occurs in the optic nerve just behind the retina. In each of the subsequent stages, the brain fills in more, sending the rudimentary image deep into the circuitry, where it passes through the neuronal filters of memory and emotion before reaching the seat of reasoning in the frontal lobe.

There, the image—as filtered—is finally resolved, even as it is further contextualized and interpreted. But with this resolution, Jay's potion darkens, becoming as murky as the others. Now, we are left with none potent enough to break through so much magic. What Jay offers seems especially disappointing, a half-truth powerless to explain away V2 and V3 seeing—and the brain's filters operating at every nodal connection of its electric rhizome. Wired together, the preconscious and the conscious are as tricky as they are dynamic. And the whole truth about the image seems clearest in what the brain imagines.

Somehow, a century before Jay, Cezanne understood this imagination and argued throughout the post-Impressionist period that the eye is not a camera, the mind not a mirror. And we are curious about the wisdom of a provincial painter—willing after so many disappointments to be taken in this time by the truths of his still lifes. Perhaps it is not a laboratory but a sunlit studio that locates the work of distilling what we see of an image and how we imagine it to (mis)represent an exterior world. Stepping into Cezanne's airy studio, with its gray walls and bright apples, its shelves of still-life objects, we spot the well-worn easel and can imagine the artist working by the light of the great north window. He is silent, unblinking, intently studying the objects arranged on the table that centers the room—a rum bottle, green vase, ginger pot, and several apples nestled among the white and blue draperies.

We stare as well, recognizing objects that center so many of his familiar compositions, including *Still Life with Apples* (1893-94) currently exhibited at the Getty Museum. We can follow his gaze—fixed on the apples—and imagine him squinting at them, apparently for hours on end, watching them slowly dissolve and taking his eyes back to their essential contours, contrasts, and edges. For Cezanne, it is a matter of objectivity, a drive to understand the subjectivity of sight by capturing its V1 beginnings in paint and color. As the image appears before us, we learn that his methodical immersion and disciplined focus result in what has been called a "flat-depth" aesthetic—which also opens up a constructivist science based on deconstructing and reconstructing those apples. Cezanne is not interested in questions of illusion or abstraction, certainly not in the "pseudoscience" of Impressionism, as he puts it. He seeks the truths of a reality that is constructed, and thus, made more real.

Cezanne offers us the work of his sustained perceptual act as an invitation to enter the still life. Entering will require more than simply apprehending its flattened composition with a perceptual act of our own. To enter is to penetrate it deeply by participating in a creative act that reconstructs what he has deconstructed. We must see his work with our imaginations, not with our eyes, and using his simple strokes, his bare edges and contours, we will create the apples and make them our own.

Cezanne's invitation includes a lesson, one we must absorb if we are to understand there is no objective "out there," but only a subjective "in here"—V2 and V3 seeing filtered through what we believe in and hunger for, what we remember and dream about. Indeed, his images are the reports given, but not of an exterior world. These are the reports (mis)representing an interior life animated by the intertwined processes of imagining and constructing our realities—the rhizomic connections tangling our truths and lies.

Somehow, Maggie, a returning student in her mid-thirties, understood the art and science—the trick—of Cezanne's *Still Life with Apples*. She did not say if its visual language spoke to her or stood as a question that explained something of her world. Perhaps she saw the still life as a signifying artifact, a means for making and taking worlds of meaning. Or perhaps it was a triadic fusion revealing the painting's truth of being, its parts, its whole encoding and decoding Cezanne's own being—maybe even Maggie's as well.

No, she said nothing of magical codes or what such grand theories may have revealed. Instead, she spoke of a simple postcard, a small reproduction of a still life very similar to the Getty's that had captivated her at age seventeen. Staring long and hard at her postcard, Maggie had dedicated herself to deconstructing and reconstructing the work of the master as faithfully as she could.

Now, reconnecting with Cezanne as a prospective art teacher and artist in her own right, she had pulled up *Still Life with Apples* on her computer screen, manipulating the image to create two of her own—a diptych testifying to the power of deep penetration, of seeing with the imagination, and of connecting inner and outer worlds. In the image on the left, an arm reaches into the still life, the hand about to snatch one of the apples. On the right, an apple core stands among the drapery folds. A line above the pair reads, "Eating Cezanne: making him me, me him." Elaborating further, Maggie said, "When I stood before *Still Life with Apples* [at the Getty], I sort of imagined that if I took a bite of the apple, it would enable me to paint like Cezanne. . . . Maybe I would know all that he knew." In Maggie's hunger, we understand the drive to connect, to empathize: Our own lives compel us to reach and imagine, to see and remember—and to know the trick of the image that nourishes the inner world and constructs the outer.

Other artists seek the truth of connection in their images. Video artist Bill Viola's quest has led him to treat the image as a bridge or "intermediate zone" between our interior and exterior landscapes. As he says, images—and art in general—connect the "deep feelings we have . . . of being in the world with the external world." It is through this zone that such feelings are "brought forth" into the world in a "tangible, physical way" others can experience.

Images deliver the stories of heart-pounding fears and heart-hurting disappointments we have all known and recount scenarios about frustrations and anxieties that wrench, triumphs and thrills that tingle. They tell us what we desperately need to hear: that we are not alone in a world roiling with emotion.

So, still searching, we jump into a video zone and are immediately immersed in a collective experience. There, we share emotional stories of all genres, national narratives, for instance, brought forth by video footage of that September morning when bodies fell from dying towers, by images beaming with election results on November evenings when different histories were made.

There are many among us who dive into video games, forming close-knit "massive multiplayer on-line" communities and adventuring into mythic realities where the characters come to life and tell yet another story of connection. One community united around Aerith, the flower girl in *Final Fantasy 7*, grieving and raging together when this beloved character was killed at her altar—an act so unthinkable, so unacceptable, that it prompted a petition demanding her resurrection. Viola's video art captures the metaphysical in all of this, real feelings recognized in a zone magically constructed.

Images, it seems, hover above theories in a zone between biology and culture, staking out the territory between a visceral world throbbing with emotional impulses and a social world built on a drive for order and the urge to control. They tell us about the truths and lies of both worlds. If we listen, images will also explain how we are lost *and* found in the middle of a biocultural existence—and how their intermediate zone (mis) represents and mediates this existence, even as it makes our lives more bearable, if not entirely comprehensible.

The zone they create is never neutral, never an open space. This avalanche of images encloses us in that familiar air pocket, the biocultural bubble that floats us into a shared topography of emotional peaks and valleys. We recognize each other in the jagged terrain, among the vibrant stories churned up—what we take to be real—and the very ones we use to grapple with the ambiguities and complexities of all that is (mis)represented. Still, this terrain and the age of images it celebrates beckon to the possibility of what primatologist Frans de Waal calls the "age of empathy." We must explore this territory more assiduously if we are to claim de Waal's age as our own.

For now, it is the neuroscientists who accept our charge. They are the pioneers willing to open new territories of human consciousness, to explore a headscape full of prospects for a more empathic age. Theirs is an expedition to determine how the mountains of images we keep in our heads can be mined, the rich ores used to crack the mysteries of empathy and human thought. These speculators have discovered that images deep in the head—distortions of the world around us—serve to focus our thoughts and tell us what we can imagine about ourselves and others.

Among the explorers, Antonio Damasio takes a step further into this territory, asserting that "imageless thought" is not even possible for our species. The way we come to know, to reason, to understand the world and our connection to its inhabitants, he says, depends on an ability to extract images and display them on our mental screens. What's more, thought depends on the process we devise to order these "pictures in the head"—assuming, of course, that we can stop their internal avalanche, at least for a moment or two.

Damasio is convinced of the neuroscience, the research evidence that structures his argument. Thought is "imagistic," he claims, and has little to do with the detailed descriptions of another process put forth by Western epistemologists of the seventeenth and eighteenth centuries or by the Greek philosophers millennia before them. Thought, says Damasio, cannot be based on their top-down, disembodied process of manipulating sets of propositions according to prescribed rules of logic.

Based on our own experiences, we may be inclined to agree. To many of us, twenty-first-century thinking does not feel like such an abstract, cut-and-dried undertaking, nor is it necessarily a linear one. If, in fact, we are thinking with images that by their very nature are nonsequential, then our thoughts must be free to branch in any direction, to crisscross and create complex, even rhizomic patterns. Streaming across our screens, these thought patterns can be vivid indeed. Surely, they light up the mind.

Damasio digs deeper still, unearthing another genre of internal images. In addition to the familiar mental representations—those movie reels and still pictures in our heads, jumbled together in catalogs and albums, but always available to the mind's eye—there is a second category, what Damasio calls *neural* representations or "body images" that are much less familiar to us, but fundamental, nonetheless, to our thoughts and personal identities. For Damasio, neural images are like maps whose topographic features and organization represent all manner of physical sensations—the "patterns of stimulation"—occurring throughout the body.

We have all felt what these maps capture—our twinges and flutters, chills and sweats, hiccups and goosebumps. We might remember a racing heart, a lump in the throat, a knot in the stomach. Neural maps preserve these patterns and cast them into the body's reservoir of fluid experiences and working memory. Their splash brings up various "somatic markers" and "emotional states" from the depths. On the surface still rippling in wider and wider circles, new images form and re-form, spilling into our thoughts and influencing our decisions—our very being. Like images of the external world, these too are dynamic, internal maps that shape and reflect what the body values—and determine what is important to us inside and out.

In Damasio's scenario, the stimulated body generates images and the industrious mind displays and organizes their constant stream. With its generative, even commanding powers, the body achieves a status equal to, if not higher than, that of the mind. So, it is that Damasio rejects the centuries-old Cartesian model that privileges the mind over the body by severing the head's "elegant rationality" from the body's "base instincts." Now, privileging science over philosophy, Damasio embraces a newer, more balanced view, one based on research implications that would rejoin rationality and instinct. Thought, he says, *requires* feeling, and feeling requires the *body*. What we think and who we are cannot be determined in and by the mind alone. The self is not ensconced in the head, says Damasio, but widely distributed throughout the body, and thus, is determined by the neural maps that are constantly skewing our mental pictures.

Damasio the scientist strides still deeper into this ontology, blending thinking, feeling, and being in ways that open a door to empathy. Because we can represent the body "on line, all the time in the brain," he says, we also have the possibility of generating our own *simulated* body states at will. Using what we remember of fading maps, we can reconstruct the topographical features of an itch and the bliss of scratching it; we can recall the feeling of bone-weary despair, the memory of a hopeful heart. Because we can generate our own body states, says Damasio, we also have the possibility of generating those of others, all the way from the emotional state to the muscular-skeletal. As he sees it, we can go from the body of the self to the body of another and through the body *into the mind of another*.

Ah, but these body maps are clever indeed. Even as they remain unseen and largely unacknowledged—peculiar patterns hidden deep—these internal images trick us into believing we can leap outside ourselves into another's mental theater and recognize what's playing on that screen. Ever cunning, body images appear to be benign but demand much of us. We are expected to grasp their imagistic propositions and manipulate their slippery possibilities, all challenging us to deduce—conclude—that what begins in one body carries a secret code for an empathy unlocking all minds.

But where is the logic in this proposition? We are left to wonder if it is science or magic that explains such a tricky philosophy. Images of the internal world, though, will not help us decide, not this time. Still, one thing is certain: Despite their conniving, these are not the images to bewitch us nor capture our attention. That imperative belongs to the dazzling images of the external world alone. But if we are so distracted by the outer, then what possibility do we have of cracking the code of the inner?

Meanwhile, focused neuroscientists such as Damasio have come to rely on the certainty of state-of-the-art imaging technologies to take on the pesky questions popping up in the territories of an ever-expanding headscape. Now, mountains of brain scans have created a glittering image-world for them to explore. Digging into what the scans capture with legendary precision, these miners have been delighted to pick through images of the head, searching for the gems that would explain images in the body.

Serendipity offered up a motherlode of explanations and put the speculators on a stronger footing in this geology. The accidental discovery of mirror neurons in the mid-1990s yielded precious evidence, fine-cut proof, that unseen images in the body exist to tell the cellular story of empathy in the head. In fact, the neurological basis of empathy had been revealed—pinpointed first in area F5 of the brain's ventral premotor cortex. With this, and subsequent discoveries in other regions of the brain, Damasio's maps acquired a precision of their own. And in the intervening years, mirror neurons have had much to tell about empathy's locations and working mechanism.

Yet, they remain a mystery—a "strange and wonderful class of neurons" still dazzling neuroscientists to this day. Despite the latest, most powerful scanners, mirror neurons have not given up all of empathy's secrets, leaving Marco Iacoboni, for one, to describe them simply as "those cells in the brain that create some kind of magical connection between people." Like the others busy in the mine, Iacoboni remains intrigued, willing to drill deeper, especially as the mountain of MRIs grows ever taller. For now, the magic prevails, and the science raises many more questions about the code hidden in the mirrors.

Still, much has been retrieved from the depths; nuggets the neuroscientists carefully polish to highlight what they have learned about the mechanism behind the mirroring magic. Staring into gleaming images of the motor cortex, they have discovered that some of our simplest movements—reaching and grasping with our hands—can fire up what appears to be a simple mechanism. For Iacoboni, the way empathy works—how we mirror each other—can be summed up in a single line, an interview soundbite: "When I see you grasping something, the same cells in my brain are activated, so it's almost like I'm in your mind."

If Iacoboni's "you" is generic and includes us all, then it seems the "magical connection" is created when one of us executes an action, such as snatching an apple, and an observer experiences the snatch through the visual and motor systems. Even the most casual observer feels what it is like to snatch. What this also means, says Vittorio Gallese, is that "We don't just perceive with the visual system, we perceive also with the motor system." Offering his own line, this colleague of Iacoboni's points to the magic within the magic that transforms the meaning of perception altogether.

Suddenly, the mechanism behind it all does not seem so simple after all. Indeed, the dual-system approach of the neuroscientists—a mirroring manipulation—challenges the very foundation of the theoretical approaches put forth by the wizards of perception. Gallese and the others are undaunted, persuaded by the wisdom of the scanner whose truths offer what theories cannot. Brain scans dazzle them, but unlike other images, would never (mis)represent the empirical certainty these neuroscientists crave. They are confident in their own wizardry, claiming that every one of us can experience—*can perceive*—what others experience, both in mind and body.

Scanners hum, and neuroscientists around the world pore over the images—each more mesmerizing than the last—to fully understand the nature of motor perception and the precise circumstances in which it occurs. As it turns out, our motor neurons fire even when we see a hand disappearing behind a screen where we know an object, say a wine bottle, is hidden, and we are left to imagine the hand grasping its neck. Simply staring at a static hand frozen in a two-dimensional image triggers these cells, suggesting that we imagine this hand in motion. Images of a lone hammer or screwdriver—tools a hand might use—will activate the motor cells along with images of the strokes the letters a hand might make. So, it seems the perceptions firing our neurons are also firing our imaginations.

What's more, images trigger what the motor region perceives and prompts us to imagine. In these circumstances, we find ourselves rethinking the image and its power to tell us who we are and how we are connected. Take Maggie and Cezanne, for instance. We might recall or imagine the young Maggie studying the postcard, but now, we imagine her motor cells lighting up, perceiving the master's brushstrokes, imagining the brush in his hand. And what of her diptych? Had the digital images awakened our own motor regions, prompting us to imagine the hand grabbing Cezanne's apple? But the scanner's empiricism has not yet said, and we are more anxious than ever to see just what the cells of an activated imagination look like. How long must we wait before an MRI pinpoints an imagination always implicated, but never depicted—the very one Cezanne understood we all share, the one putting us in each other's minds, the fountainhead of empathy?

Perhaps scans of the "strange and wonderful" neurons are like other images after all. They too burst from their frames to claim more than they can. Yet they are merely the "reports given," the insistent substitutes used for firsthand experiences, in this case, of "some kind of magical connection between people." Apparently, they (mis)represent the certainty of their own precision. Left to speculate about what these images may or may not imply, neuroscientists like Gallese can only offer inferences, much like Damasio's "possibilities" that would have us going from the body of the self into the bodies—and minds—of others, sharing experiences, and imagining what electrifies a collective cortex.

Not all neuroscientists agree, but for his part, Gallese theorizes that we experience other people—their movements and gestures, say—at an "abstract level of representation," through what he calls an "embodied simulation." Such a simulation, he says, "allows our body to resonate along with the bodies of others."

Now, we are the ones left to speculate, to wonder about the magic embodied in Gallese's simulations, in Damasio's possibilities, and in the tingle of rhizomic resonance. We are the wizards in search of explanations, the ones outside the lab who investigate the images capturing what the scanner cannot. Eureka! We find our resonating bodies amply represented in images of synchronized swimmers and pirouetting dancers, in the choreography of scrimmaging athletes and high-stepping marching bands—in the music of rippling laughter and full-throated choirs. Our bodies feel the resonance in a kiss, an embrace, and a hall resounding with bravos and exuberant applause. We see, hear, and feel what our neurology makes possible, what takes us from self to other and synapse to society. This neurology is existential, with a philosophy built in that reminds us we are not freestanding individuals but a wired-together collective living among the cross-connections of a vast rhizome. Again and again, its tenets insist: There is no "I," only "we."

Like Damasio, we might use our empirical evidence, our imagistic reasoning, to challenge Descartes's mind-body duality, along with his enduring proposition: "I think, therefore I am." Our counter is strong, based on eyewitness accounts of the cultural experience and grounded in the science, the magic of the mirroring mechanism. Our logic is sound: "We resonate, therefore we are." Equally valid is the corollary—our proposition that, "We are, therefore we dance . . . and imagine . . . and tell stories."

Two centuries after René Descartes, the philosophers Giles Deleuze and Félix Guattari, also French, use the rhizome's crisscrossing connections to envision the collective experience that informs our ways of thinking and being. Their rhizomic model stands up to refute Cartesian "top-down, disembodied" views of individualistic thought, theory, and culture. Maps are also part of their model, and Deleuze and Guattari use them to chart how we, as members of the collective come to know how we understand cultural influences and how we come to be in a "milieu" they believe is rhizomic.

In this milieu, say Deleuze and Guattari, knowledge and culture are constructed within a network ever-growing and rippling with grasslike lines or "ligatures" free to connect any point to any other point. We might be tempted to picture a backyard choked by the randomly cross-connecting roots and shoots of crabgrass—and we would not be wrong *per se*. But in this case, it is more accurate and far more preferable to look to the digital network we find flourishing on our screens. We log on to the Internet—itself a rhizome—to immerse ourselves among the "ligatures" that free us to connect any data point to any other and to do so in any dimension. These ligatures seem exuberant, uninhibited, and we will encourage them to cross-connect our ways of thinking and being with Facebook posts and research databases, LinkedIn invitations and world news events. And we've only just begun.

For their part, these energetic lines urge us to pay attention to different ideas and perspectives. For instance, they could entangle political and economic ideologies that focus our thoughts on capitalist imperatives and socialist sensibilities, or show us where community activists are busiest, organizing protest movements either for or against immigrant rights, voting rights, or abortion rights. They are insistent, these ligatures that expect us to connect different genres, and we will oblige them by browsing among Amazon's titles in search of a critically acclaimed collection of contemporary poems and a best-selling work of historical fiction. Thanks to their rhizomic enterprise, we have become quite comfortable with character-driven novels and movies that tell their stories from multiple points of view. We think nothing of comparing the online menus of different area restaurants, the schedules of different movies playing around town, and the reports of traffic conditions on different surface streets before heading out to navigate the network that cross-connects different communities and cultures.

Deleuze and Guattari are quick to point out that growth in networks online or on the street is not willy-nilly. In their model, wriggling ligatures are guided by principles of "mutualism" and "multiplicity" that steer them toward unlike genres, theories, values—the disparate data points that, once connected, establish a mutually beneficial "unity in multiplicity." Such guidance, say the philosophers, results in what we experience firsthand: Knowledge that is nonhierarchical, and culture that is unpredictable. Both are multifaceted and flexible, each offering us troves of fresh, if surprising, possibilities.

Sure enough, we construct such knowledge and culture as citizen journalists who write all manner of blogs, informative in their own way. We are also citizen scientists who work on massive projects helping to map brains and stars. The Smithsonian puts out an appeal, and we become transcribers helping to chronicle the history of American slavery. Visual and cultural information is extracted with zeal from the galleries appearing on Pinterest and Facebook, what is always matched by the information-studded collections we curate ourselves. Music pours from car speakers, filling the streets and informing us of its hip-hop or Latin presence while the earbuds of our iPods answer with a different tune. We listen to TED Talks and consult Wikipedia, even as we decide which restaurant—Vietnamese? Indian? Vegan?—sounds most appealing, which film—French? Israeli? Disney?—looks most promising, and which route—through Koreatown? Little Lithuania? Little Italy?—will be most interesting. All that we construct must surely abide by Deleuze and Guattari's principles as we entangle ourselves in networks that are unorthodox, dynamic, and open to serendipity's unifying impulse.

What's more, Deleuze and Guattari's rhizomic model allows us to climb in and out of the network at any point during the always ongoing construction process. We take full advantage, coming and going even as the data are represented and interpreted. This is our twenty-first-century network with no beginning or end but always a middle from which it grows and in which we are called into being. Our ways of thinking and feeling—resonating—are validated, along with the imagistic reasoning and collective identity they make possible. We trace

along the multidimensional ligatures that open new pathways
and promote interactions between power structures, semiotic
signifiers, social struggle, and the arts and sciences. They are
entangling, indeed, and persuade us to bridge across rival
theories and diverse perspectives—and to participate in a
dialectic always in the middle of creating a "unity in multiplicity."

Cartesians imagine knowledge and culture of another type,
as if branching from a mighty oak whose rings map history's
chronology and whose roots tap tradition's hallowed ground.
Relying on its vertical lines, the trunk draws strength from the
canons, sending the wisdom and authority they codify straight
up into the canopy. Handhold by foothold, individual "I"s are
expected to climb into this hierarchy, gradually moving higher
and higher among the branches, whose forks demand either/
or decisions. These, we realize, represent the data ordered
as discrete and dualistic categories, the ones labeled either
"subject" or "object," "cause" or "effect," "mind" or "body" that
also determine what interpretations are permitted.

On their way down, climbers descend from leaf to limb
to trunk, guided by a singular, if principled, line of inquiry.
They must dedicate themselves to the search for sources, for
beginnings and endings. Highly focused, this search seems to be
fueled by an epistemological energy flowing throughout the tree
of knowledge and into the arboreal structure of culture. This, we
might imagine, is the energy needed for building such a culture
among the boughs, where various tree forts and social values
are established—where individual inhabitants become cultural
beings by tracing along chronological lines to find the cause, the
origin of what Deleuze and Guattari call "things." We might also
imagine the tree dwellers—ourselves among them?—picking up
fallen acorns, a few of the tiny things that mark the beginning of
something huge, something predetermined, but wondrous still.

Deleuze and Guattari swing their ax, Damasio his as well,
but the gnarled old tree stands its ground. Unlike the rhizome
and its resilience, the aging oak is strengthened by its resistance,
by the roots reaching deep into human stubbornness and our
blanket refusal to abandon the search—especially the search for
the "things" whose cause could reveal how the world works and

whose origins could explain our own. We are insistent, indeed, as if driven by some sort of personal and cultural need to get to the bottom of "things," to know how the story begins and ends.

There are many among us whose very livelihood depends on this search: the civil engineer who must pinpoint where the stress fracture occurred, the radiologist who does the same; even as the seismologist finds where the fault lies, the obstetrician attends another birth, and the coroner determines the cause of death. And there are historians investigating who fired the first shot, sociologists what triggered the riot, and humanitarians still discovering how to eradicate hunger at its root.

We pull together, investing in research aimed at finding the cause of cancer, in projects analyzing the building blocks of life in the human genome and on the Martian surface. And just as history tracks the beginnings of social upheaval, and the outbreak of war, science targets the V1 as the beginning of sight and area F5 as the basis of empathy. In the museum, we expect to see works of art—originals only—exhibited in chronological order so that we might trace the beginnings of aesthetic upheaval and the outbreak of another "ism." At the multiplex, we expect the prequels and sequels to reveal more and more about the characters, but mostly about where they came from and where they are going. Oh yes, we need to search, and like the cultural beings we are, we need to look to the stories for answers, taking some comfort in our colorful creation myths—tales of Adam and Eve, or Father Sky and Mother Earth—that explain how it all began, but not how it will end.

We search on, enlisting the aid of the Internet, a most expeditious and rhizomic means of unearthing our own beginnings. With a few clicks, we have results taking us back in time and down through the generations to the very roots of the family tree. Or perhaps it is a search more intense, arduous, to find the missing birth parent or long-lost sibling who will heal the broken branches. More than a curiosity, a retiree's project, or adoptee's resolve, this is the call of identity, an oath sworn to find answers to the perennial question of the Western world: Who am I, and where did I come from? The need to know spurs us on, and we find ourselves clicking link after link, tracing family names and relationships further and further from the trunk until we are swaying among the smallest of branches. But these appear to be more like ligatures now, the crisscrossing roots and shoots that reach into unexpected dimensions and connect us to other families' names and relationships.

Indeed, we are back in the rhizome, discovering just how closely related we are to George Washington or George Clooney and how few degrees separate us from Kevin Bacon. Just like that, the Internet that allows us to trace along chronological lines to the source of genealogical "things," is the tool to plant us—iris lovers and tree dwellers alike—among the exuberant, if unruly lines connecting us to a multiplicity of other beings. Identity, we realize, is constructed in the context of an ever-expanding network resonating with stories, with questions about how these stories fit together and where our own fits in. We also realize that the work of civil engineers and radiologists is situated within the puzzle of interconnected parts, that the seismologist must probe the pattern of slip-strike and thrust faults crisscrossing subduction zones and edging tectonic plates.

Historians and sociologists, like the humanitarians, make their discoveries in light of the political, economic, and social conditions that surround hunger, unrest, and war. We pull together, like flash mobs and citizen journalists, learning more about unities in multiplicities, participating in projects of ridesharing and yarnbombing, crowdsourcing and crowdfunding—in stories with no beginning or end telling of lives shared in the middle.

The rhizome and tree metaphors are apt, and their images succeeded long ago, digging their way into us, despite the admonitions of Descartes, Damasio, and Deleuze. We need both, the crabgrass and the craggy oak, and remain unconflicted, even as we stand in the middle ground between their "we" and "I." This is the space we claim, open and devoid of philosophical bickering; a place neither terrifying nor reassuring that lies beyond wizards' labs, artists' studios, and neurologists' scanners, where our naked toes explore the grassy ligatures, our backs rest against the massive trunk in the shade of spreading limbs. Here, we are unconcerned with truths or lies yet free to contemplate the images of Sontag's image-world and Viola's intermediate zone. Jostling for our attention, these are the extensions of things that (mis)represent our world and the feelings we have of being in it; the images that show us the cause, the origin of "things," when they are the "things" of storytelling that multiply the connections—feelings—we share in tangible ways.

They tumble down, brain scans and still life paintings, resonating bodies living and dead, images of Moonstone Beach and Tahrir Square, of Jeanette and Aerith, and pipes that are and are not. They spill their stories and create the setting for ours.

Though they murmur about empathy, these images cannot confirm its role as narrator. If, on the other hand, we are the ones to narrate this story, is empathy a character strong enough to shape its arc?

Chapter II

Blowin' in the Wind

You likely have your own way of characterizing empathy, as I have mine. We scratch at its essence, searching for a core, but find . . . what? So, we settle for a sketch, a few attributes, a role it might play. Perhaps we draw from a biblical verse—*Love thy neighbor*—forever drifting on the edge of a Sunday school memory or snatch song lyrics from the ether—*He ain't heavy, he's my brother,* for instance, or *No man is an island, no man stands alone/each man's joy is joy to me, each man's grief is my own* . . .

Or maybe empathy comes to life in a vision, costumed in a gauzy metaphor, something symbolic that captures what words cannot, a circle of clasped hands, say, or a high five, a poignant tear, a simple smile. Maybe we catch the whispering of empathy's voice in a newborn's cry, a Salvation Army bell ringer's plea, or a campfire chorus of "Kumbayah." Whatever the attribute, the ideas it embodies can be added to the others put forth over the years, each another attempt to grab a handful of empathy out of the air—valiant efforts all to pin down its elusive nature and give some color and dimension to its character.

Searching among their promises, though, we will find neither a consensus nor the hierarchical ordering we seek. Like the scuttling leaves, the flapping candy wrappers, and plastic bags caught in a sidewalk wind devil, empathy sucks up suggestions but is unable to point to any patterns in their swirl—and unwilling to blend them together. We can pick them out, the sentimental and the cynical, the stereotypes and the insights. And there are the academic efforts, the newest ideas offered only recently by the neuroscientific community, now joining the old chestnuts gleaned from the philosophical and psychological traditions. Also in the whirl, we can spot the contributions of historians, politicians, and cultural critics. Each bestows its color but does little to define, or stop, the spin. In this story, empathy embraces its role as tiny tornado, an invisible force we can feel, even as it swirls around an invisible core.

Still we identify them, Iacoboni's "biological drive," and the mirror neurons that magically connect us to each other. And there is Maurice Merleau-Ponty's concept of "lived experience," an existentialist empathy whirling in his words: "I live in the facial expression of the other, as I feel him living in mine." We spot some of what psychology has to offer, a definition distilled from Daniel Goleman's research on emotional intelligence, hurtling past us as "an ability to read emotions in others"—an ability that includes "understanding their concerns and taking their perspective." More lyrical is psychologist Martin Hoffman's metaphor that sees empathy as "the spark of human concern for others, the glue that makes social life possible."

We see Alexis de Tocqueville's "habits of the heart," defining empathy in nineteenth-century America as a national resource vital to the survival of the fledgling democracy, a description chased, we notice, by then Senator Jeff Sessions's conviction that empathy in twenty-first-century American politics is a partisan issue, a kind of zero-sum game dictating that "empathy for one party always means prejudice for another." Gusting past us now, we see Sontag's critical discourse casting empathy as a foolhardy, even failed, enterprise—not a zero-sum game, but rather a mug's game. Also in the cyclonic swirl, we pick out writer-critic Jonathan Lethem's claim that empathy invokes a fundamental sense of "neighborliness," which is all we have, all that remains when the great critique is stripped away.

And here comes de Waal's "fellow-feeling," an "innate, age-old capacity that has been naturally selected for"—his claim that empathy is all we've *ever* had, all that ensures our "synchrony," our very survival as a group-living species. In the midst of all this churn is economist-activist Jeremy Rifkin's "evolution of empathic consciousness," what he believes is the whole story of human history. For him, empathy is "the very means by which we create social life and advance civilization." Attributes spin, and now we feel the tension but cannot be sure if empathy's force is weakening or gathering strength.

We step back, surveying the detritus that characterizes empathy as a hodgepodge of conflicting "drives," "abilities," "capacities," "resources," "games," and "means" serving all manner of ends. Even at this distance, the attributes carried in the clutter remain distinct, and we cannot see how they could ever be connected. What we are given is a flurry of academic ideas, caught up like confetti in a never-ending cycle of rancorous debate. And if cross-connecting ligatures are nowhere to be found, then we are the ones to sort through the bits of color, to search the swirl for empathy at the beginning and to trace any straight lines that could lead us to its core. So, we stand by, waiting for the churning to stop, ready to inspect what is dropped at our feet—ready to search for causes and sources, for patterns of similarity, some semblance of order that would resolve the conflicts and unwind the cyclone on the sidewalk.

Until then, we can only review what is already apparent. Empathy is elastic and expected to wrap around the partisan and the neighborly, the foolhardy and the existential. Such flexibility appears to allow its size and scope to be scaled up or down. Empathy can be something small and intimate, an interpersonal relationship based on one individual's concern for another. Or it can be something grander and all-encompassing that takes in the sweep of human history, the evolution of civilization. Large or small, empathy stretches across domains, as some descriptions root it in a biological world of innate drives and evolutionary "synchrony," while others give it a home in a cultural sphere held together by "habit of the heart" and social "glue."

Empathy is so agile, so amenable, that it accommodates dualistic ideas—those focusing on the feelings and concerns that sketch its emotional demeanor and those establishing thoughtfulness, understanding, and perspective-taking as features that shape its intellectual character. This divide, as we might suspect, has been described at length by the academics who envision an "affective" empathy that focuses on a person *feeling* something due to the thoughts and feelings of another, and a "cognitive" empathy that focuses on a person *understanding* another's thoughts and feelings in a given situation.

As if to reinforce this bipolar vision, *Webster's Dictionary* states in no-nonsense terms that empathy is "the intellectual *or* emotional identification with another." And we are not surprised to learn that it is both, according to a holistic approach favored by Goleman, de Waal, and Damasio, among others, who argue for a nimble empathy and an "embodied cognition" that has always reached across feeling and understanding. We are witness to empathy's gymnastics, what it must perform in a swirl of controversy, twisting and turning among rival lines of inquiry.

We are also not surprised to discover that academic wizardry is involved in the project of building boxes that would contain empathy's contorted energies. To be sure, analysts have been hard at work, classifying the descriptions and definitions amassed over the years—all making claims on empathy's character, even as they follow different lines of inquiry. Methodically, these wizards scrutinize each idea, affix color-coded labels, and hammer together the two-by-fours of a typology rigid enough to organize what is an impressive and eclectic collection indeed.

As it turns out, the typology requires four boxes to accommodate the number of approaches used to explain empathy—to calm the fluttering and make it manageable. One approach, labeled "phenomenological," packs its box with first-person accounts that describe empathy as an affirmation of self-identity. Perhaps this would include Merleau-Ponty's "I," affirmed in his lived experience of another's "I."

A second, or "behavioral," approach relies on third-person accounts focusing on "perspective-taking," and assumes that the ability to read minds—based on having a "theory of mind"—is not just an abstract idea or theoretical possibility, but a human reality and requisite condition of empathy. Goleman's thoughts about perspective-taking appear to belong in this box.

In the third, or "functional" approach (the one most likely associated with Iacoboni's "magical connection" and Gallese's "embodied simulation"), empathic behaviors are related to the functions of various neural systems. This includes the functions of the mirror neuron system and possibly those of some neurotransmitters, such as oxytocin.

A Neo-Darwinian evolutionary approach fills the fourth box, and like de Waal, envisions empathy as the product of a dialectic that intertwines the evolution of neural systems and social systems.

Four boxes are required, say the wizards, and if we understand what lies inside their claims, then empathy is as elastic as ever—a phenomenon related to self-identity, and a behavior involving mind reading, and a function of particular neural systems, and an evolution of entangled neural and social systems. With one hodgepodge still whirling in front of us, we seem to be staring into another—and neither identifies a core.

Sure enough, we soon spot the typology's labels caught up in the currents, their emphatic colors clearly visible, adding what they will to empathy's churn. But their block letters, once boldly precise, are now too dizzied to specify what the typology signifies. We cannot see if its four approaches are meant to branch from one central trunk or if they are rooted in different grounds, each nurturing another kind of tree. Empathy spins and will not follow arboreal lines of inquiry; nor will it yield to any chronological lines that might lead to one cause, one source, one core.

Stepping closer to this devilish wind devil, we catch details in its flickering debris and notice the terms tossed about—words like "connection," "compassion," "concern," and "understanding" perennially flying around empathy. Perhaps their meanings and derivations offer some clues, and their etymological lines trace from roots tangled in empathy's essence. Or perhaps these are rhizomic lines, the cross-connecting ligatures that hold empathy together. Either way, we are encouraged to find that different dictionaries appear to agree on the subject of lineage.

So, we trust the consensus telling us that the word "connection" comes from the Old French, "connexion" (or "connexionen" in Latin) and traces from the Latin, "connectere," meaning "to fasten together, to tie, to join together." Referring to a "close union," a "binding together" in today's usage, "connection," we see, remains true to its roots, "con" (together), and "nectere," or "nexis" (combined).

"Compassion," we are told, is also from Old French and Latin ("compassionem") and also seems straightforward—its roots "com" (together), and "pati" (to suffer), appearing again and again, still sustaining definitions such as "suffering together with another," "participation in suffering," "sympathy," "fellow-feeling," "feeling pity," and the "desire to relieve suffering." And "concern," we notice, is a Middle English word, but traces from Old French and Latin to "concernere," meaning "to sift together, to mingle."

From this point, though, the path appears to be a convoluted one. Despite sharing a root with "connection" and "compassion," "concern" runs astray, abandoning any ideas of "togetherness," (sifted, mingled, or otherwise), while acquiring meanings more ponderous and orientations more individualistic. Today, we find definitions such as "a matter that relates to or affects one," "regard for or interest in someone," and "an uneasy or troubled state of mind." Turning to "understanding," we find a word lacking French or Latin roots altogether. From the Old English "understanden"— when "under" meant "between" or "among," rather than "beneath"—we find that the word we use today reflects some, but not all, of its roots. Dictionaries tell us that "understanding," defined as the "faculty of comprehension, reasoning," traces from roots meaning "comprehend, grasp the idea of" and "stand in the midst of." We are caught, indeed, standing between and among— "in the midst of"—etymological lines that may kink or snag, yet spiral smoothly around empathy's invisible center.

And what of empathy's own etymology—the one it appears to share with compassion's synonym, "sympathy"? What the dictionaries will confirm for us is that the English word "em-path-y" was only invented a century ago, while its older cousin, "sym-path-y" has been in use for many more. We are told that the root they share is derived from the Greek "pathos," meaning "feeling," and that "empathy" was coined to mean "feeling in, or into," while "sympathy" long ago captured a sense of "feeling with, feeling together." Today, the dictionaries fall silent, refusing to distinguish the two terms any further. The dust of confusion flies up, clouding the tiny tornado and any ideas we might have of unwinding its tightly twisted lines.

Again we step back, this time knowing the spinning will not stop—only further entangling empathy in the knots and loops of "feeling together," "joining together," "suffering together," "sifting together." We are left with this "entanglement"—this "confused medley" or "circumstance that confuses or complicates," something so "interlaced" that "a separation cannot be easily made." Driving home the point, the Oxford English Dictionary tells the story of entanglement's Swedish origin, "to disorder," illustrated by the image of a boat trapped in shallow water, the oar caught in the seaweed. Though we cannot see how empathy would play either the oar or the seaweed, we know it leaves us stranded, staring at the shore so near, yet so far. No, empathy cannot follow the lines, not even the lines of its own script.

So, it is not easy discovering what makes empathy *empathy*. Perhaps the project requires a nonlinear approach, one daring us to visualize empathy's essence (*What color might it be? What form might it take?*)—an impatient approach expecting us to snatch glimpses of its character in our vast stores of images (*How might empathy be unmasked? On whose face might it appear?*). Such an approach puts its trust in images of the interior world, knowing their vivid wisdom always informs images of the exterior. Our challenge is to make an unconscious process conscious; to develop a visual literacy that pushes us to read the body maps we use to picture both worlds. We are also charged with opening channels that will ensure a smooth and steady flow of the inner structures or "schemas" we use to make sense of the abstract and the idiomatic—what surely must include empathy.

Such are the demands; but even if we should agree to master—trust—this imagistic approach, there are no guarantees that empathy will be revealed in all of its guises. And we may be unable or unwilling to understand how our corporeal and perceptual experiences build the recurring structures of internal images—the very ones commanding our interpretations of the external images that (mis)represent what we see of the world. Still, we will respond to their visual cues—the bewitching stardust they toss into empathy's swirl. And we just might recognize empathy on a city street splashed by mud puddles or in a verdant valley devastated by war and flood. Maybe we will acknowledge its presence in a New Testament parable, a humble pair of shoes, or a crinkly tangle of yarn. We may see how images stretch with empathy, accommodating its reach across self and other to affirm one in the other. Empathy whirls around us, scattering our images in all directions. We just might gather up a few.

Perhaps you would be interested, as was I, in my students' unflinching efforts to capture empathy, put it down on paper in what could be called "analog drawings." Such drawings rely not on graphic symbols and their neat, agreed-upon meanings, but on messy, sometimes meandering scratches and squiggles that are always raw—and quivering with ideas of their own. In pen and pencil, chalk and crayon, this group of prospective art teachers tapped into a hidden reservoir of maps and schemas to call empathy from the depths—and make it concrete, if only in an abstract sense. Drawing quickly, easily, they seemed to know their task was to reveal what already existed—obliging empathy's demand to be presented in smears of red and blue or streaks of blue and orange. Several drawings suggest that empathy blends the reds and blues to show its true colors in the shades of lavender that result. Several more begin with color opposites and situate empathy in strips of blue on one side of the sheet, orange on the other, both sides sending out the squiggly lines of an energy that seeks to radiate across a neutral center. Empathy is also caught in a couple of mirror images, symmetrical drawings that were folded over to show a tangle of chalky lines reflected in the shadowy print of another. One drawing offers up a set of crisp horizontal lines stretching across the paper's center to wrap around two circles that could be the rollers of a conveyor belt delivering empathy as a continuous loop. Another drawing is a portrait giving empathy the face of an expressionless clown, while the last depicts empathy as octopus tentacles, some twining together on the page, others drifting apart.

An eclectic collection, to be sure, the drawings pledge their sincerity to yet another hodgepodge, this one perhaps more colorful than the others already confronting us. Like the scientists, psychologists, and etymologists before them, the students describe attributes of an accomplished empathy able to blend, radiate, mirror, loop, and intertwine, but unable to take on more than one of these roles at a time. Still, the collection scripts a unifying paradox meant to persuade us that empathy orders a chaotic snarl by doubling it, while its uncanny clown maneuvers us into the bittersweet, where we wriggle between a smile and a frown.

Exploring each other's drawings, students saw no irony, even as their words floated up to explain and to reinforce the paradoxical *mélange*. Empathy, to some, is "uplifting," when to others, it involves "low self-esteem" and "sadness." Some said empathy is about "value, but not necessarily validation," clarifying this to mean "having value" or "being valued" but not "validated." It is about "enlightenment," "freedom," and a "generosity of spirit," one group declared, while another was equally convinced of empathy's penchant for "weakness" and "sense of unaccomplishment"—an invented term whose meaning they believed requires no clarification. Students also spoke of "unity" and "the communal," of "giving and receiving," and a "balance of emotions." Empathy means "I feel you," some said, when to others it promises "support, comfort" and "being alongside." No one spoke of the paradox connecting words and images or questioned the spinning in the room. All accepted empathy as the maelstrom it appears to be.

Their oars free of entangling seaweed, the students paddled on, but unlike them, we are caught in a whirlpool on the high seas. Scanning the open sky, we search for new images to navigate by—

the brightest ones that could light the way out of our spin and fill the void between the black and white of empathy's "freedom" and "low self-esteem," its "enlightenment" and "weakness," "value" and "validation," "giving" and "receiving." We cannot be sucked into empathy's Bermuda Triangle, lost in the turquoise mystery of a "generosity of spirit," "balance of emotions," and "sense of unaccomplishment." Empathy is relentless, but will release us, we feel certain, once the luminous images set a course taking us beyond the lavender of red and blue collaborators or the no-man's-land between adversaries cloaked in blue and orange.

On this voyage, empathy's face could reappear, rendered not in the blank makeup of a clown this time, but among the wise wrinkles of a patient grandmother, say, or in the misery of her granddaughter, a ten-year old tomboy seated beside her. We would see that empathy's looping conveyor belt has been replaced by the neat, interlocking loops of the grandmother's knitting, her busy needles working rhythmically, taking up the soft pink yarn that grows into a perfect baby sweater before our very eyes. We would also notice how relaxed she is, serene even, enjoying this sunny afternoon, while the granddaughter squirms and struggles with a pair of brand new number eight needles, jabbing and poking at the snarled yellow yarn meant to feed her sad practice square.

So pleased and proud to teach her grandchild, the grandmother receives more than she gives, but the child feels ashamed and overwhelmed by her own "sense of unaccomplishment" and the wretched hole that appears in the square. Perhaps this is what a "balance of emotions" looks like, this empathy on my grandmother's couch that summer day so long ago. Now, I see her "generosity of spirit" as she leans over and, without a word, rips out my rows of frustration—erasing the hole and restoring order to the chaotic loops. Sailing through the Triangle, I received more than she gave.

A painting lights the sky and steers us into the next scene of this story—what appears to be a timeless one transcending first- and third-person accounts and carrying us into a kind of "narrative empathy" where we imagine ourselves within the chapters and identify with the characters, inhabit their roles. This story means "I feel you" and promises "support," "comfort," and "being alongside"—a promise kept by Jean-Francois Millet's *The Knitting Lesson*, painted a century and a half before my students' wisdom filled the classroom, a century before Grandma's generosity schooled my clumsy needles.

Millet tells of yet another young girl's search for affirmation—validation—in the snarling yarn. She could be Henriette, one of his younger sisters, who is seated alongside an older sister, possibly Millet's beloved Emilie. The two wear the blue of their native Normandy and work in the gathering dusk of the family's rough-plastered farmhouse, where we are drawn to Henriette's face, brightened only by the light of the fire in the great hearth.

We see how intense she is, even fierce, holding the knitting close, staring into her moment of vindication when the needles will begin again—working rhythmically this time—and determined to banish the memories of an errant stitch and so many ripped-out rows now tangled in the pink crinkly yarn piled in her lap. In this moment, Emilie turns from her sewing to reach for her young charge, nearly upsetting the basket on her own lap. We feel her, the teacher whose calling is to support, and share her instinct to oversee the redemption so critical to the lesson. But we also identify with Henriette, who must free herself of the tangles. Tied up in their knots, we search for ourselves, but Millet leaves us on empathy's edge, looping between accomplishment and unaccomplishment.

Paintings shine with stories that guide us into an empathy the students' analogs did not. Less roiling, perhaps, this empathy is more demanding and presents us with the rigors of running a tight ship. We must clear the shallows choked with tangles and tentacles and set sail for the deep unknown, well beyond the faintest beacon of mirror neurons signaling us to resonate with others. We must prepare for rough weather ahead, brace for a plunging bow that slices the spray, smashes the chop, and finally delivers us to the open water, where imagination takes over as empathy's first mate. Though we are still woozy, hurling over the rail, neither officer shows any mercy—and both order us to work inside, where we are to search our souls, plunge deep into self-reflection's honesty. We will only be permitted to reappear on deck, they bark, once our self-awareness and personal insight are well-developed. As the captain insists, insight and imagination are what equip us to interact with others, what allow us to project ourselves into their stories and wonder about the circumstances of their own journeys. *Where have they come from, and where are they going? What has life been like along the way? What will their tomorrow bring?* Aye, aye, cap'n, we mutter, as we are dismissed, banished to the darkness inside, where we can only grope and are bound to stumble on the journey within.

Still, wonder and imagination chart the course—the one that, in psychiatrist Jody Halpern's view, defines empathy as "a spark of natural curiosity" which prompts "a need for further understanding and deeper questioning." To keep this spark alive, along with Hoffman's "spark of human concern," we must begin by questioning ourselves and, as Goleman says, by bringing intelligence to our own emotions so that we might regulate ourselves and understand the emotional lives of others. But we are blind, we whine, hardly able to focus on a flickering spark. Comforted only by the glow of the smartphone's screen, we return to the tweets and texts, the satellite signals and Facebook posts that light our way. Running up the red flag, Goleman warns that people who lack self-awareness also lack imagination. Their myopia can leave them foundering on the rocks with the personalities of Mr. Spock and Data. The danger approaches, but in our bleary fog, we will focus on *Star Trek* fantasies playing on Netflix instead.

Narrative empathy returns to take control, and, ordering us to come about, we head into the winds of a different story. This one seems curious, telling about a thirty-year voyage of self-discovery and homecoming prompted by a painting's deepest questions. Empathy rekindles the spark, and now we must have more—chapters and chapters about what we learn was Henry Nouwen's encounter with Rembrandt's *The Return of the Prodigal Son,* painted in 1669. Ah yes, we are curious about the Dutch painting and the Dutch professor-turned-pastor; made to wonder about Rembrandt's probe of the parable and Nouwen's search for a safe haven, the lasting home for his weary soul. We agree to lose ourselves in the story's details, inside the triad of characters glowing in the painting's divine light, where Nouwen would eventually find his calling.

We too notice the father, old and bent, but wearing a sumptuous red cloak and a small smile, his arthritic hands clasping the exhausted prodigal dressed only in humble homespun and a broken sandal. This is the younger son who kneels to lay the shame of a shaven head against the forgiveness in the father's welcome. We are well aware that Rembrandt inserts a third figure into the light, the older son who also wears the crimson cloak but stands stiffly in the back, clasping his own hands—the darkness in his eyes piercing the spectacle in front of him. We know he is the dutiful one who stayed home, working long and hard without reward—not so much as a single goat— while the squandering nomad is celebrated with the family's fatted calf. Rembrandt gives no clues about the setting, allowing this story to unfold anywhere. But we know we are somewhere, stuck in another of empathy's triangles—and feeling the terrible tension among resentment, repentance, and redemption. But this tension is what released Nouwen and revealed the reconciliation that brought him home—and into the L'Arche community, where he works with disabled adults.

Again, narrative empathy calls out and, again, directs us to wonder, to test our imagination and self-awareness in yet another story rooted in homecoming. Heidegger takes over here, challenging us to imagine a protagonist, the unseen wearer of the old work shoes presented in Van Gogh's 1887 painting *A Pair of Shoes*. We look closely at these shoes, take in the certainty of their laces and the hob-nailed sole of the one upturned—what we sense gives the two a quiet dignity and their "truth of being." But we cannot see the ghost who put them on and stood to receive their gifts. Our story remains untold, while Heidegger's, we learn, begins and ends with a farm laborer—the peasant woman—in whose world the shoes "find protection." She is "certain of her world," even as she stands in the muddy divide between its natural and (agri)cultural hemispheres.

Heidegger hears the grand narrative she articulates and uses its eloquence to (mis)represent the certainty of ours. Looking beyond what we took as visual cues, he elaborates further, "From out of the dark opening of the well-worn insides of the shoes the toil of the worker's tread stares forth . . . The shoes vibrate with the silent call of the earth, its silent gift of the ripening grain, its unexplained self-refusal in the wintry field . . ." The woman worker is at home in the field; she stands in the shoes that stand for us, harvesting the grain for the bread of an urban world. We are deaf to what she hears and must labor that much longer to renew ourselves—that much harder to find our truth of being and a lasting home in the human community.

For all that he envisions, Heidegger sees little of Van Gogh himself—the other ghost in the painting's narrative—who, we learn, was another wearer of the shoes. Now, we are the ones to take over. We can picture the artist haunting the stalls of a Paris flea market, where he is said to have purchased the shoes. He stops to hear their call, and, looking past their polished outsides, stares into the "well-worn insides" that reclaim his own story. Perhaps the vibration of the shoes lifts him out of the city's unhappy bustle and roots him in the Dutch countryside where he once lived among the peasants—his fellow potato eaters— who seek the certainty of a lasting home on land reclaimed from the sea. We understand why the shoes send the dislocated painter into a Paris downpour stomping through muddy streets to execute his solemn oath to restore their dignity, recover the truth of their being—this, after another unseen character in the story has stripped their soles of the earth's protection, shining the shoes for an alien world. Empathy flares and dares Vincent— us—to wonder about the circumstances of the shoes' demise. Who was the one to wipe away the "wintry field" or the last to stand in Heidegger's story? We might imagine an anonymous farmer, but empathy demands more—a scene, perhaps, situating the life of an old man, leathery in the sun despite his straw hat, who coughs and is easily winded now but faithfully tills the rich bottom land of the Marne River Valley, still pledging its ripening wheat to the hungry capital nearby.

Perhaps it was not a farmer at all but a Marne quarrier whose calloused hands grip first the pick, then the shovel to open the black earth forced to give up the last of the burr stone coveted by the miller's wheel, what was needed to grind the whitest flour for the Parisian baguettes. Van Gogh splashes, and urban mud puddles do what they can to settle him, but he is certain their world is not his. We might imagine the shoes accompanying him to Provence, where in the last chapter of the story, they return to their protection—and he reconnects with the sweat of the peasants and the certainty of labor in the rolling fields.

The shoes may be gone but vibrate still, and what began with Heidegger does not end with Van Gogh. Perhaps it is their soles, unwavering in their grip of the earth, that call us back— return us to the Marne, where an unlikely character emerges to take up the story. This latest protagonist—a sailor serving with the American Expeditionary Forces far from home—is certain of this chapter and does not apologize for its irony. It opens in December of 1918, just weeks after the armistice ending World War I was signed at Versailles, and he is on leave, riding a train though the valley once known for the whisper of its wheat fields, and now, for the hiss of its battlefields. Though its earth lies moaning, gashed open by too many bombardments and trenches, too much machine gun fire and too many graves, the young man hears only its silent call.

Gazing out his window, he takes note of the river, no longer silvery and serpentine, but flooded with anger and mud, and its imperative to smother the remains of the German Army's "barb-wire entanglements" still defacing the valley floor. Yet, he looks beyond the Great War and peers into a scene greater still that recalls his roots in the American Midwest, capturing a life of uncertainty on the Missouri dirt farm where he grew up. In front of him now, all he can see is the French farmers returning to plow the gentle slopes, their freshly turned plots creating a "checkerboard effect" and readying the wintry field for its most unexpected self-renewal yet. Sharing his story in a letter home, the sailor—who would become a New York attorney and the grandfather I remember—declared this to be "the prettiest valley [he] had ever seen." What he leaves us all is an approach to defining empathy—an imagistic, if ironic one, like Van Gogh's and Heidegger's, Nouwen's and Rembrandt's, Millet's and my students' that finds the lines and traces them into an empathy spinning around certainty and uncertainty.

The winds of empathy rise, composing the music that howls and whistles on the dance floor where Certainty and Uncertainty are locked together in an unending tango. Certainty is aggressive and tries to lead, but Uncertainty appears to be the one more practiced and executes the steps with surprising skill and precision. Still, the two dance toe to toe, ever fierce and so focused on countering each other's moves that they are unaware of the other pairs on the floor. Their passion fascinates us, and we watch wide-eyed as Certainty and Uncertainty seize the night, swooping, sweating—and stealing the scene from those who came to waltz. We will not turn away, even as our star performers crush a couple necking in the corner, leaving the two known as "Self" and "Other" shattered and barely recognizable on the floor.

The music screeches its protest, but Certainty and Uncertainty do not miss a beat. They are the furious ones, and in their oblivion, circle even wider—as if to secure their imperial reign at the ball. In no time at all, the pernicious pair crumples a couple of fox trotters called "Self-preservation" and "Self-sacrifice," reigniting their bickering and driving them further apart. Worried about the fallen, a Good Samaritan steps from our midst, only to be swept aside by the tango's *tour de force*. No, the star-crossed bullies will not be other-oriented nor heed Empathy's calls for fairness and justice on the dance floor. Now, they stomp on a pair of theories, scattering the debris of two schools of psychology across the room. Again they strut, unconcerned with the chaos left in their wake. Spinning free of Empathy's whine, Certainty and Uncertainty know full well what they can inflict upon us. Yes, they have been around and around together many times before.

Queasy now, we have seen enough and whimper for Certainty to save us—to be the one to rewrite the scene. *Please banish Uncertainty from the realm*, we beg, *and teach us the lullabies that will hush Empathy's unsettling screams.* What we imagine and hunger for is pristine, a gala shining with order and civility. We have faith and believe mightily that Certainty will prevail—oh, but it must become the authority we can count on to give us the confidence we need and the answers we want to our most vexing questions about the meaning of selfhood and personal responsibility. Faith alone persuades us that Certainty's unmeasured strength will lift the mysterious burden of otherness from our shoulders. We are more and more convinced of Certainty's fine-tuned precision that will balance our need for self-preservation against Empathy's demand for self-sacrifice.

Certainty is noble, pure, and so righteous that we know it must be our miracle worker—the one to bring the light to human conflict and finally resolve ancient tensions between the individual and the collective that strain us so. This is the belief we hold sacred and why we will always look to Certainty for our truths, why we trust it to choose the psychology, the philosophy that defines our empathies. Most of all, we look to the day, the moment, when Certainty will dance with us in a world soothed by the music of rules that tell us what is fair and just and how to behave accordingly. Then we will know what is right—and what is not.

Touched by our devotion, Certainty rises and, in an instant, commands the pulpit. Steely eyed, Certainty looks our eager congregation in the face and promises to save the world for us—but only if we sit through a sermon on that most important rule of all, the golden one ordering us to treat others the way we ourselves expect to be treated. Wagging a finger now, Certainty translates, "This means you must *be nice*." Then we hear the pedantic preacher's call, "Say it with me now," and know our response should be a resounding one. But all we can manage is a tentative nod.

Resolute, Certainty launches into a description of the Silver Rule, warning us away from what we ought not do. Raising a fist—as if to punch the sterling phrase higher still—Certainty booms, "Don't treat others in ways you would not want to be treated." The call comes—*Don't be nasty*—but this time, we will only slump in our seats and roll our eyes, like the surly adolescents Certainty believes we are. Gold or silver, it is clear that our preacher expects us to abide by these rules of reciprocity and, of course, we know we should always behave ethically. But in the face of so much nastiness—violence and betrayal, prejudice and greed—we also know it is not so easy to be nice.

Certainty slams a fist on the podium and continues to rail, "This is a universal code of ethics—an ancient one at that. If you people ever want to waltz in a well-ordered, twenty-four-carat world, then it is about time you practiced it." The breathless diatribe grows shriller, less convincing. "This is the code that arose among the earliest civilizations—in China, India, Greece, Judea—the one adopted long ago by the great religions— Confucianism, Taoism, Buddhism, Hinduism. Why, the Hebrew verse, *love thy neighbor as thyself*, appeared as early as 1300 BC, and the English phrasing of the Golden Rule appeared in 1567." Panting now, Certainty seems desperate, anxious—well aware that Uncertainty sits in the back. Uncertainty will usher us out now and return us to the known world, long tarnished and still spinning between the grit of what is and the gold of what ought to be.

We turn to leave, but the winds of Empathy snarl and bang at the windows, unnerving us so that we stumble in the aisle. When the front doors slam shut, we know we are trapped between Certainty and Uncertainty once again. Certainty seizes the opportunity and tries to stabilize us with a fact-filled lecture about the psychologists who translate the Golden Rule to mean *empathizing with others*. Mildly curious, we wriggle from Uncertainty's grasp to hear about "empathic behavior" that is moral and just and explained by Daniel Batson's "empathy-altruism hypothesis."

As if taking over himself, Batson preaches that people do not simply mirror behaviors but will stand up to *help* if they have feelings of "empathic concern" for others. Chiming in, Certainty declares, "They will help, whether or not they stand to gain from their actions."

"So, there is no expectation of reward?" we ask.

"Only the hope that others would do the same for them," Certainty confirms.

Restless, Uncertainty breaks in. "Where does 'empathic concern' come from? And why aren't such feelings distributed more equitably?"

But Certainty, ever masterful, deflects the question and directs us to the Good Samaritans who act out of compassion to alleviate the suffering of others. Still, we feel Uncertainty's breath on our necks and rise to challenge the assumption that selfless "other-oriented" behavior is soaked in a soul-crushing empathy of pain, suffering, and vulnerability. "If we should act to help the sufferer, are we vulnerable to this empathic darkness?"

Uncertainty glares at the podium and hisses, "Tell them—or I will."

Certainty sighs and then shouts over the howling winds, "Empathy does not require pain and suffering!"

Uncertainty snorts, "Nor does it always lead to altruism—tell them."

Certainty gazes off and says stiffly, "There are different theories that explain—"

But Uncertainty surges ahead, interrupting and screaming, "And their credibility?"

Head bowed, Certainty sighs again and mumbles, "We cannot be sure." We glance at the front, at the back, longing to share but a moment of grace, an easy, guilt-free smile. We wonder if a more luminous Empathy might ever brighten our sanctuary.

Too late, we realize that Certainty and Uncertainty are hell-bent on reenacting the nasty debate among nice psychologists who fire missiles at each other. We can only dive into the naked neutrality under our seats, shielding our eyes as theories white-hot with controversy explode around us. Fallout on the floor glows with plutonium's half-life that will fuel their assumptions about what motivates human behavior for years to come. Though warheads whistle overhead, it is Certainty's sudden reversal, loud and cynical, that we find frightening—and more penetrating.

"Altruism does not exist," Certainty blasts. "People will give aid and comfort to others only when the benefits of doing so outweigh the costs." We choke on the tirade's radioactivity, but Certainty spews more, "Giving does not speak of empathy. No, giving says more about—and I'm quoting here—'the redemption of the giver and less about the liberation of the receiver.' No, you will not give freely of yourselves." Our one-time preacher's sentiments are clear, but we are bewildered by this abrupt abandonment of Batson's hypothesis and quick embrace of the enemy's "social-exchange" theory.

As a zealous convert, Certainty condemns us now, calling us "calculating," self-interested creatures ruled by the question, *What's in it for me?* Apparently, we are beings who look for rewards after all, or at the very least, reciprocity.

Brows furrowed like our own, Uncertainty is now the one to point a pedantic finger. "Isn't that what you told them to do—live by the tit for tat of the Golden Rule? An eye for an eye, tooth for a tooth?"

Purple faced, Certainty looks down at the pages and pages of notes lying in shreds and in frustration, flings them into the toxic haze. We feel the convert's stinging humiliation, and though it is not in our best interest to do so, we crawl out into the open to rebuild the broken pulpit. Batson, unfazed by it all, steps forward to affirm that people will act out of concern and "a true interest in the well-being of others."

Certainty seems not to hear and, gripping the podium once again, stands before us, tall, composed, and eager to issue a new proclamation—what must come quickly before Uncertainty can poke the irascible self-sacrifice/self-preservation conundrum again. Throat cleared, Certainty launches the edict, "Human motivation may or may not explain empathic behavior, but human *development* definitely structures it—along with sympathetic responses, I might add."

We are wary now and take cover, as Certainty has lobbed another missile into the fray, this one carrying the controversy of Martin Hoffman's developmental theory. Hoffman, we learn, delivers a different punch—an explanation powered by the assumption that empathy and sympathy are not only closely related but also hierarchically arranged.

Uncertainty fires back immediately, "What distinguishes sympathy from empathy?"

Impatient, Certainty barks, "Remember the roots—'sym/pathos,' meaning 'feeling with,' versus 'em/pathos,' meaning 'feeling into.' "

"Yes, but how is the Greek translated into the language of behavior?" comes the follow-up strike.

Fingers drumming now, our lecturer is even more condescending, saying, "Look to the definitions," and before

Uncertainty can ask, "Which ones?" Certainty rattles off, "Sympathy is 'the capacity for sharing the feelings and interests of another,' and empathy involves 'identifying with the thoughts and feelings of another.'" Like Uncertainty, we are left pondering the differences, semantic and behavioral, even as Certainty presses on, saying, "Hoffman recognizes empathy only as a *precursor* to sympathy, one that is necessary but less cognitively and morally demanding, and thus, lower ranked on the hierarchy of human development he envisions."

Safe under our seats, we prepare for Uncertainty's barrage, what will surely be a furious interrogation aimed at piercing the blur of a hierarchical vision. Still, we flinch as the questions fly: "Isn't it true that identifying with another—even a character in a painting or novel—and seeing through their eyes, feeling what they feel, speaks only of empathy—with no mention of sympathy?" Certainty's face reddens, but Uncertainty is relentless. "And isn't it also true that empathy does not necessarily lead to a sympathetic response? Just as sympathy does not necessarily begin with empathic concern?"

Wheezing now, Certainty is ashen, with eyes as dull as Uncertainty's are sharp. "Is it more demanding to share the Hallmark sentiments of a sympathy card with a bereaved widower than to identify with his grief—to feel the knife of sorrow and loneliness that cuts to the quick? And is it—"

But Certainty gasps, "Enough," and falls to the floor crying, "You've made your point." Psychology's war has taken its toll. We are exhausted and so numb that we cannot feel *with* or *into* anyone. In this air unfit to breathe, we will not revive Certainty.

Uncertainty is the one to identify with Certainty's plight; the one willing to share the pain of confusion so familiar. Though Certainty is still dazed, the hand Uncertainty extends is clear, along with the realization that survival depends on the close working relationship the two must forge. They exchange a knowing look and agree that Certainty can speak with authority, but only about the uncertainty of a world littered with competing interests and tarnished truths. Uncertainty can become an eloquent orator speaking only of the certainty that life's journey will be a convoluted one made messier by a world spinning with the meaning of ambiguity, contradiction, and complexity. Together, the pair must find the way forward, a path less treacherous that takes them and delivers us into the existential quiet of a gladiator-free arena where selves are neither sacrificed nor preserved.

This is the place to encounter the philosophers who believe the Golden Rule means treating strangers as neighbors, others as second selves. Here, the neuroscientists will greet us as well and offer their assurances that we will find not missiles but mirror neurons firing—each magical cell exploding with possibilities that can take us from the body of the first self into the body of the second, and from that body, into the mind of this other self. When Certainty and Uncertainty check us into the arena filled with neighborly strangers, we will find it made of earth and concrete, as well as crabgrass and broken glass; a place situated within the clatter of the practical world where lives are lived and in which possibilities are grounded. We must stand in this world and hope to find our protection in its muddiness.

So, we put on Van Gogh's shoes and prepare to walk across the great wintry field. Certainty and Uncertainty will accompany us, as always, and with every step, pepper us with questions about what it would mean to stand, or walk, or even dance in each other's shoes. "Remember," they warn, "survival depends on finding your unexpected self-renewal in the self-renewal of the other."

Empathy is meant to stare from the dark opening of the shoes, and yet it is not the vibration of another's tread we feel but our own pinched toes and blistered heels. What if the shoes of the other hurt more than our own? Still, Heidegger's field beckons, and joining the procession, we are hypervigilant, ever in search of comfort, the right fit for marching with—in—the soles of others. But there is so much footwear to size up, we whine, a thousand pairs to try on—some canvas, others calfskin, or alligator, ostrich, *peau de soie*, patent, and suede, shoes that are hob-nailed, high-topped, wing-tipped, open-toed, steel-toed, stiletto-heeled. We notice the pairs that are beat up and spiffed up, the ones branded Nike, Gucci, Oxford, and Ugg that slip on, strap on, lace up, buckle up, and zip. There are the storytellers—

the flip-flops and Florsheims, penny loafers and pumps—that take us to school and work; the broken sandal that brings us back home. We also recognize the ballet slippers and our *pas de deux* yet to be danced, the combat boots trained to approach the other as the enemy. They are signifiers all, flashing the wearer's identity up and down the ranks, but sharing none of it with a second self.

Through all of this, where is Empathy, knifing through us, its windy churn cold, shrill, and too exasperated to feel for us much longer? Will we catch the Iraqi sandals flying about a Baghdad square struck by yet another bomb blast? Or pay attention only to the Toms shoes flying off the shelves in yet another retail outlet—sales that put shoes on the feet of others with every pair we buy for ourselves? Are these the comfortable shoes we have been looking for? The ones that let us believe we walk with the Ethiopian mother through parasite-infested mud to wash clothes at the river's edge and pretend we accompany the Argentine child to school now that she wears the required shoes? What shall we take from our great march but that shoes fit all of us and none of us—and ground Empathy's rule-bound stories of a silver self and golden other in the need for redemption?

It is affirmation we seek, and Empathy is more concerned than ever that our need for redemption will remain ungratified. Still, the winds die down, and Empathy tries again, this time whispering of a different story—the one told by Les Christensen's contemporary sculpture, what we see in a monumental pair of wooden wings whose delicate feathers are defined and detailed by hundreds and hundreds of pointy-toed shoes, their "run-down" soles turned outward to confront us with the march of those who have gone before. Dirty, worn, the soles of the unseen wearers give us the proof we need that our shoes will execute their daily pledge to connect us to the earthly world, even as they protect us from the concrete and broken glass—and lift us beyond its noisy call. It is the soles we must have to show us where we stand and what we might reach for. They create the space for us to imagine there is something kinder, more authentic, even transcendental still to be encountered. They position us to discover the courage we need to stomp down our fear of otherness in the world we know and in the one we do not. We read Christensen's title *Why Should I Walk if I Have Wings to Fly?* But before we can respond, Empathy's impatient winds howl with questions of their own: "Will you walk with these wearers? Dare to feel the pinch of their toes? Or go forward carrying their stories in your souls?" We blink, but Empathy is relentless: "On whose wings will your dreams be carried?" We are tired of walking and tired of braving the wind chill of an Empathy that expects so much yet spins our heads with conflicting demands. This Empathy is not the wise, compass-carrying pathfinder we need, but a stormy, contrary presence that confuses us and then watches as we stumble. And for what? All we can expect in return are endless opportunities to further refine our sense of unaccomplishment and play the mug's game with greater skill. No matter the approach—and we have tried them all: phenomenological, behavioral, functional, etymological, imagistic—Empathy will not be revealed as our affirming mentor nor speak definitively of its own essence or intentions for us.

On our own, we have discovered little but the rancor of contradictory claims that appear to blacken the tornado's core. Some would have us believe that Empathy's force is strengthened by an ancient rule still too difficult to apply. Others argue about its spark, the synaptic arc that fires the neurons telling us to cooperate, even as other neurons drive us to compete. Still other claims envision the spark flickering with curiosity meant to prompt questions about other human beings—the very interrogation that begs the larger question about protecting ourselves. In this darkness, we wonder if Empathy's sputtering spark is but a pinprick of light offered up to the vagaries of human concern. There is also the hypocrisy of an Empathy all too certain of its altruism and compassion while its tentacles entangle us in guilt and suffocate us with our own cynicism. Ready to escape the rocky, exasperating conditions on the ground, we look beyond Empathy's turbulence to the sleek, silver wings of a Boeing 777 or Airbus A380 that will carry us into the clouds.

Buckled up, we settle back, and upon leveling off at ten thousand feet, we put on the noise-canceling headphones we hope will block Empathy's frantic attempts to get us to listen to the music of its new claims—what sounds like polyphonic promises to build our capacity for understanding others. But we have heard this overture many times before and immediately switch to another, more entertaining track. Empathy finds us and tries a different approach, this one meant to appeal to our pragmatic nature and promising to tame the tornado—unravel its impossible mystery by revealing what it purports to do for us—all that it makes possible in our world. Unimpressed, we flip through the in-flight magazine, glance at the safety instructions card, but Empathy will not be ignored. As we fill in the first squares of the magazine's crossword puzzle, the persistent whirl of Empathy gives up its gifts.

Like gusts of air blasting from the vent above our heads, they stream into our laps and spill into the aisles—mysterious puffs packaged in the simple practicality of brown paper and clearly marked "language," "culture," "the arts," "meaning," "context," "trust," "intent," "thought," "emotion," "theory of mind," "world of objects," and "world of others." With no room to stow any under the seat or in the overhead bin, we do what we can to stack and juggle the inconvenient gifts. When the captain turns off the seatbelt sign, we know we will not be free to move about the cabin. No, we are trapped with an Empathy bent on bringing us back to earth.

Our ears pop, and the pilot confirms that we have begun our descent and will be arriving at the gate shortly. Empathy has diverted the flight indeed. Just like that, we are beneath our precious clouds, left to circle the worn-out dreams only too familiar—what appears below in a few open fields and wooded lots soon to be swallowed up by the sprawl of cookie-cutter houses and suburban parking lots that give way themselves to the grid of anonymous city blocks and the gridlock of traffic choking every major thoroughfare. We could be landing anywhere (everywhere) disappointment spreads.

The flight attendant tells us where we can claim our baggage but says nothing about where we might reclaim ourselves. When she hands us customs declaration cards to complete, we know Empathy has something else in mind. The wheels touch down, and while the plane taxis, we struggle to zip bulging backpacks, stuff Empathy's outpouring into extra shopping bags—and stuff our feet into the pointy-toed shoes we are forced to wear. Just as the jet bridge is connected, Empathy takes the microphone and welcomes us to Hong Kong—but also to Johannesburg and Tokyo, to Nairobi and Sydney, and to London. Now, we are overwhelmed and so confused that we beg Empathy to come with us—help us negotiate the bustle of these international airports among the world's busiest.

But Empathy reassures us, says we are carrying all we will need. In protest, we point out that we have no pocket dictionaries and do not speak Mandarin or Cantonese, certainly not Afrikaans or Japanese or Swahili. "How are we supposed to make ourselves understood?" Empathy counters our panic with patience yet remains firm. "You must develop a fluency in the one language everyone understands." Still, we cry, "What about the cultural differences—how will we—" But Empathy insists, "You're going to be fine. Just remember to bear left when encountering others—and smile."

The airport world closes around us, and, in an instant, we are caught up in its rhythms. The sights and sounds, we realize, are repeated across the globe; the rituals and patterns are most familiar—and clearly understood. There we are, standing in long lines—queuing up to collect bags, to use the restroom, or check out of shops with our purchases of water, coffee, overpriced trinkets, and airport souvenirs. There we are too among the seekers gathered around the all-knowing board, clutching our boarding passes and searching for information about connecting flights. When the electronic letters spell out "Delayed," or worse, "Canceled," we droop in our collective despair just as we all brighten up when the board proclaims, "On Time." We recognize this place of placelessness where every one of us—those who get their bearings on the left and those who get them on the right—intends to be somewhere else. Sojourners all, we arrive as strangers from every corner of the earth and despite our disorienting jet lag, use our transitory togetherness to fashion a culture—shape the limbo we share. We master the language of oneness that is spoken here.

Our waystation creates a context, and in it we understand the meaning of the text written on the faces and in the bodies. It is as if we can read the thought balloons above the heads—proof, Empathy whispers, of the prevailing "theory of mind" that also builds our trust and makes the intentions behind our actions clear. So yes, we will step aside for the frantic traveler racing through crowded corridors because we know he still hopes to answer a final boarding call. We will feel for the parents camped in the waiting area, too exhausted themselves to console the baby who screams with the pain of ears clogged by too many takeoffs and landings. Happening upon the terminal's grand piano, we will pause to appreciate its resonance—take solace in the Beethoven, hum along with the Broadway tunes that flow from the effortless fingers of another wayfarer taking solace. We will catch ourselves when, distracted, we mistakenly—instinctively—bear to the right, nearly crashing into an oncoming stranger. Yet, the two of us will exchange smiles—one, a sheepish flash of embarrassment to say, "How silly of me, I forgot, so sorry," and the other a sign of reassurance offered to forgive a minor and unintended transgression. And how convenient for us that Empathy will gather up the brown paper that once covered its practical gifts.

Now, Empathy smiles, persuaded that we have graciously accepted its gifts and will build on their simplicity—use them to venture into the complexities of a wider world shaped not by shiny sights and sounds but by the life-giving rhythms of redemption and affirmation that beat with the possibility of finding our self-renewal in the self-renewal of others. In this world, the giddy Empathy imagines that we will give more than we receive. Exuberant, confident, this is the Empathy that believes we are ready at long last to take wing and dance—soar— as a group-living species sharing an earthly journey.

Surely, we will fly around the world with more than our airport etiquette to answer the call of others still struggling to get their bearings. Well aware that we have too often delayed, or even canceled such departures, Empathy is now certain that we will find our way and arrive on time—in time—to bring comfort and the gift of selflessness to those stuck in the limbo of a Congolese refugee camp, or trapped in the rubble of a Syrian city, or on a Filipino island ravaged by a typhoon. And it is true; there are some among us—the aid workers and Peace

Corps volunteers and doctors working without borders—who find Empathy's destinations on the board and rush off to their gates more than ready to embark on this mission. We know they must be Empathy's favorites, the reliable ones willing to spring victims from their traps and offer them care and a much-needed compass. But does Empathy realize that they are our surrogates—the very ones who absolve us of our guilt and allow us our cynicism? Does Empathy not see them tightening the jaws of inertia's selfish trap? We can only guess, but it seems clear that Empathy expects more of us—holds out hope that one day soon, we will find our own true north and be called to give . . . what? We cannot be certain.

Empathy sighs and stops dancing, forced now to launch yet another appeal, this one a campaign designed to blanket us with images, clear and concrete examples intended to show us what giving and receiving look like when they become so blurred that one cannot be distinguished from the other. And there on a video conference call, we see Jeanette, the Haitian bank teller, reconnected with her liberators some months after her six-day imprisonment in the earthquake's darkest dungeon. Jeanette thanks them again and again, these members of the Los Angeles-based Urban Search and Rescue team, and asks if there is anything she can do for them. They are grateful—elated—just to find her again, vibrant as ever, and to see for themselves that she is doing well in Miami, her bandaged hands healing after the amputation of her crushed fingers.

Then it comes to them. "Would you sing your song for us?"

"In French?" she asks.

But the melody, the lyrics just flow, and Jeanette sings as if drawing from a well deep within. It is clear, even to us, that she never lost her bearings. She is grateful for the gift of life, and understanding their need, graciously, she gives it back to the men of the USAR team. Her song fills us all with . . . "But wait," shouts Empathy, "There's more." We are directed to images of children who cannot yet read a compass but still know the way, their busy hands true, unwavering, reaching across great distances to clasp the hands of others. Of course, their gestures so earnest, their mission so noble, make us proud. It is gratifying indeed to learn of their empathy flights—one bound for Port au Prince, for instance, that took off from Los Angeles carrying local children's impulses to help Haitian children piecing a life together in the shattered weeks following the earthquake. On board were the ten- and eleven-year-olds' drawings and letters, candy, and a hand-drawn comic strip, some school supplies, and the $1,732.33 they had raised themselves.

In return, the Haitian kids—homeless, shoeless, attending a makeshift school under a tree—were determined to send what they could, which was all they had: a song, clear and heartfelt in its recording, pen pal letters written in their best English, and a toy car built of juice bottles they had salvaged from the ruins, its impressive working wheels made of bottlecaps. Like the fifth graders on the receiving end, we too unwrap this outpouring of creativity, ingenuity, and grace to reveal the gift of selflessness. How was it possible, we wonder, that the Haitians who had lost so much—an older brother, two sisters, a favorite cousin—could understand the American children and what they might like to receive? Again, Empathy sighs, but, this time, stares at us in utter disbelief. "And still, you demand explanations?"

Empathy is tense, agitated now; its notorious winds whipping up. "Look inside yourselves. Trust your impulses. Reach for your own ingenuity!" When, unpersuaded, we stare blankly, Empathy screeches, "Look deep in the marrow." But we are caught in the whirl once more—circling with our questions about the core still unresolved. We will ride the blustery carousel until we grab the answer still blowin' in the wind.

Chapter III

We Sing the Body Electric

Empathy's mystery begins in the body, say the scientists and poets, the philosophers and artists who search doggedly for clues in its sinewy birthplace. Detectives all, they find their evidence in the ebb and flow of the body's humors, in the black bile of its earthy gall bladder and yellow bile of its fiery spleen, in the phlegmatic water of its rational brain and airy courage of its deep-red blood. There is more to be gathered from its sweating skin and dancing limbs, hints offered by the ripple of its muscles, the gestures of its hands—and all they might hold. Magnifying glasses in hand, the dedicated detectives study the body's secrets and glean what they can from the many faces it wears and the many selves it constructs. Some probe cracks and fissures in its mind, others dig for the seat of its consciousness, so desperate are they to discover the precise constellation of brain cells—"neural correlates of consciousness" (NCC)—that will crack the case and explain the mystery of empathy's corporeal universe.

These are the detectives who follow the footprints, dust for fingerprints, and report what they have found thus far. Walt Whitman, for instance, sings of a body electric, one charged full with the "charge of the soul." Deleuze is convinced of the body's authenticity, what focuses his search for "the real." Nietzsche proclaims, "There is more reason in your body than in your best wisdom," while Damasio testifies that, "The mind is embodied, not just embrained." Filling her canvases with what the body feels, Frida Kahlo paints the "biological truth" of her sorrows and rage. Still, the case remains open, and Pert's mind-body search for the "Molecules of Emotions" goes on.

Empathy, for its part, would redirect the investigation altogether. Once again, the single-minded Empathy tells us all, detective and nondetective alike, to look deep in the marrow to discover its essence. And once again, we are unable—perhaps unwilling—to grasp the directive's metaphorical meaning, leaving us to comply only in the most literal sense. Indeed, a hip can be punctured, its white bone forced to give up a blood red sample of what lies at its core. In exchange for the discomfort, we expect to witness the birth of Empathy's first cells, to follow the tiny ovals as they venture out into the pulsing stream to deliver the oxygen—courage—we must have to keep our systems alive. But we can see nothing, not even with the aid of the hematologists' microscopes; no sign of Empathy at the center of these nonnucleated cells. We wonder how Empathy could ever perfuse the lifeblood of a species left to the cowardice of its lies.

The detectives, though, say this is not the question to be addressed. More determined than ever to locate Empathy's organic hideout, they push us aside and launch new probes meant to pry open the quivering heart. Perhaps the cardiac surgeon's scalpel knows which chamber Empathy inhabits or which artery it clogs. The transplant team perhaps has caught Empathy in the race it runs between the donor's lifeless heart and the recipient's waiting cavity. The anesthesiologist must be questioned as well; perhaps there is information to be had about Empathy and what it feels while the body sleeps. So too the pathology lab must be thoroughly inspected, scoured for evidence of Empathy among the cultured cell colonies. Perhaps its DNA can be found in a single cell, one containing the code that will crack the case.

The yin-yang of the feminine body and masculine body must be sliced apart to determine if Empathy camps on the border between them. Perhaps the gynecologist's hysterectomy will be useful if Empathy is found embedded deep in the fibrous walls of the uterus that could not be saved. Maybe it is the body's maleness that Empathy prefers, and it is the urologist who understands what enlarges the prostate and what withers it away. What will the post-op exams reveal about male and female bodies that have been surgically altered or about the bodies whose gender has been reassigned? Surely, they must know Empathy's touch—feel the massage meant to soften surgery's scars.

But no, there is nothing to be felt, no evidence found. The state-of-the-art operating theater is sterile indeed, its cold stainless steel offering no refuge to Empathy or any of its sensibilities—none that would recharge its authentic soul or enlighten the reason of its embodied mind. There is no biological truth the fugitive could ever know. Perhaps the beep of the monitors meant to track Empathy's flatlining rhythms is too much, as is the glare of the lights flooding the depths of its living mystery. What if this is the light that blinds us to its truth hidden—shivering—in plain sight: Empathy is a fibrous strand easily missed but doing what it can to hold us together. Or is it the most gossamer membrane, one easily damaged by scalpels and distorted by microscopes whose precious permeability would allow a back-and-forth flow between selves and others? Apparently, neither the detectives nor we possess the delicacy needed to pluck the truth from its pulsing lifeworld.

We regroup, try another tack. If the elusive Empathy cannot be made to shine despite, or perhaps because of, our best clinical practices and highest standards of care, then it seems clear we must return to the torchlight glow and forgotten wisdom of an earlier era. Perhaps we could rediscover the Renaissance, say, and the time when Leonardo conducted his own investigations under the cover of darkness. Expert archivists take over for us now and with hands gloved, they examine the carefully transcribed notes—the precious pages documenting what the artist-scientist found in the dangerous dissection of his thirty cadavers. The notes are encrypted, and, like the archivists, we cannot decode Empathy's corporeal story, not even when the mirror reverses Leonardo's forensic secrets.

So, we turn to the archaeologists, perhaps their studies of the hunter-gatherers' fertility figures have traced Empathy to its earliest origins and discovered its nourishing milk flowing from the Venus of Willendorf's ample breasts. Perhaps their studies have found Empathy buried in the canopic jars alongside the mummies—what the orderly Egyptians believed would vitalize the afterlife for a civilization too stiff and stylized to frolic in its first life. On the grimacing faces of Roman citizens caught vacationing among Pompeii's noxious pyroclasts, was it Empathy the archaeologists saw? Perhaps they believe Empathy was behind the sacrifice of an Inca princess or spurted from the heart of an Aztec slave. Now, will their research tell us how Empathy is embodied by any culture? Will it identify just what of an enculturated body is passed down through the ages to the children of every civilization?

With this, investigation gives way to speculation, and different detectives push different scenarios. They quarrel over questions still unanswered—still unasked. Whitman, though, is certain of the body nonetheless. *O my Body!* he exalts. It sings of itself—neck, jaw, limbs, joints—and its rhapsodic parts are never to be doubted, never to be deserted, but always celebrated for their melodic perfection. *O I say, these are not the parts and poems of the body only, but of the Soul . . .* This, he knows, is the body that cannot be corrupted, this perfect, sacred Body.

For us, Whitman's lyrics conjure images, not of angels, but of Adonis and Nike: what we see in the kinetic poetry of an athlete's body—the glorious gliding of Olympic ice dancers and long-distance hurdlers, the intricate choreography of World Cup goalkeepers and waltzing wingers. *O*, we say now, mesmerized by the image of a perfect body diving into Viola's video *Five Angels for the Millennium*, the art that positions us at the bottom of a pristine pool where we find ourselves looking up though the sparkling liquid layers and cascading bubbles to embrace the diver's sensuous, slow-motion plunge.

Whitman reaffirms our reverie, even as he sings of perfect bodies plunged into slavery. They are the bodies he remembers standing atop the New Orleans auction block, and he affirmed, *The man's body is sacred, and the woman's body is sacred.* His love for the strong, sweet, and supple qualities of the well-made body is unbound and looms so large that it cannot be contained by any pool. Ever rhapsodic, it swims free . . . *as if in a sea.* Yet, it seems his love song is chained to the slaves' unanswered question: *If the body were not the Soul, what is the Soul?* We wonder if Empathy will ever respond.

Kahlo is just as certain of the Body, the one made sacred by its brokenness. It mourns itself, and what was the poet's rhapsody becomes the painter's requiem. The notes screech of her body—its pelvis violated by a runaway bus and heart brutalized by a love betrayed; its spirit torn between two cultures and self-presentation toying with a third gender. We see its image, raw and pure, bear witness to the biological truths laid bare in portraits bleeding with fetuses lost and choking on a necklace made more perverse by its sacred thorns. Beneath their ferocious unibrow, the eyes stare straight into the question of empathy.

We cannot blink now, and, turning to the ones who seem so certain, ask the uncomfortable: What about the sacredness that whips the body and scars the soul? Or the body corrupted by war? Damaged by disease? Diminished by the ravages of time? What can any of the detectives tell us about the rational body drowning in the phlegmatic waters of a disembodied mind or even the vomiting body consumed by the fiery bile of a bad-tempered spleen? Are these less-than-perfect bodies the ones that are out of balance? Or could they be the ones experienced enough to build on Empathy's less-than-perfect foundations? The bodies to take Empathy in and offer comfort, when in return, Empathy can only offer . . . what? The detectives, for their part, offer no answers, no new scenarios, and, staring straight into their files, do not blink.

Still, our quest continues. Mindful that the experts' techniques have not located Empathy in the milk of ancient bodies or in the marrow of sacred ones, we will try a different approach. Ours will be strategic, a matter of identifying the conditions in which the fleeting phantom must take shelter to rest its soul, and thus, make itself most vulnerable to capture. Perhaps we will catch Empathy among the lepers, for instance, where it has been at home for centuries—what the nuns of St.-Lazare's twelfth-century leprosarium must have found flourishing in the infectious lesions. Surely, it reappeared in the twentieth century at Lambaréné where the limbless bestowed their dignity upon Dr. Schweitzer and his jungle hospital. Surely, it was Empathy reaching out from the *Buddha Shakyamuni*—the armless ninth-century sculpture that cradled Alicia, the sobbing student who grieved for the lost infant she would never cradle in her own arms.

It must have been Empathy appearing on *Saint Cecilia*'s face, its likeness captured in Guido Reni's 1606 portrait—what Gina, an embittered student took from the eyes, transfixed, and gazing heavenward. These were her father's eyes, also transfixed; the ones Gina had seen imploring the heavens, begging for a miracle to save him from the killer cells' metastasis. It must have been Empathy spreading throughout the classroom and running down the cheeks of Gina's classmates who mourned the father and the faith she had lost—the sacred truths that scarred her soul.

And what of Empathy's face? Will it show itself to the plastic surgeon whose chin implant dares to define it? Or to the makeup artist whose foundation and eyeliner make up the character it will play? Was Empathy reflected in the still water of Narcissus's pond or in the jealous queen's mirror on the wall? Did Leonardo paint its mystery on Mona Lisa's face, and does the Renaissance diva smile, knowing she has kept the secret of his midnight discoveries for five hundred years? Is it Empathy we see today, splashed across the covers of the glossiest magazines and stuffed into the pages of the grainiest tabloids, its countenance fused with celebrities and frozen forever at the supermarket checkout line?

Or is Empathy more fleeting, glimpsed only in a flash across the face? What we might catch in a desperate look, a furtive glance, a knowing leer that cannot be captured by the detectives' mugshots? Perhaps Empathy hides among the smallest details, in eyebrows, for instance, bushy or plucked that shoot up with such surprise when their secret is revealed at last. Could Empathy be lubricating the colorful contact lenses that tint what we can see of its world? Or does it adorn the ring piercing the nostril that flares with disgust each time we fail to recognize its splendor? Perhaps Empathy lives on the lips, the tender ones chapped and cracked that long for the kiss of softness. Or is it more comfortable on the luscious, collagen-injected lips made to quiver and droop by a kiss rebuffed? Where, Empathy, where is your face?

We must look deeper, dig beneath the skin-deep beauty of every face. Perhaps Empathy will be found among the facial muscles, the forty-three or more of them that control the countless (dis)guises in which it could appear. Surely, high-powered magnifying lenses will be needed to detect the twitch of tiny fibers making huge decisions about the look of scorn or doubt it might wear, the wide-open grin or clenched-jaw resolve it might show. The lenses must also be strong enough to focus on face-to-face encounters and distinguish Empathy from what some detectives call "mirror mimicry"—the phenomenon they say occurs when the cheek muscles used for smiling in one face are activated by the happiness dancing on another or when the brow muscles used for frowning respond to the etched furrows of another's scowl.

These are busy muscles, indeed, all tensing, relaxing, mimicking—and working hard to mask Empathy in one moment, unmask it in another. We take a breath, consult Merleau-Ponty, the existentialist detective willing to meet the muscles and to live face to face in a world unwilling to lift the mask. What has he revealed? Was it Empathy when he came to live in the facial expression of the other? Or when he felt the other living in his? What might these lived interactions between selves and others signify?

Perhaps Danesi, the semiotics detective, has found signs of Empathy hovering in the interpersonal space between faces. As he is quick to point out, this is a restless, often confusing space cluttered with signs of gender and culture that compete for attention even as they are difficult to read. For instance, Danesi continues, men tend to grin, women tend to smile; men make funny faces, women maintain their facial composure. Southern Europeans make more eye contact—and hold their gaze longer—than Northern Europeans. What's more, American professors like me often find that Asian students, especially those who are newly arrived, will defer to authority and avert their eyes altogether.

Staring at Danesi's report, our own eyes glaze over, and we peer dumbly into the messy awkwardness of the interpersonal space it describes. Where is Empathy now, we wonder, and is it up to the task of reading so many signs and cutting through so much complexity? Is Empathy the one to bridge the gap between grins and smiles? Or fill the void between funny faces and faces that remain composed? Is Empathy bilingual, able to translate one language spoken by the steady gaze of Greeks and Italians, say, and another spoken by the quick glance of the Swiss and Germans? Will it find a common language that could ring true, ring out in the valley between Chinese teachers and students? Between American professors and Korean students? But mostly, we wonder if Empathy is willing to speak up and create a space open to the lexicon of every face.

Viola answers with another video, the slow-motion aesthetic of this one meant to create a hypnotic space in which to study facial expressions more intently—patiently—and possibly, to discover the biological truths their interactions signify. It was in such a space that viewers crowded around a small screen at the Getty Museum one Sunday afternoon (I among them)—all of us riveted by the face of an actor (Viola's model), whose expressions were changing ever so gradually, almost imperceptibly, from joy to sorrow to anger to fear to awe to a dreamy, trancelike state, and back to joy, sorrow, and the rest.

In a trancelike state of our own, we looped around and around with the anonymous face, fascinated yet determined to name the exact moment when one expression ended and the next began. Again and again we tried—or did we prefer to stay within the loop's eternity, losing all sense of time? If we had found the moment, what, exactly, would we call joy that turns to sorrow, or sorrow to anger, anger to fear? Was this the biological truth of Empathy revealed?

What if Empathy should live in that turning—and die unnamed in that most elusive moment? The actor's face never deviated from the script and, caught in the timeless loop itself, offered no new clues. We did our best to hold on to Empathy's moment with hands searching our own faces—fingers feeling for the critical muscles that mirrored the actor's. What did we find but that the six expressions and forty-three muscles blurred together, as if to prove there is only one face. Could this be the face of Empathy? Was this what the man in the plaid shirt saw in the blur—his face pressed so close, an inch or two from the screen? Or was this most intense viewer more like Merleau-Ponty, the one among us to live in the facial expressions of the actor and feel the actor living in his? Had viewer and actor carved out a tight space that signified Empathy? Could we squeeze in and read the signs?

What of other evocative—provocative—images, the videos and photos that jolt and trigger involuntary responses deep in the viscera? They catch us off guard, and we cannot predict which ones will grip us, thrust us into a space raw with the pain and suffering of others depicted in pernicious and untenable situations. Such images refuse to be held accountable for what they inflict and thus will continue to target us on screens large and small, hit their marks in living rooms and movie theaters and art museums—and leave us gagging, with hearts pounding, stomachs twisting, adrenaline surging. Perhaps they are the eager volunteers, serving mightily as analogs for Damasio's body maps and Iacoboni's brain scans, all intended to show us Empathy's interior world.

Could they also illustrate the corporeal story of Suzanne Keen's "narrative empathy"? What must be a cliffhanger, like the one her own body recounted in response to news footage of the Bosnian War. Was it Empathy that stunned her with the unexpected ache of her arms, stretch of her calf muscles, and knot of her anxious stomach as she watched the horror story of a refugee's panicked escape—a mother seen stumbling, about to lose her balance, carrying her frightened child down a steep and treacherous hillside? Was it Empathy that shook me with a sudden and violent urge to vomit when, shortly after the birth of my second child, I saw *Sophie's Choice*—and witnessed the Nazi brutality that forced Meryl Streep's title character to choose one of her two children to be saved?

Is it Empathy that induces intense "embodied responses" in the art museum—what gallery attendants observe in visitors—in a young adult, for instance, who stood before a crucifixion wincing and crying "ouch," as if her own ribs were pierced by a Roman spear? What about the kindergarten child seen raising her hands, a gesture more embodied than innocent, one mirroring the woman in Ana Mendieta's video art who raised her hands, bloody as they were? Could these be the hands of Empathy, sacred and profane as they are? How are we to know?

Accustomed by now to the stony silence surrounding questions of empathy, we start when a voice rings out, announcing, "What your gallery attendants describe is called *Einfühlung*." It declares, "Of this, I remain convinced. *Jawohl!*"

Wide-eyed, we wheel around, anxious to locate the mysterious speaker, a German man it would seem, and we are even more anxious to learn—possess—what makes him so certain. Perhaps the voice belongs to a new detective, clear-eyed, fresh-blooded, who will step from the void with new evidence that could take the stalemated investigation in a new direction.

But there is no one—not a soul to be seen—and it is only the disembodied, if authoritative, voice that rushes on: "I myself have experienced many objects of art physically—internally, as it were," it tells us in a thickly accented testimonial. "This is because 'I transpose myself into the inner being of an object and explore its formal character from within,' " it explains.

"And this is Ein-füh-lung?" we ask, carefully enunciating each syllable, surely the way to get control of the unfamiliar term if not of the bizarre situation in which we find ourselves. How odd, indeed, that a speaker unseen and unnamed might convince us of what convinces him; eerie too that his internal connection with art could be made present when he himself remains absent.

"Nein, nein!" interjects another voice, also insistent, also German. Again, we search for its owner and again discover nothing but another phantom male. "You must think more broadly—go beyond the limits of the object! Consider the phenomenon I call inner imitation," he barks a bit too imperiously. "Permit me to ex—"

"I beg to differ," says a woman's voice just as imperiously. We detect an English accent as the speaker issues this proclamation, "'Tis aesthetic sympathy that is described."

"Rubbish," snorts a fourth voice, a man's, his accent identifying him as her countryman. We gasp, incredulous that yet another phantom as outrageous and opinionated as the others has joined the fray. "The proper term to be applied," it asserts, "is *empathy!*"

"How can you be so certain?" we explode. Heads throbbing now, we have had quite enough—enough of this dialectical mystery and its competing assertions put forward by invisible speakers who have shown themselves only to be arrogant and downright rude. "And just what *is* empathy? Or *Einfühlung?*" we spew. "How about inner imitation and aesthetic sympathy?" Hissing now, we demand to know which of them is most credible. "How will we discover the *one* that solves the problem of empathy?"

Maddening indeed, debate among claimants so strident yet so shadowy is also unsettling, and we worry that we may be hearing voices in our heads. "Who *are* you anyway?" we screech, our own voices stretched tight by anxiety and frustration. "And *where* are you, the whole lot of you?"

"Calm down," advises yet another voice in the cacophony, this one gentler though and vaguely familiar, as is another still that whispers, "Take a breath."

"Certainty?" we ask tentatively. "Uncertainty, is that you?"

"Here to explain," they assure. A feeling of relief overtakes our anger, and though we could never have imagined ourselves welcoming the return of Certainty and Uncertainty, we are thrilled now—and all ears.

"These are the ghosts of history," says Certainty, "and their theories were very much alive in the late nineteenth to early twentieth centuries—"

"Theories that were heavily debated in their time," Uncertainty interrupts.

"And the echoes remain," Certainty continues.

"Still influential today," Uncertainty acknowledges.

"But why have the ghosts come back to haunt us now?" we demand.

Certainty sighs, and Uncertainty says, "You might want to pull up a chair, make yourselves comfortable." Then they tell us unconvincingly, "Try to relax."

Then Certainty says simply, "The ghosts are here to help us understand the body's authenticity . . ." before trailing off.

Uncertainty takes over when a second, even more wistful sigh escapes Certainty's lips. "But mostly, they are here to confirm that Empathy's journey—from the body to the brain to the object to the other—has been a convoluted one."

"Like history itself," Certainty picks up. "Empathy travels across time, inhabiting worlds of ambiguity, contradiction, and complexity along the way." We roll our eyes in lieu of screaming, "Yes, we are well aware of this!"

"The ghosts will settle down," Certainty says more convincingly now, "if you would simply agree to hear them out—pay attention to what they have to say about authentic corporeal connections."

Uncertainty says, "Much can be said about them. You will want to listen carefully to each of their stories."

With this, it appears certain that we will be learning more about the body's so-called "authenticity" and more still about Empathy's contentious past. But we are uncertain about what more of the reverberations could possibly add to the present debate.

Certainty and Uncertainty lean forward in their chairs and launch into the story of *Einfühlung*, which begins in 1873, we learn, when the German philosopher and aesthetician Robert Vischer coined the term, meaning "feeling into" or "in feeling," to capture bodily experiences with works of art. Our storytellers pause to remind us that Herr Vischer is the ghost who claimed to project—to "transpose"—himself into the "inner being" of a work. Hence, "feeling into," they add. We nod and are not surprised to hear that Vischer was also embroiled in a rather spirited debate of aesthetic issues raging in his native Germany at the time.

He argued that the appreciation of art itself *depended* on the viewer projecting him or herself into a contemplated work and experiencing its formal properties internally and thus, authentically. This was the viewer who felt the weight of its compositional mass, the mood of its warm or cool palette; the viewer whose own inner being raced with the energy of its object's kinetic lines and danced among its rhythmic patterns, soared in its open space, and hunkered down in the closed space. Vischer appears to have prevailed, as it was his kind of physical intimacy and corporeal connection—his *Einfühlung*— that persisted in Germany for some twenty-five years. We try to take it in—the full sweep of this history—even as Certainty and Uncertainty promise there is plenty more to come.

They turn to the other German ghost, Theodor Lipps, who they explain was also a philosopher interested in the relationship between a work of art and its viewer. Lipps is known to have written about Vischer's *Einfühlung* as late as 1897, but soon after, expanded its meaning to include visual illusion and then broadened his thinking to encompass the relationship and corporeal connection two people might share. If individuals could project themselves into works of art and experience their inner being, he seemed to reason, then they could also project themselves into other individuals and experience *their* inner being as well.

It was not long before Lipps abandoned *Einfühlung* altogether and replaced the term with what he called "inner imitation." We nod vigorously, spurred by the memory—the bark—of his imperious insistence. In 1903, our storytellers continue, Lipps published a treatise that defined inner imitation as the process by which one individual feels his or her own emotions stir when observing the emotions expressed by another. In effect, Certainty and Uncertainty now agree that two individuals share an authentic connection when feeling the same emotion at the same time. Or we could say their bodies are "feeling with" one another. As for the philosopher himself, they pick up, Herr Lipps believed the corporeal experience of "feeling with" inherent in inner imitation fit well with the long-established definition of sympathy. His work focused on such sympathetic experiences and explored the psychological processes that could explain how one human being discovered the self of another.

Certainty and Uncertainty sip some water. So it was, they resume, that within a period of about six years, Lipps transformed

Einfühlung into inner imitation. "Feeling into" was replaced by "feeling with," the self projected into a work of art became a self discovered in another human being, and what had been the sole province of philosophy was repositioned within the fledgling field of psychology. No wonder, our storytellers add in an aside, Lipps is said to have been the philosopher most admired by Freud. How curious, Certainty and Uncertainty muse, glancing at each other. It was Lipps's inner imitation based on the old idea of sympathy—"feeling with"—that found a home in the new psychology. To us they say we will be leaving Germany now but that we have not heard the last of Vischer's *Einfühlung* and the idea of "feeling into." Curious indeed, we think.

The scene shifts to England, where we find Vernon Lee (also known as Violet Paget), an aesthetician and writer who, at the beginning of the twentieth century, was active in London's *avant-garde* and a member of the Bloomsbury Group. Certainty and Uncertainty confirm for us that she was the female phantom arguing for "aesthetic sympathy." Like the Germans, Lee concentrated on embodied responses induced by objects of art— the changes in bodily posture and breathing that occurred when, as she believed, the viewer *merged* with the object. Merged?

We wonder, brows furrowed; and seeing our confusion, Certainty and Uncertainty elaborate further. Lee believed such physical changes were the result of what she described as "a tendency to merge the activities of the perceiving subject with the qualities of the perceived object." Still not satisfied, we ask if this tendency could encompass more, perhaps a merger between the aesthetic of Vischer's "feeling into" and the sympathy of Lipps's "feeling with?" If it could, would the resulting hybrid, already aptly named "aesthetic sympathy," be authenticated by the world of psychology or by the world of philosophy?

Impatient now, our storytellers hurry on and deftly transport us to America—Ithaca, New York—before we can ask any more pesky questions. It is there that we learn of Edward Titchener, the English-born professor who established and directed the first psychology lab at Cornell University. Certainty and Uncertainty note that Titchener was the fourth ghost—the assertive one interested in accuracy and precision. And in the proper application of the term "empathy" we supply, indeed they verify. "You see, Professor Titchener was an empiricist looking to identify the 'basic units' and 'mental structures' that make up human consciousness. So, of course, it would be important to him to define terms and differentiate one psychological process from another, say 'feeling into' from 'feeling with' for instance."

In 1909, they continue, Titchener came up with the term "empathy," an English word he derived from the Greek roots "em" and "pathos" that captured *Einfühlung's* German meaning "in feeling" or "feeling into." The new term was neat, precise, Certainty and Uncertainty claim, and cleaned up the confusion surrounding "inner imitation," "aesthetic sympathy," and *Einfühlung* itself. What's more, they emphasize, Titchener's "empathy" acted as a counterweight to "sympathy" and created a kind of parity that allowed the two to be compared directly and their labels to be applied accurately. This is Titchener's gift, our storytellers declare, and what enables us to clearly distinguish one from the other.

"To clearly distinguish one from the other," we mock, barely able to choke back an exasperated sneer. "Distinguish empathy from sympathy and sympathy from empathy—is that right?"

Certainty and Uncertainty say nothing.

"A label will enable us to do this?" we spit sarcastically. "And this is a gift?"

Still no response.

Giving up, we smack our foreheads. "Unbelievable!" comes our bitter scoff.

Certainty and Uncertainty flush now and look away, too embarrassed, it seems, to admit they have overreached. How could they not remember the blur of Empathy's devilishly persistent wind devils churning with the likes of compassion, understanding, and *sympathy*? Or the tangle of its rhizomic roots and shoots—the nodal connections where "feeling with" becomes "feeling together" becomes "mingling together" becomes "suffering together" becomes . . . ? Who could forget the nuclear nightmare of missile-lobbing psychologists clouding the air with arguments about altruism and the hierarchical arrangement among empathy and sympathy? Not to mention the absurdity of Empathy itself, its metaphors too hazy, its questions too pointed.

Recomposing themselves, our storytellers stand and turn to leave. But in the doorway, they stop to reconsider Titchener, who, they say, would have been most gratified to know that late in the twentieth century, Empathy's "basic units" were precisely identified with the discovery of mirror neurons in Giacomo Rizzolatti's lab at the University of Parma. Then, reaching for the knob, Certainty and Uncertainty offer their parting words, saying, "Look to the neuroscientists, the ones who appreciate Empathy's elegant circuitry and its valiant attempts to structure human consciousness."

Certainty and Uncertainty may be gone, but they have opened a door, and we realize that neuroscientists at work in their labs— mining the gold to be found in mountains of brain scans—are the detectives we have been looking for all along. They have the evidence and much to report about the magical cells that allow "our bodies to resonate along with the bodies of others." These are the detectives, Gallese and Iacoboni among them, who can explain what the ghosts of history could only describe. Hard evidence of the mirroring mechanism at work is robust, authentic, indeed, and validates the earlier treatises asserting that individuals could transpose themselves into or merge with objects of art and feel their own emotions stir when observing the emotions expressed by others.

First discovered in area F5 of the premotor cortex, mirror neurons have been giving up their secrets, and our detectives have since learned that their mirroring mechanism can be found in other areas of the brain. As for area F5 itself, detectives have now determined that there are at least two, and possibly— probably? certainly?—three types of motor neurons lighting up as if intended to illuminate the depths of Empathy's corporeal mystery. These include, we are informed, the "classic" mirror neurons originally detected in the mid-1990s, the *canonical* mirror neurons *and* the still elusive *super* mirror neurons.

The detectives pause, perhaps to reflect on what clearly fascinates and inspires them. "Just imagine," they seem to say, eyes bright, gazing off, "the 'mirroring function' of these remarkable cells . . . the characteristic 'pattern of activity' that defines a whole *system*, the mirror neuron system that allows every human being to navigate whole *worlds,* especially the world of objects and the world of other human beings. Well, this is just stunning. Simply profound."

Rapture gives way to responsibility, and our detectives return to the task at hand, anxious to provide details about area F5's classic mirror neurons. Their presentation is earnest and replete with evidence of just how sensitive these particular cells are to the human hand. These, we learn, are the cells excited by dexterity; fingers and thumb that grip a hammer or stroke a cheek, flash a gang sign, or guide a pencil's diligent scrawl. Oh yes, say the detectives, these neurons are "specialized" indeed, "coding" for the hand's articulate actions and firing both when one person's hand executes a grasp or signal or caress and when another person perceives such actions.

"And get this," the detectives seem to insist, "this built-in mirroring mechanism has quite a bit to do with a shared capacity for motor perception and motor cognition." Excited now, they explain that these neurons allow us to perceive—and not with our eyes—the hand's many "motor behaviors" and to recognize what these behaviors signify. We want to take this in, think hard about the neurons that allow our hands to resonate along with the hands of others. Lost in thought, we imagine how busy these tiny cells must be, the very ones enabling huge TV viewing audiences to perceive and understand quarterbacks firing footballs thirty yards up field or resonate with pop singers gripping their microphones, occasionally passing them from one hand to the other for effect. It is not just the star performers' hands our neurons experience but also the hands in the live audience itself, clapping, high-fiving, fist-bumping, and waving at the TV cameras, also for effect.

Still excited and apparently unaware of our pensiveness, the detectives rush ahead to the canonical mirror neurons. This type, they emphasize, is specialized for "*object*-related hand actions," coding not for the grip or the grasp but for the object itself, "like the football or microphone" we retrieve from our thoughts. Confused for a moment, the detectives seem to sputter,

"Yes, well, the hammer or pencil, any graspable object," before hurrying on. Unlike their classical neighbors, canonical neurons fire at the very sight of a graspable object, they say, and trigger the "motor plans" that instruct the hand, telling it how to take hold of the object it seeks "to apprehend."

We think about such objects, the toothbrush and coffee cup, cell phone and car keys "apprehended" each morning without fail and the countless others "apprehended" throughout the course of a day, every day. They are familiar, ordinary, the icons of a busy, if routinized, lifestyle. Yet, each is made special by its resonance, the detectives would have us believe. Thanks to the canonical mirror neurons, objects become extraordinary, exquisite even, and create a world we can navigate with ease, say the detectives. We think about this world and the material culture it endows, the shared identities it constructs. We think about the burgeoning Amazon warehouses and Walmart stores that contribute to the churn within the mighty world of objects and wonder when the exquisite becomes the excessive. Then we remember the objects cluttering our attics and taking over our lives, the very ones that overwhelm our landfills and choke the planet's oceans. Have these castoffs lost their resonance?

The detectives, though, want our undivided attention and proclaim that there is more about the canonical mirror neurons we should know. These neurons also fire, they tell us, at the sight of letters, even simple strokes or marks made by a pencil or brush or other graspable instrument. Detective Gallese steps forward to explain that simply observing these traces of the hand's activity, or what he calls "static graphic artifacts," induces a "motor simulation" of the same "gestural act" required to produce the artifact. He says we can imagine the hand making the letters, the marks, and our own hand matching them stroke for stroke.

The good detective is right of course, and we are able indeed to imagine the marks on a wall as, say, the traces of the toddler whose clumsy crayon left them on what had been a freshly painted surface. We can also imagine the same child a few years later who forms the letters of his or her name ever so painstakingly only to become the adult hurriedly scribbling a signature legible to no one. We have been this toddler, this child, this adult. Our canonical mirror neurons fire away, hardwired to remember the "gestural acts" required to produce a lifetime's worth of "static graphic artifacts."

Our wonder widens, and we imagine hands around the world, generations and generations of them collecting and trading objects, making and using tools. We think about the centuries—millennia—of mark-making, all to reiterate the messages "we were here" and "we mattered." Like graffiti scrawled on city streets and tattoos inked on wriggling bodies, these traces and artifacts are stylistically and culturally different, and we wonder if they still induce in us "motor simulations" of the same "gestural acts" needed to produce them. And how about the marks of today?

Are the canonical mirror neurons activated in the same way, say, when we observe graffiti's aerosol art sprayed on New York's buildings and on LA's freeways? What about when we study the strokes and symbols etched on a proud Maori warrior and when we study the teardrops and gang name identifying a hardened prison inmate? There are the alphabets too—Greek, Cyrillic, Hebrew—as well as the Chinese, Korean, and Japanese characters to think about. How do our neurons respond to these artifacts? To the marks made by all human beings to identify themselves and their statuses, their places in the world?

Again, the detectives try to grab our attention, this time to have us imagine how important, how vital these canonical mirror neurons were to the survival of our ancestors, the earliest hunter-gatherers whose hardwiring resonated with the flint to be sharpened into blades and pulsed with the reeds to be fashioned into baskets. Again, we take off wondering about the biology of activated neurons that led our tribes into the culture of signifying objects. How were the processes of motor perception and cognition tied to the processes of toolmaking? How did it happen that reeds were later used to carve cuneiforms into clay tablets, what would enable the ancient Sumerians to decipher the culture they shared? What about the Egyptian scribes and their hieroglyphics, the Chinese calligraphers and their characters, the medieval monks hunched over their manuscripts? Were theirs the "gestural acts" that tapped a biological resonance strong enough to establish a clear cultural presence?

Stick became stylus; stroke became signifier. Blades and baskets are still in use, but now, keyboards and screens have become important to our survival as a tribe foraging in the jungles of material culture. These are among the objects that teach us what is vital, lessons about utility and value, possession and power. No object is innocuous, none inanimate. All vibrate with the synaptic energy that fuels the social order and makes our lives comprehensible. We know which objects are handmade and which commercially produced, which are keepsakes, which junk. There is no doubt about which objects are to be stockpiled, which to be safeguarded. We know which items to share with others, which to snatch from their grasp. Above all else, we know who is among the "haves" and who is among the "have-nots." But we can only wonder how the resonance of area F5's neurons reaches so deeply into the world's economic and political systems. What is it again that such resonance has to do with empathy? Or *Einfühlung*? Inner imitation? Aesthetic sympathy?

Though we have hardly begun to grapple with questions hidden among the classical and canonical mirror neurons—thorny issues related to capitalism and consumerism or existential concerns about having more and *being* less—the detectives are already focused on super mirror neurons, the last of the three types. Some seem uncomfortable with this type, and we are aware of a tense murmuring, no, argument in their ranks. The evidence is circumstantial, they say, and many will only agree to report that the existence of these neurons is hypothetical at best. Oh sure, the naysayers admit, these neurons are implicated in motor behaviors involving hands and objects. The moderates are willing to go further and suggest that these controversial cells are also implicated in interactions between human beings. It appears we have yet another question to grapple with.

For Detective Iacoboni, there is no doubt that super mirror neurons clearly exist and can be pictured as a "functional neuronal layer 'on top' of the classical mirror neurons" that controls their activity, increasing or decreasing their firing rates. In theory, this layer controls the hand's motor behaviors and prevents us from behaving inappropriately as social creatures attuned to the hand gestures and object-related actions of others. True enough, our hands do not mimic every gesture we perceive nor grab for every object we desire, not even the most coveted. We seem to know when to lend a helping hand or keep our hands to ourselves; when to welcome others with an open hand or warn them away with a clenched fist.

Essential to our development as an object-toting, group-living species, super mirror neurons—or something like them—must surely be linked to motor perception and motor cognition. Look at their socializing function and all they have taught us about sharing time and space with others. Super indeed, these specialized, if hypothetical, neurons must also be instrumental in setting up the most fundamental of human relationships and represent what Iacoboni describes as a "wonderfully simple neural distinction between self and other." But other detectives shake their heads and shake our confidence that empathy—or something like it—could ever be identified in self/other relationships developing from cells that remain unidentified themselves. We cannot be sure, and what might have seemed "wonderfully simple" is once again terribly complex.

Still, Iacoboni admires the super mirror neurons and imagines their "functional neuronal layer" developing in the earliest face-to-face encounters between babies and their parents or caregivers—the layer's pedagogic pattern of activity at work even, perhaps especially, in these rudimentary self/other relationships. We can picture these intimate interactions and understand how important they must be to babies just learning to distinguish themselves—the coos and smiles of their own being—from the other beings cooing and smiling in front of them.

But we also know that not all nurseries are created equal nor are parent-child interactions universal. They are context bound, as confirmed by studies indicating that mothers interact differently with their infant daughters than they do with their infant sons. Also, the cries of French babies, as recorded and analyzed, are heard to imitate the "up-speak" said to characterize the French language, while the cries of German babies match the "down-speak" characterizing the German language.

Are the super mirror neurons implicated, their synaptic pedagogy responsible for such differences? If these secret cells develop along gender and culture lines, then what is or can be known about the functional layer they form—not the neuronal one Iacoboni envisions, but a *socializing* layer sitting "on top" of human interactions? Could such a layer explain why adult women—treated differently as infant daughters—score twice as high as their male counterparts on paper-and-pencil measures of empathy? Could this layer control other behavioral biases? What if it increases and decreases not only the firing rates but also the *smiling* rates of men and women, for instance, or the eye contact made by Northern and Southern Europeans? Could it be that the mystery the super mirror neurons represent—Iacoboni's simple distinction between self and other—has complicated the search for Empathy all along?

For once, the detectives seem interested in at least some of our questions, none, though, pertaining directly to the controversy clouding the super mirror neurons. They search their files and retrieve two bright, shiny studies—hard neuroscientific evidence, they boast, of gender and cultural differences in the brain captured by advanced imaging technologies. Even as we wonder how or if the super mirror neurons might be implicated in the results of either study or both, the detectives launch what appears to be their serious-minded mission of reading the jargon-filled reports as dispassionately as possible.

In the first, they announce, electro- and magneto-encephalography were used to measure the neuronal response in the motor cortex of male and female subjects who were directed to observe two different test conditions displayed on a screen. All subjects observed the random movement of a simple dot in one display, and in the other, the actions of a hand deemed to be gender neutral. Results indicate, the detectives report crisply, that mirror neurons in the motor cortex of both men and women were equally activated in response to the moving dot. But the response to the hand actions was quite different, with the women's mirror neurons becoming significantly more activated than the men's.

Interesting, we mumble to ourselves, only to wonder what conclusions can be drawn from this finding. What, exactly, is happening in the heads of the female subjects—or not happening in the heads of the males? What does the gender-neutral hand have to say to both genders that the dot does not? More to the point, what do the hand and the human connection it implies have to say about the super mirror neurons and the functional control they imply? Are these cells bent on teaching the classic mirror neurons when to fire, and thus instructing us all, men and women alike, on the circumstances of empathy? We cannot be sure; maybe no one can. But it seems clear to us that this study, in spite of or because of its clean design, sophisticated instrumentation, and definitive results, offers only a description and not the answers we hunger for. Perhaps we can only conclude that the connection between empathy, gender, and super mirror neurons is simply too messy, too crude, and too ambiguous to be captured by neuroscientific research.

The second study, announce the detectives, clearly intent on moving forward while maintaining their scientific objectivity, was designed to investigate the neuronal response to "culturally specific hand gestures." In particular, we learn, it tested the hypothesis that the mirror neurons of American subjects or participants would become *most* excited when observing an American actor performing the gestures commonly used in American culture, become *somewhat* excited when observing a Nicaraguan actor performing American gestures, and become *least* excited when observing a Nicaraguan actor performing the gestures commonly used in Nicaraguan culture.

"As expected," says Iacoboni, taking over as spokesperson, "the participants' cells became very excited when observing the American actor performing the familiar American gestures—a 'thumbs-up' sign, the 'V' for victory, for instance. But an interesting, unexpected finding was that these cells became *more* excited when the participants watched the Nicaraguan actor performing the unfamiliar Nicaraguan gestures than when they watched the Nicaraguan actor performing American gestures."

We want to ask in our own dispassionate way if the super mirror neurons explain this "interesting unexpected" finding. If they do, we will also ask about the implications for motor perception and motor cognition. Mostly though, we burn with questions about the chances for empathy—and the chances for answers. Iacoboni spares us, interrupts what surely would have been another of our precarious interrogations teetering between the realms of objectivity and subjectivity. He is already presenting an explanation of the results: "It is like [the participants] were understanding that there was some kind of harmony between the actor making the gesture and the gesture itself." With this, Iacoboni steps away.

"Some kind of harmony?" we echo in disbelief. But Iacoboni does not hear, and we cannot ask what he intended the musical analogy to mean. Alone now with only our thoughts, we are left to grope for a way, a word to translate the lovely, lyrical figure of speech offered as a decidedly unscientific, jargon-free conclusion.

"Some kind of *authenticity*?" we try. "What the American participants were recognizing in the Nicaraguan actor's performance of the Nicaraguan gesture?" We think about the participants and try to put ourselves in their places. Though they did not understand the cultural meaning of the gesture itself—surely, most Americans would not—somehow, these participants seemed to understand something more. Perhaps they were "feeling with" the actor who was "feeling into" the gesture.

"Some kind of resonance?" we blurt in spite of ourselves. Again, we ponder, lost once more in the stream of never-ending questions. Perhaps the participants and the actor were sharing a specialized biological resonance that bridged the cultural gap between them, we guess.

"Some kind of . . ." we trail off, unwilling now to utter the word, to pronounce "empathy" as first intended for fear these three syllables could blister the lips. We have already been burned by Empathy's own mystery and nearly drowned by torrents of unanswered questions.

About to be overwhelmed anyway, we close our eyes, try to imagine the unseen harmony or authenticity, the invisible resonance or empathy—or other essence still unnamed—the *something* that must have been picked up by the participants' motor perception and cognition, making everything clear to them and nothing to us.

We listen for "some kind," *any* kind of harmony to ring true in the musical mist. What if Iacoboni's analogy turns on something other, something more than the mirror neurons, super or not? Could it be nonneural, a harmony unconcerned with "wonderfully simple" distinctions between self and other? A harmony so resonant, so authentic that it fills the social gaps opened by terribly complex distinctions between selves and gestures, selves and objects, selves and others?

Is this the kind of harmony—simple, complex, neural, social—my students were understanding in the arts methods classroom, what they recognized in Christina's connections to the irises, in Gina's to St. Cecilia, in Alicia's to the Buddha Shakyamuni? Was this a harmony so resonant, so authentic that it filled the gap between a lonely white iris and the riotous purple ones, all springing up in the tumultuous garden of life? Was this the kind of harmony riveting Gina's classmates, their own eyes so transfixed that they saw what connected St. Cecilia's heavenward gaze, Gina's bitter stare, and her father's imploring look?

How about Alicia's classmates? Were they "feeling with" the bereaved mother whose arms ached with loss, even as she was "feeling into" the armless Buddha's wisdom? Had one of these classmates captured this story of harmony when a week after the tearful class presentation she wrote, "The [sculpture] reached out to [Alicia] with compassion and got her in touch with a void that could be filled by connecting with the universe . . . The piece also opened her up to receiving some healing and a connection with the community"?

And there was Maggie, who hoped to paint like Cezanne, to be him, and know what he knew. Was her connection to the painter and his *Still Life with Apples* (1893-94) a resonant one strong enough to transcend Gallese's claim that a still life is really a "moving" life vibrating with the strokes, the gestural traces, of the artist's brush?

Could this also be true of another older student, Deborah, whose connection to what she described as the "boring" still life,

White and Pink Mallows in a Vase (1895) by Henri Fantin-Latour, seemed to vibrate beyond its smooth surface and imperceptible strokes? "Boring" or "moving," where was the harmony? What connection were the younger students sharing when two weeks after Deborah's quiet presentation, they identified the "plain, but meaningful" painting, its flowers or "mallows" glowing pink and white against a flat gray background, as one of the most memorable in their class? Was it authenticity they had recognized when they said Deborah's story "fit well" with the mallows—the tall flowers with strong fibers planted in the back to give height and definition to French gardens of the day?

"I am happy to remain in the background, not needing attention like my more dramatic friends," Deborah had told the class. Like the mallows, her fibers "ran deep," making her strong, "hard to break," she said. Most of all, Deborah was always there to support the ones she loved, maybe even give some definition to their lives.

And the artist himself? Had Deborah and her classmates resonated with Latour's story? Had they recognized that it "fit well" with what he once said about remaining in the background behind the more dramatic painters of the Impressionist and Post-Impressionist movements? Were his fibers also strong, unbreakable, even as he understood his "boring" work would never define the art world of the late nineteenth century? Still, there must have been "some kind of harmony" defining the students' world, a quiet kind waiting to be discovered in the early twenty-first century that would support classroom connections and make them memorable.

What connects other artists to their work, gives authenticity and definition to the ideas they manipulate, the materials they transform, the traces they leave? Take, for instance, Jasper Johns, leader of the American Pop Art movement. What did he reveal when he said, "Take an object. Do something to it. Do something else to it. Do something else to it"? What was the "something" to be done, and did it leave traces of harmony, resonance, or authenticity? Was Johns "feeling into" the object when doing whatever he did to it? Working during the Cold War's nuclear arms race, had he felt something for the targets and flags we see in his iconic paintings of the mid-twentieth century? Are we also doing something, "feeling with" the target's bull's-eye, the flags' stars and stripes—understanding a harmony so shrill, so jarring that it reawakens old fears of being targeted by Soviet-era missiles and stirs a constant need for rallying around the flag? Does Johns's cultural commentary close any biological gaps between gesture, object, artist, and viewer? Between feeling and doing? Between unharmonious but resonant ideologies?

What about Johns's friend, Robert Rauschenberg, the Neo-Dadaist who also explored gaps over the course of a long career, most notably the gap between art objects and everyday objects? What did he find? Was this the place of harmony, or resonance, or empathy? Is this the place where we connect art and life, resonate with what Rauschenberg may or may not have transcended? Is it empathy we feel, something like Vischer's *Einfühlung*, when we read his artist's statement on the gallery wall—Rauschenberg's public declaration that he "felt empathy" for things, the "objects in a junkyard" that called out to him as if begging to be given new lives as the found-art sculptures and assemblages we see rising from the gallery floor? Had he given these objects a chance to transpose themselves into his inner being, and if so, do we take a chance, transpose ourselves into the objects, and like Vischer, explore their character from within? Or would we be exploring the artist's character, as it were?

And what of the philosophers to follow Vischer? How are they connected to such things, Heidegger, for instance, who talked about the "thingliness" of things—the thing that allows objects and the questions attached to them to be understood? Was he speaking of authenticity? Of resonance, or "feeling into" objects of art and life? Does his "thingliness" attract us, lure us into a material culture that opens as many gaps as it closes even as it burrows into our inner being? Is this the "thingliness" that drives us to make culturally iconic objects personally significant? Or is it the other way around, and we take our intimate experiences and make them iconic? More pressing still, what might assure us that these are the questions attached to such things? Who can tell? If our questions remain unanswered, or worse, are unanswerable, then how will we understand the things of "thingliness"?

Merleau-Ponty described his own encounters with objects, spoke of experiencing them directly, deeply, physically. As he explained, "Things have an internal equivalent in me. They arouse in me a carnal formula of their presence." What are we to make of his calculus and the formula that would take us back to the body we may overlook but can never leave behind? Is this the formula that Johns understood, the one Rauschenberg applied in the junkyard, the students in the classroom? Perhaps the very formula we could use to solve for the unknown—all we do not know about harmony or empathy, about opening or closing gaps that might be neural *and* social, "wonderfully simple" *and* terribly complex? Would authenticity appear in the solutions we derived? Might we see how objects become "internal equivalents," how they acquire a "presence," a personal significance, an iconic stature?

Is this the same formula students used to make extraordinary connections to each other through the "thingliness" of ordinary objects? Not a math major among them, had they understood a different calculus, the presence of connections made authentic and memorable? How else would they have remembered another student, Cindy, and her story about a simple cell phone like any other stashed in the backpacks around the room?

A story arousing much more that would be recognized as Cindy's hard-won independence, her freedom to pursue her own goals as long as she kept in close contact with her parents, overprotective and anxious about "dangerous" freeways and a long commute into a world they knew nothing about. A story that aroused in Cindy, in her classmates, a "presence" of the stamina required to juggle responsibilities to parents and professors, to self and others.

What about the students in another class who clearly recalled Roberto and his connection to McDonalds's iconic arches, one forged in a rural Mexican village where he had spent the first twelve years of his life? A Big Mac and fries were the rare and luxurious meal to be savored at the end of a hot and dusty journey three hours long, they heard him say. They had nodded and smiled knowingly, Latinos, Asians, and Anglos alike, at his shock upon arriving in Los Angeles and finding a McDonalds on every other street corner. They understood how disappointed and foolish he felt to learn that his new friends and acquaintances consider a Big Mac to be nothing more than cheap, unhealthy fast food. What had made this classroom connection resonant, present, and one of the most memorable? Had it found its "internal equivalent" in an external borderland, its "carnal formula" in a cross-cultural experience?

In yet another class, what was it when Marvin held up an image of the Gap's iconic logo—what carried the students beyond its resonating letters and strokes, beyond the gestural traces of the designer's hand? What swept these hipsters past the brand of "cool" clothes sporting the popular label and sucked them into a story of brutality, oppression, and desperation?

For his part, Marvin had told the class about the unfair labor practices, the sweatshop conditions his mother and aunts were forced to endure, their backs aching, fingers bleeding, as they sewed the clothes for retailers like the Gap. He had been serious, seething even, and as one of his classmates later remembered, "His face showed a fierce, determined look, as if to say 'this is enough!' "

The students had been riveted as Marvin explained that his mother and her sisters were from El Salvador and were "forced to leave everything behind" when they fled to this country. They had been trapped between government and rebel forces, he said, and still somehow managed to escape the violence and corruption of the Salvadoran Civil War, only to be trapped by another kind of violence and corruption in LA's garment district.

Shaking the logo in the airless room, Marvin had urged his classmates not to buy the clothes made to support "corporate greed" and to suppress "workers' rights." The class had exhaled, said they never knew that conditions were so bad, and in a solemn show of solidarity, pledged to honor his request. What was the formula for their pact? Were Marvin and the others understanding a solemn kind of harmony? Of authenticity? Of resonance? Empathy?

What is the formula, "carnal" or otherwise, for understanding connections between self and other? This is the question we float, surely an important one, if a bit earnest. But this is the very question that tugs and strains and, finally, escapes our grasp altogether. There it is, flickering and buzzing in the air like an old neon sign atop a roadside motel in the middle of nowhere. Though they sputter on and off sporadically, the letters are bright and do what they can to pierce the darkness that wearies us so. Occasionally the letters form a word, "SELF" or "OTHER," for instance, but never light up, we notice, to spell "E-M-P-A-T-H-Y." And just when we might think the power has gone out or the neon has given up for good, the word "AND" blinks and comes to life, valiant and reassuring in the night sky. We blink as well and conclude that there will be no formula lighting up, none that would solve for the unknowns, "self" or "other," none for "self *and* other."

"SELF" flashes on again, still without explanation, still without "EMPATHY." The letters are bolder this time, crackling so loudly and glowing so intensely that they overload our senses even as they enshrine their mystery. With yet another flash, our eyes blur, and for a split second, we think we might read the word "SELFie." Or wait, could it be "SELFish"? Dazed, we wonder what is going on and if there is some connection between the two. Is there a message or an implication that we are selfishly obsessed with taking selfies? So many—too many—selfies? Rubbing our eyes, we look again, and there, writ large, is an answer none of us would care to receive. In the dead of night, the word "Self-CENTERED" glares at us clear as day.

Defensive now, we want to object, point out that there are selfLESS souls among us, the steadfast ones who minister tirelessly to the needs of others. They are like the self-STARTERS, also in our midst, highly motivated, though not by a sense of self-RIGHTEOUSNESS, but by their own self-AWARENESS and a call to succeed at what they do. There are the psychologists working diligently to boost self-ESTEEM, to cure a nation's angst one patient, one client at a time. We might also point to the philosophers methodically investigating the meaning of self-CONSCIOUSNESS and to the neuroscientists desperately searching for its location in the ooze of the brain.

"And-and," we stutter, groping for more examples of nobly dedicated selves. Ah, yes, of course. How about the artists and their self-PORTRAITS that carefully preserve their faces in perpetuity—Kahlo having painted some seventy, Van Gogh, how many? Oh, but wait, we muse. On second thought . . . well, it looks like these portraits might be part of a long, long line of SELFies, all speaking of self-OBSSESSION.

However reluctantly, we must agree to concede that yes, there are some egomaniacs in our ranks—the politicians, for instance, who are always looking for photo ops and appear to be as self-SERVING as they are calculating. They are fund raisers, not public servants, who act out of their own self-INTERESTS rather than on their constituents' behalf. And yes, truth be told, there are the celebrities, who, like adolescents everywhere, seem so self-ABSORBED, concerned only with their self-IMAGE and self-PRESENTATION.

"But-but," we sputter, unwilling to give any more ground. Remember, we insist, there are the selfless souls. Still, we are deflated, trapped by our own circular, self-DEFEATING argument. We look down at our shuffling feet, then up at the victorious sign. "SELF" it burns without apology, without mercy. We bow to its intensity, admit that some of us, well, most of us, are a bit too SELF-interested. Certainly, there is plenty of evidence to be found in our own vocabulary—and plenty of neon to be used in advertising our own obsession with SELFHOOD.

What is this obsession and the "SELF" it bestows upon us? Do we know what reveals the "I," the "Me" that stares back at us from the mirror's glossy surface? Or what endows us with a personality, an identity? Is the Self found in the mind? The body? Does it make us think or make us feel? Is it projected on the face, what others locate among the features and expressions, or in the flush of its aspirations and scars of its disappointments? Are there different Selves, a private one known only to our inner world and a public one ready to confront the outer? Or perhaps, as psychologist Daniel Kahneman describes this duplicity, there is an "experiencing Self" and a "remembering Self"—the former living in and for the present moment, the latter existing only to recast the moment and insert it into a storied past. What story does this or any of our selves tell? If it is fictional, then who or what is the subject of the tale, and in whose reality will the past, as rewritten, collide with the future as imagined?

"NotSELF" flares across the sign now, and in the next instant, "secondSELF" lights up the sky. The two alternate, one on, the other off, each blazing with the energy of a red giant, each vying for control of our keenest attention, and neither focusing on the definition of a true Self. The pulsing, strobe-lit effect is too much, and we feel dizzy, barely able to decipher their neon message, let alone grasp its subliminal implications. The most we can come up with is a literal translation—"notSELF" to mean "anyone but me," or "not me" ("I"), and "secondSELF" to mean "anyone like me," or "another me"—provided of course that "ME" ("I") is reasonably equivalent to "SELF."

Whatever their meaning, it is clear that "notSELF" and "secondSELF" are locked together in an electric duel, a rapid-fire debate too exasperating for us to handle. To put an end to it, though, we must choose one over the other. Only then will we prevail and bathe in the glow of a steady stream—shine with the light of a single idea. But how are we to decide, given that "not ME" and "another ME" appear to stand on opposite sides of a great and mysterious divide? Even setting aside the larger, more complex ideological questions this raises, the truth is we find it a struggle just to clarify the subtler, more nuanced differences between the two. Clearly, we are most unprepared to choose and most unwilling to negotiate the divide.

The wiring begins to smoke, and the sign—perhaps on the verge of its own meltdown—begins to fade. When the flashing stops altogether, we are relieved, glad for any reprieve. It manages to relight, though, and immediately reestablishes its dominant position above our heads. What it says goes, and once again, we have no input—and none to give. Laserlike, the sign stabs our eyes with the white-hot light of "OTHER," an intense word, to be sure—one that contains a broad spectrum of meanings, some generic enough to transcend any divide and others specific enough to answer any questions about who or what the "NOTself" and "SECONDself" represent. They are "OTHER," the sign informs us, and as the object of its conquest, we recognize that we are too. *How does it feel?* the neon seems to mock.

Our selfhood ebbing away, we fumble for the language—another list of hyphenated terms—that might capture what it means to be objectified, branded as "other." The old sign relents, throws us a new word, and in an instant, "otherNESS" flashes across the brain. We have heard the term before, recall that it refers to a state or condition of being the "other"—the one marginalized, if not excluded altogether by mainstream Movers and Shakers, the ringleaders at the center of a dominant circle of Selves. A condition emphatically defined, indeed. Who but The Other is forced to check the box marked "OTHER"?

Oh, but wouldn't it be more accurate to describe "otherNESS" as the condition that results when one is *made to feel* like "The Other"? Made to feel like the outsider? An outlier? The object of scorn? The object of pity? Or made to feel like the kindergartener who is the first to be left standing in a game of musical chairs or the fourth grader chosen last to play any sport on any team? How about the middle schooler singled out by the bullies lurking online or the high-school stutterer who cannot make it through a valedictory address? Now, we are made to shiver in the creeping chill—the adults who still remember and would rather forget.

We also remember whole groups of Others, children who grew up black in Mississippi or brown in Arizona, generations of Catholics living in Belfast, of Sunni in Baghdad, Shia in Baghdad. What about Palestinian citizens hunkered down in the Gazan rubble, Syrian refugees camped across the Turkish border, Ebola victims quarantined in Liberian huts? There are those Others without proper ID who cannot vote, those without proper documentation who cannot stay, and the unwashed without an address or even a place to clean up, the unremembering without a voice to speak for themselves or a mind to call their own.

This "otherNESS," like most, represents more than marginalization or exclusion. This is what festers beyond the box marked "OTHER" and can only be described as the condition that results when Others are made to suffer at the hands of Selves. Might this condition be related to an attitude? Or to a history whose only subject is the SELF, one shaped by a worldview envisioning the "NOTself" as "anyone but ME"?

Empathy, were it ever to light up, would surely remind us to welcome others into the group, a group that suffers together just as it rejoices together and always resonates as one. Of course, we know we should be more inclusive, more "other-ORIENTED," as the sign tells us now. But if we were to take this advice—admonition—to heart, would it also mean that The Other must be seen as a "SECONDself" and treated like "ANOTHER me"? If indeed this is the expectation, then where would we find the strength to heave our baggage across the divide and the grace to land on the side of otherness?

No need to find what you already have, insists evolutionary biologist Frans de Waal. We are all Others, he wants us to know, tiny specks in a great collective that minimizes the individual and maximizes the oneness, the survival of the human troupe. In the early days, says de Waal, it was "synchrony" and "attunement," "mood convergence" and "bodily correspondence," even "yawn contagion" and a "herd instinct" that kept us going—the evolutionary processes that regulated and coordinated our activities and movements and allowed our species to flourish.

Still we laugh and cry together, eat and play—and, yes, yawn together. We are the synchronized swimmers, the choreographed dancers, the ones marching in step. We cheer for the players on the home field, boo at the visitors, erupt in "bravos" for the orchestra in the concert hall, rise in a standing ovation for the actors during the curtain call. In a grand show of "bodily correspondence," we line up together, a herd driven to seek food and drink and use the restrooms during halftime at the stadium and intermission at the performing arts center. Where have all the Selves gone? How long will it be before they return? When they do, will we know how to balance Selfhood and Otherness at last?

The neuroscientists have already assured us; we are equipped, they say, with the hardwired mechanism that enables us to mirror each other's actions and behaviors, what endows us with a built-in capacity for sharing thoughts and feelings. "When I see you grasping something, the same cells in my brain are activated, so it's almost like I'm in your mind," says Iacoboni. Gallese, who would remind us that "embodied simulations" allow "our bodies to resonate along with the bodies of others," also points to a parallel resonance in the brain's temporoparietal junction that allows us to negotiate boundaries between Self and Other.

Encounters with others are embrained and embodied, say the scientists, their evidence lending credence to the philosophers who speak in corporeal terms about "lived experience"—Merleau-Ponty, for instance, who would have us believe that it is possible to "live in the facial expression of the other," as we "feel [the other] living in [ours]." Existentialism unites them, the scientists and the philosopher; they are a force to be reckoned with, but still, we hesitate. What holds us back now that they have revealed the mind and body, even the face, of the Other who turns out to be our Second Self?

The existentialists persist unconcerned, their arguments sound, and mean to cajole us into believing there is a close, if not reciprocal, relationship between Self "AND" Other (or shall we say "Second Self"?), one that represents more than what the isolated motel's rooftop sign could ever express. This relationship is based on "interdependence," as Iacoboni and Gallese point out. Self defines Other, and Other defines self. You can't have one without the other, they say. So, it would appear that the "MEness" of Self can only be understood in relation to the "YOUness" of Other and vice versa. Because You activate my being and I activate yours, "We" emerge—the very "we" who resonate together and are "biologically wired and evolutionarily designed to be deeply interconnected," says Iacoboni. What's more, our sense of interdependence—"sense of us"—is shaped in and by what Gallese calls our "shared, we-centric space."

The key, it seems to us, is found in the body. We must learn to trust the biological mechanisms to do the work and to resist the cultural pressures swaying us to think in blunt, binary terms. It is up to us to reject a stark either-or, on-off relationship between Self and Other. The fullness of lives lived in the "we-centric space" cannot be captured by a checkerboard pattern of black and white squares and maybe not even by a tessellated design of colorful shapes, each defining the other.

The project at hand is to find a better analogy and claim interdependence for ourselves. What if we were to envision a sphere, simple and elegant, like a bubble glistening in the air? Light, iridescent, this bubble would be unlike those frothy others, so sugary and fizzy that they were lost in the foam. In this new vision, we would know that the bubble's pressure inside and out was perfectly balanced, the surface tension just strong enough to configure an interdependent whole with only a thin membrane to separate the inner and outer surfaces of Self and Other.

If conditions should change—the balance shifts, and the tension builds, and the analogy pops—what then? What happens to interdependence and to the resonant Self and Other who rounded out the "we-centric sphere," what they once shared, if only for a moment? Without a "sense of us," what becomes of our biological wiring and evolutionary design? And if, in the void, both our Selfhood and Otherness are swallowed up by cultural forces, would we then be made to suffer alone in a frenetic crowd, trapped in a relationship based on alienation?

What will become of us when, slogging through the desert, we are too alienated even to acknowledge a shared plight? How will we keep the wind at our backs when the mind wanders off course, too numb and inhospitable to take in the undefined Self, the anonymous Other? Where will we turn when the mirror is shattered and the Self we thought we recognized is obliterated, its shards left dangling and splinters too jagged to gather up? Will we change our ways, stare into the face of redemption long enough to discern a Second Self glittering in the ashes?

No doubt, heads will spin, searching for answers even as we are confined to an empty room. If only we had paid attention when the walls were closing in, or better yet, if we had studied the white ones that contemporary artist Michelangelo Pistoletto adorned with twenty-two ornately framed mirrors—twenty of them gashed by his own sledgehammer. What might we have discovered in this piece, *Twenty-two Less Two* (2009) and in its thousand reflections still sparkling with the remains of a private Self defined only by its public cracks? Or would it be the other way around, that the public Self was disfigured by too many private horrors? In the pair of unbroken mirrors, might we have caught the ghosts of a Second Self and the Self it made whole?

What if our bubble of interdependence had not been left to drift in dangerous skies? Or if the resonance of biology had guaranteed a stronger membrane? Surely, a precarious sphere would be more secure on solid ground, tied to the culture of asphalt where we could climb aboard, put on a seatbelt, and barrel through Life as a private Self on a public highway jammed with other private Selves. Doors locked and windows up, GPS on and music playing, isn't this where Selfhood begins? Where it will end? Isn't this how we define Otherness—not as sad individuals marginalized or made to suffer but as fellow travelers, all of us fuel-injected with a sense of freedom, of independence—all made to feel safe sealed inside metal bubbles? Surely, this is the analogy that works for us.

When the road rage builds and the bubble's protective membrane is punctured, what then? What happens to the Selves who are tangled together with only their insurance information to exchange? What becomes of us, when, there in the turning lane, we see the broken glass that marks the place where our analogy breaks down? Was the stoplight to blame—the point of no return where the restless Selves had sat too long in the red glare becoming ever more alienated, ever more anonymous? Like these Selves, will we also squander this bit of shared time and space and then fail to negotiate the intersection where biology and culture come together? Will we speed off in different directions when the light turns green, biological instincts driving some of us, while others follow cultural traditions? Will we ever cross paths again or are we the Selves connected only by a longing for the open road?

If only the windshield could be kept spotless, streak free, then maybe we would see clearly enough to appreciate the irony of a shared predicament—the very situation that contemporary artist Sheela Gowda would have had us "behold" in her 2009 installation of the same name. We might have been struck by the scale of the piece and its twenty car bumpers mounted on a massive white wall, their metallic gleam intertwined with the jet-black loops of a python-thick rope. Or we might have responded to the sharp contrast between the bumpers' cold steel polished mirror-bright and the rope's intricate texture braiding together four thousand meters worth of human hair. What might entice us even now? What shall we take from the biology that ropes us together and the culture that keeps us apart? Do we appreciate the one snaking among us, coiling tightly around our Life journeys, or the other working car by car, bubble by bubble to protect us from the strictures and soften the blows?

What if we were to abandon the car altogether and make our way into the world of public transportation crowded with time and space that must be shared, biology and culture that must be blended? Would we be as restless as before—find ourselves in the synchronized rush of multitudes running to catch the subway? Would we count ourselves among the mindless, faceless commuters—de Waal's Others—stepping over the tattered, barefoot soul who has fallen unconscious on the stairs? Or would we be among the handful who eventually break from the herd and stop to help? What would it take to wake us up— break us out of the alienating "urban trance"?

First, we must *notice*, says psychologist Daniel Goleman. If, indeed, we are to become a responsive Self ready to aid the suffering Other, we must repair our "collective blind spot," he says, and then "notice what we don't notice." Goleman says he is optimistic, but we are not so sure. What if we noticed but were not moved to help? What if we can't feel what we can't feel? Would this leave the Self and Other in a swamp, still separate, yet drowning together in the murk of independence, never to inhale the oxygen of interdependence?

Will we ever notice? Ever stop treating the Other as an "It" and objectifying the Self? And if we would rather not answer, then how will we ever breathe new life into the relationship between Self and Other? How will we understand Martin Buber's philosophy or learn to envision a Self as the "I" who encounters and reveres the Other as the "Thou" of his "I-Thou" relationship? Will we ever again feel a need for "social communion," what Alexis de Tocqueville found to be so present in early America?

Yes, we might, we could, says psychologist Carol Gilligan. But it all depends on how we resolve the "conflict" we so often feel between our responsibilities to the Self and our responsibilities to the Other. The resolutions we come up with are critical, she says, because they influence our activities and the ways we behave toward others. What's more, they determine what world views we hold and how we judge our own self-worth.

If we should accept our responsibilities to the Other, then the Self will be defined by the actions it takes to connect with others. This Self, says Gilligan, will measure its worth against an "ethic of care" and locates its being in relation to the world. If, on the other hand, we should give the priority to the Self and avoid responsibilities to the Other, then separation—separateness— will define the Self. Gilligan says the isolated Self will assess its worth using an "abstract ideal of perfection," along with other standards of "character and status." In this case, the world is positioned in relation to the Self.

Will we accept or avoid the truths of these responsibilities? Are we meant to live with such absolutes—the black and white of self-sacrifice or self-preservation? Of caring or not caring, noticing or not noticing? Or are we the relativists, the contextualists who will find ourselves dancing along a continuum somewhere between selflessness and selfishness? Pirouetting at different points between EMPATHY and NOTempathy? Who are we but the ones who think we can dance, who will always dance with the stars, dance in the rain, and splash in the murky grays of a world's worth of shifting sands? It all depends, we will say, and waltz through some situations, salsa through others. Yes, there are contingencies, but in the end, we can always be counted on to dance around Gilligan's responsibilities and Goleman's optimism.

We tango and twirl around the solitude of Selfhood, two-step and twist around the synchrony of Otherness, knowing all the while that dance must be our metaphor. Beyond analogy, this is what embraces our gyrations and lets us pant or glide; the vision that sees us dancing among the bubbles and between the bumpers. We are free to dance with the mirrors shining in the brain and the mirrors shattering on the wall. So, we cavort and sing the body electric, even as our skin sweats and muscles groan—and heels mash the expressionless face.

No, we are not the angels dancing on the head of a pin but the mortals who dance with the black of our secreting bile and the fire of our coursing blood. Though our hearts beat faster and faster, Empathy will not unravel any more of its corporeal mystery. Left to our own devices, we will choreograph other stories, find the rhythms that let us dance with the black swan and with the sugarplums in our heads. We will tell about the Carnival's samba, the bayou's zydeco, repeat the story of the Raven dance and the Lion dance, and we will not dance alone.

Chapter IV

Storytelling and Something More

S o, here we are, dancing with our stories, you with your tall tales and fairytales and I with my fables and folklore. We are the Selves who hear their melodies in a major key and select them again and again like the most frequently played songs in an old-time jukebox. How delighted are we to collect them—bedtime stories, horror stories, cautionary tales alike—and count them among our favorite keepsakes, the little gems tucked in a velvet-lined jewelry box.

Stories sparkle with a wisdom we find comforting. Of course, we would; they do not require us to master their life lessons. We will not learn what they have to impart about growth and transformation, forgiveness and redemption. Oh, but we will always expect them to teach the fine art of living risk-free, especially throughout their most frightening of passages. We need not worry; we are safe with our stories as they are with us.

Most of all though, we prize the stories that know how to read us, know when to pump up our sagging hearts and smooth out our rocky lives. They are talismans of authenticity, what we rub to hear the music that keeps us dancing. Look, there we are, each of us strobe-lit by the disco ball's sparkle, each of us hearing whatever jazzes us and whirls us beyond the starkest questions of morality and memory, myth and mortality. The dance floor is boisterous and crowded with our dazzling delusions.

Though yours differ from mine, and mine from yours, our stories are similarly credible, every one of them authentic and shining with dependability. This we believe and is the credo we share. Surely, our stories will tell us who we are, where we came from, and where we are going. Their surprising plot twists and loveable characters, no matter how flawed, will never disappoint. We will not be left hanging, and, in the end, even the characters long dead will live on in us. They are loyal and their stories will never trouble us with rumors of how it all ends for us. We are the heroes who will not be deceived by the truth of our own demise.

This much we know, the separate Selves united by a shared destiny to dance across boundaries and romp in the borderland between myth and reality. This is where we thrive, a species habitat perfectly suited to our rhizomic ways—one entangling us in story arcs linear and circular that we will trace with gusto and follow into any genre we like. It's a wild ride to be sure, so we must hang on tight to our Kindles and paperbacks, hunker down in our video games and theme parks, where crisscrossing arcs abound.

Still, we search for something more in our Adventureland, something given by a second or third life or bestowed by crafty worlds of war and mines. Surely, we will find the "more" in tales of historic expeditions and post-apocalyptic futures or in bodice-ripping romances and bloodcurdling mysteries. Until then, we must rely on the stories we know, the kind that still transform familiar places into open spaces and vice versa.

We live through our stories, act them out as if rehearsing the different and better Selves bound to emerge in so much unfolding. These are the stories we practice again and again, each time taking comfort in all they reveal—and in all they do not. They give us the scripts, and we stand on stage, ready to play the parts, gratified only by the best roles recurring throughout the opening acts of human history. If only we could do them justice, give the performance of a lifetime, then everyone would see that we walked across the sands of time and left our mark.

Perhaps we will take our places on the grand stage with the generations who came before, all of us inheriting the creation myths that explain the beginnings of time but not the contradictions of culture. Or we will look to coming-of-age stories to start us on the winding path that eventually finds a way forward without worrying us about the responsibilities of adulthood. The most comforting role of all, though, may be played in the magical realism of stories delivering us into worlds so wide that we expect to fly with all manner of spirit beings who will not judge the singular truth of our mortal soul.

We dance on delighted and unaware of the onlookers—three of them we would later count—who can be seen shaking their heads in the video that came to light. In the disco ball's glitter, we are too busy to notice their angry eyes nor could our ringing ears hear what these strangers have to say. Later, we would learn that the trio was fixated on what it called our "plunge into Nostalgia's paradox"—the busybodies' label for what they believe had landed us in a "deafening playworld" where we expected to hear all about the journey ahead.

Apparently, they had studied our "sorry case" like a panel of judges handing down rulings and taking themselves very seriously. Here is their evidence, transcribed from a security camera recording all that transpired on our dance floor:

"Look at them spin," begins one of the spectator judges—a fiction editor by day, it turned out. "There we have our sweet dancers, so desperate to prance into Selfhood, so anxious to reveal something more in their lives. And still they deny the bitter truth of their sparkling cage: They are going nowhere, revealing nothing."

The other two, a social worker and an audiologist, step out of the disco ball's glare and tear themselves away from its mesmerizing mirrors. One coughs, the other gulps, and both fix their gaze on the fiction editor, whose own eyes appear to darken and drift off.

"If only they could find the still point," muses the editor, "and rediscover the ancestor Selves from whence they came." Deep in thought now, the editor seems lost in all that is left unsaid. "If only they would awaken to the characters whose truths have carried them along the way—whose wisdom peels back the layers . . ."

The other two cock their heads, but give a polite, if tentative, nod. Looking beyond them, though, the editor does not notice their quizzical expressions.

"Yoo-hoo," calls the social worker to the fiction editor. "You out there, come on back. We're right here in front of you."

"Could you explain," the audiologist urges the editor.

The fiction editor starts, mumbles a "sorry," but becomes even more wistful. "Would our friends hear us if we told them? Would they turn down the music and hear—really hear, as if for the first time, that they are the descendants of Adam and Eve, the children of Father Sky and Mother Earth, the followers of Vishnu and Shiva?"

The social worker and audiologist blink and look at each other, their eyes asking if a response is required. "It seems dubious," continues the fiction editor, confirming that the questions were rhetorical and part of an ongoing monologue. "The dancers are too dazzled and will not soon discover who they are, how far they have traveled, or how far they have left to go."

The three of them look down at their feet, none willing to confront the strange, if pernicious, pall now hanging above their heads. Finally, a throat is cleared and the audiologist blurts, "Let me see if I have this right. You say these people are dancing in the dark. It's exhilarating, but it's also frightening—not to mention dangerous. The problem is if they turn on the lights, the fun disappears with the fear—and worse, they will be forced to see the true shabbiness of their smoke-and-mirrors carnival ride."

The audiologist pauses to let the other two visualize Playworld's run-down ride and reflect on Nostalgia's paradox—and the absurdity of it all.

"And no, they probably would not hear us—or anyone else for that matter," says the audiologist. "I suspect their hearing is damaged, particularly in the range of 300 to 3,000 hertz, what we call the human voice range—an impairment likely due to severe tinnitus, the result of too many loud parties."

"Sounds serious," says the social worker. "But tinnitus might explain a lot. Their poorly developed interpersonal communication skills, for instance. An unwillingness to listen to others."

Blank faced, the fiction editor does not acknowledge the audiologist's stripped-down assessment of Nostalgia's paradox nor the technical explanation of what ails the carnival riders trapped by the smoke and mirrors. Nor is it clear that the social worker's words registered.

"These blissful dancers are tilting at windmills," says the editor. "They are the fourteen-year-old adults still coming of age, still pretending to be Huck Finn and Tom Sawyer on the Mississippi. How exuberant they are, the children still growing up with Dorothy and Toto in their own Oz."

The audiologist and social worker wait politely, if expectantly, for more evidence, perhaps indictments, gleaned from nineteenth and twentieth-century literature, American or otherwise. But the fiction editor only sighs and murmurs, "Like Holden Caulfield, they are lost in the rye," before drifting off again.

"Excuse me," says the social worker, clearly annoyed. "I couldn't hear. You were turned away. Could you please repeat that and maybe rejoin the group? I'm sure you don't want to be rude."

"I could fit you with a hearing aid," says the audiologist to the social worker.

The fiction editor is taken aback, unable to stifle a gasp. The audiologist, who has caught the Salinger reference, seeks verification now. "Are you suggesting that they are stuck in limbo, maybe like Dave, rocketing further and further into the silent emptiness after HAL's demise?"

"Or they are stranded on an uninhabited island like Robinson Crusoe," says the social worker, picking up the thread and ignoring the audiologist's offer.

"Yes, well, if we are talking about islands," begins the fiction editor, still distant, perhaps wandering in the noir of an imagined netherworld, "it would be rather like *Lord of the Flies*, and our dancers are blind to the brokenness. Piggy's glasses are gone, along with any clarifying or corrective power they may have had. The disco people will not see the truth revealed in the hedonistic dance they do with Jack and his tribe."

"They have clearly lost their way and will need services," says the social worker, who seems a bit impatient, perhaps wearied by the island metaphor's metastasis, but more likely annoyed by the fiction editor's distance.

"I am especially worried about real-world evidence of a protracted adolescence," the social worker says, "and what comes with it—poor impulse control, for example. Now, there's your hedonism."

The social worker studies the others' expressions, but they seem equally unreadable. With a toss of the head, the social worker pushes on with the information deemed important, whether the two of them are ready to take it in or not. "A long adolescence like this also explains the failure to complete the developmental task of self-integration in a timely manner. And as we are seeing, such a failure has major social consequences."

The fiction editor blinks then inhales as the social worker gathers more steam, more determination. "Most concerning of all, at least from my perspective," the social worker declares, "is the failure to develop pro-social behaviors and become active, fully functioning members of society—the kind of adults who will help ensure that the social fabric weaving us together remains intact, if you want another metaphor."

Like the editor, the audiologist blinks, inhales, and, spontaneously, the two nod their affirmation of what clearly are the social worker's mounting and apparently heartfelt concerns.

"Can you believe it?" the social worker begins, and by the tone of voice alone, the others know this is a launch and not of an inquiry investigating the causes of a never-ending adolescence.

"There are brides and grooms," continues the social worker, voice tighter still, "who will enter into marriage—and into the larger social contracts—as Cinderella and Prince Charming, complete with an extravagant wedding in the grand ballroom of the Disneyland Hotel."

The social worker takes a breath as the other two catch theirs. "It is hard to see how these young couples will take on the responsibilities of adulthood and participate in civic life, when in fact their wedding package includes a ride in Cinderella's coach."

Imagining the cartoon image, the fiction editor and audiologist wince then brace themselves for the worst and what they hope will conclude the social worker's rant. "Yes, you guessed it," delivers the social worker, "the brides and grooms, just starting their lives together, will leave the hotel in Cinderella's coach ready only for their escape into happily ever after fairytales."

"And when the clock strikes twelve, what then?" says the fiction editor in a similar noninterrogative tone.

"I doubt our Cinderellas and Prince Charmings would even hear it," says the audiologist. "Their tinnitus would really flare up after that party. And like the other dancers at the ball, they are not inclined to power through that much ringing in their ears. That would require intense concentration, a lot of paying attention and lipreading—too much effort for them. And what would be the point? They only hear what they want to hear anyway."

"Oddly enough, they seem to hear the music," the fiction editor points out.

"It's more like they *feel* it," the audiologist clarifies. "More visceral than auditory, especially that pounding bass in the lowest frequencies."

"So, they will dally at the ball and dance their lives away," mourns the fiction editor, gazing off again.

"They keep dancing," says the audiologist, "because they are afraid. Heck, maybe we all are."

"Afraid of what?" the social worker questions.

"The long silence," answers the audiologist, "what they will hear at the end once the music finally dies."

"Meanwhile," the social worker picks up, "they will only dance with their characters, not with each other."

"Especially the women," murmurs the fiction editor.

"Oh, so you did hear me after all. Wasn't sure—you were far away again," says the social worker. "What do you mean by that?"

"I would like to hear about women and their characters," says the audiologist.

"In the world of publishing," the editor begins, "it is well known that women make up the bulk of the fiction readers. They are avid, indeed, and read novels by the truckload—certainly many more than men."

"Why would that be?" demands the social worker. "How do you explain it?"

"There are theories, of course," the editor confirms, "all related to one's capacity for empathy."

A look of curiosity crosses the audiologist's face, but it is skepticism that pinches the social worker's. "Women, as you may know," continues the editor, "are more empathic than men. Not surprisingly then, women tend to identify with the characters more often and more wholeheartedly than do men. Women will share the characters' worlds, put themselves in their situations, and feel what they feel. A well-drawn character can leap off the page any time but most often will come to dance with a female reader."

"Women must hear something in the music that men do not," muses the audiologist.

"Perchance the song of empathy," the fiction editor ventures. "What wondrous frequency might that be?"

"Well, I'm sure I wouldn't know about that," says the audiologist.

"Nonetheless, it seems an intriguing possibility," says the fiction editor. "I did read in a rather well-researched work of nonfiction—*Empathy and the Novel*, I believe is the title—that women readers have a 'busy mirror neuron system.' Do you know about this, the brain's magical network of mirrors?"

"The MNS," the audiologist confirms. The social worker nods, eyeing the editor-turned-scientist.

"Yes? Splendid," says the editor and smiles. "But, unfortunately, it is not clear which came first. Might it be the firing neurons firing women's imaginations and thus their capacities for empathizing with the characters? Or might it be the other way 'round, and women's reading habits and interests are the sparks lighting up the neurons and building a brilliant electrical grid in their brains?"

"Chicken or egg," says the audiologist.

"First, second, men, women—what difference does it matter?" blurts the social worker, most impatient now. "I want to know *why*. Why do these people invest so much of themselves in a book's characters? It's all fiction, for God's sake. A silly daydream. What do they expect to get out of this lie?"

Unsure of where this latest rant is going, the audiologist looks up at the ceiling and begins to whistle, the tune barely audible. The social worker glances upward as well, but seeing nothing, returns to the interrogation on the ground. "Why would we—I mean, they, *those people*," the social worker says, pointing at the disco dancers, "want to be like Robinson Crusoe? You know, 'put themselves in his situation, feel what he feels'? Or even worse, live on a presocial island like Jack and Piggy?"

The whistling grows louder, and now the fiction editor looks up then looks confused, as if trying to place the simple tune, a jaunty melody that seems vaguely familiar. "Complex characters thrust into unimaginable situations are a gift to us—all of us who dare to change, grow, and imagine our worlds as if they could be otherwise. These are the fraught and fully dimensional characters that allow us access to our deepest feelings of doubt and despair," says the editor, "even as they pluck our heartstrings and would have us believe redemption and transformation are possible."

Stone-faced, the social worker says nothing. "These are the characters most like us," continues the editor, "the deeply conflicted protagonists and compelling antiheroes who represent the quirks of human nature. Good writers channel them, use them to condense an uncompromising world beset by contradiction and ambiguity. We use the characters to cope wi—"

"Stop that whistling," blasts the social worker, eyes wild, darting from the fiction editor to the audiologist and back. "It's really annoying. No one wants to listen to the *Gilligan's Island* theme song right now."

The fiction editor's eyes light up. "That's what it is. Oh, of course."

"What'd you think it was," snorts the social worker, "the song of empathy?"

The audiologist's face is ashen, but the others take no notice. "Ah, but we do want to recall that fateful three-hour cruise now," says the fiction editor. "What we have is a sitcom, to be sure, a harmless, lighthearted romp that is also a parable meant to teach us about the seven deadly sins—a cautionary tale meant to show us what will happen if we let those hideous sins of commission sully our souls."

The social worker scoffs, but the fiction editor continues undaunted. "We have a zany cast of seven candy-colored characters beloved by millions. Gilligan and the other castaways make us laugh, but more importantly, they make it safe to laugh at sin—theirs and ours. And—"

"It's just a stupid laugh track, all fake," growls the social worker.

Again, the audiologist blanches in sharp contrast to the deepening scarlet of the social worker's face.

"As I was saying," says the fiction editor, "each of the characters represents a different sin."

"Ginger represents lust," pipes up the audiologist, coming back to life.

"Yes, according to most analyses," confirms the fiction editor.

"Then Mary Ann must be envy," says the social worker.

Surprised by the social worker's change of tone and heart, the other two blink but manage a nod. "Indeed," they say.

"She was always my favorite," mumbles the social worker.

"And Thurston Howell?" asks the fiction editor.

"Greed," say the others, caught up in the editor's name-that-sin game.

"That one seems too obvious," says the fiction editor. "How about Mrs. Howell's sin?"

"Sloth," responds the audiologist.

"No, no, not at all," says the social worker. The others exchange looks. "Well, maybe. I guess I could see that. She never does anything, wouldn't lift a finger. But Lovey is so damned self-indulgent. I think she represents gluttony."

"The captain is gluttony," asserts the audiologist.

"Possibly," says the fiction editor, amused by the others who appear to have such a vested interest in the characters. "What about the professor?"

"Easy," says the social worker. "Wrath. I mean, how would you feel if none of your inventions ever worked and you couldn't get anyone off the island?"

"Pride," says the audiologist. "The professor is guilty of having too much pride."

"Nope, not seeing that," argues the social worker.

Jaws clenched, the audiologist says nothing.

"Where does this leave the captain?" the fiction editor asks.

"He's wrath," says the social worker, arms crossed. "He's angry enough to hit Gilligan with his hat all the time, isn't he?"

"You just said the professor is wrath," chides the audiologist. "The skipper is clearly overweight. That makes him gluttony, as I said before."

"What about Gilligan?" asks the fiction editor, as if relishing the intense loyalties to the characters.

"Gilligan is sloth," says the audiologist, eyes flashing.

"Whoa!" shouts the social worker. "You said Mrs. Howell is sloth. You can't have it both ways."

"Well, what do you think Gilligan represents?" comes the audiologist's snide retort.

"Some have said Gilligan is Satan," the fiction editor interjects. As expected, the others' reactions are immediate and fierce.

"No way," explode the two, eyes narrow, hard.

"Ah, but he is the devil who tempted the other six, luring them with the promised delights of a tropical cruise," the fiction editor says with a bit of a smirk. The others shake their heads, nostrils flared, chins out. "The devil who holds them captive on the island, his very indolence sabotaging their efforts to escape," chortles the editor.

"See, I told you so. Gilligan is sloth," the social worker announces to the audiologist.

"You did not," barks the audiologist. "But sloth still wouldn't make him Satan," roars the audiologist.

"Gilligan is kind of an Everyman," the social worker replies.

"The most loveable character," says the audiologist.

"I still like Mary Ann," whimpers the social worker.

"Gilligan is the most like us," says the fiction editor, beginning to sway and swirl.

"Yeah, except he's kind of goofy," says the social worker, also swaying back and forth. "A big, overgrown kid living in his own world."

"And really lazy," says the audiologist. Then with a shimmy, the audiologist adds, "He's lost, aimless, doesn't know who he is yet—and doesn't want to do anything about it."

"Trapped by his flaws," says the fiction editor, and the three of them dance on.

It was the noise of their overheated argument that first called our attention—what the video would confirm. Interfering with the music, the uproar had forced us to stop dancing, and in our stillness we spotted the trio of onlookers—that panel of judges going nowhere, ruling on nothing. There they were, all right, the three of them dancing in the dark.

"Look at them spin," we had said. "Our bitter dancers, caught in Nostalgia's paradox, who will not turn on the lights. Oh, but we see what they are, the sweet hypocrites caged by their sins of omission," we said.

And what had they omitted? Which C-sharp melodies had refused to play in their jukebox? What little gems had turned up missing in their jewelry box? Was it the story of civility? Or integrity? Humility?

"Empathy," we sing now.

But what if empathy were to be located? What if it is empathy that roots us in the borderland or dizzies us under the disco ball? Could it be Empathy who tells stories meant to blur the lines between what is real and what is not? Or is it we who omit such truths? We the sinners who tell ourselves stories in order to dance—to dream? Are we the Every man, Every woman telling ourselves stories in order to feel and to feel *better?* Or find our destinies? Make sense of a world spinning out of control? Must we be the ones to spin the yarns that one day can retake control?

Damasio says we are wired to tell ourselves stories. "The brain is a born storyteller," he says, "busy constructing the narrative of our own autobiography." What is an autobiography but a tangle of short stories knotted together? We have no time to sort them, only to tell them—and tell them we must. How else are we to make sense of what gnaws at us from within the internal world or shouts at us from the external? Ours is the storytelling species, uniquely aware of what is at stake. Stories must come through for us, must reconcile the differences between inner and outer worlds and smooth out their competing demands.

What's more, the stories we tell ourselves must do the heavy lifting, give us a way to handle the brain's consciousness of time—what we remember of a lived past and what we envision in an anticipated future. Our stories are resilient indeed, and as Damasio sees them, robust enough to resolve the "conflict" between the two states that have us looking backward and forward at the same time. Better still, our stories write the permission slips that allow us to start over again after yet another of our "setbacks," as Damasio calls them. When the memories are too paralyzing, the future too forbidding, we need only reinvent ourselves and tell a different story.

Perhaps we will applaud Kathryn's storytelling efforts, her brain's response to the desperate questions of making sense, starting over, and retaking control. "My life is in chaos," said the returning student—an older woman in a class of twentysomethings. Yet, the story she told herself was clear to all. Everything made sense now that she identified with the wild, windswept branches of *The Mulberry Tree*, Van Gogh's small but intense canvas, painted at the asylum in Saint-Rémy during the autumn of 1889. Was it the yellow leaves of a lonely tree flailing against an indigo sky that spurred Kathryn to find the words? Or had Van Gogh's own turbulence explained the terrifying chapter now unfolding in her story?

Either way, Kathryn told herself that she was not alone, not "the only one going crazy"—the reconciliation she would make and the comfort she could take after the sudden death of one son, the incarceration of another, and the long-term reality of caring for a daughter with Down syndrome, alone.

The need to make sense manifests itself early on and is first expressed in the marks that fifteen- to eighteen-month-olds make on the walls or in the sand. When they *notice* these marks— embrace their magical powers—these toddlers are reborn as storytellers. They join the human community and begin the work of making sense of a world thrumming with lights and sirens and turning on sandbox rules and demanding schedules.

Finger-painted scribbles become controlled if exuberant circles that, with a few more tweaks and some added interior lines, blossom into depictions of the main character in the four- to five-year-old's story. These are the "mandala" or "big head" drawings universally recognized and understood as "me symbols"—the first representation of Self. Like the child's stories, these drawings quickly become more detailed and complex. Vertical lines are extended from the head to represent legs, and now human figures appear lined up side by side on a "baseline" at the bottom of the page, the largest of them meant to indicate the storytelling child. Through the lens of Self, the seven-year-old begins to make sense of social structures—claims a place in the clan—and a larger story told countless times through the ages is retold once more.

From the mark-making preschooler to the memoir-writing retiree, this is what we share—a species narrative bound up in a long tradition of storytelling that began in the cave. With hungry predators howling outside, we were safe enough inside, yet hungry ourselves, always craving the terrifying tales that would humble us, leave us awestruck, make us feel more alive and thus better able to face the wider world beyond. These are the same stories that satisfy us today, the authentic ones charged with emotion that rivet us, seduce us into telling their visceral truths. These are the stories we retell, each time embellishing them until they become epic, ever more mythic and absurd—the tall tales we will always find reassuring.

Today we venture out in an SUV, the cave on wheels meant to protect us in the asphalt jungle—save us from the fearsome eighteen-wheelers snarling and belching outside. How snug, perhaps smug, we are inside with audiobooks and podcasts that shape our own stories—the tall tales we tell ourselves to feel *safe*, feel *free*, more alive, and less absurd. Ours is an epic journey, so the story goes; and We believe what it tells us. On we go, barreling through the jungle spurred by the stories that embellish our everyday comings and goings. Like our ancestors, we still go out to forage, still come home to regroup. Only the most mythic stories will tell us where else we have been and could be headed.

We will use these stories to make the familiar strange and the strange familiar, which is to say, we will use them to transform place into space and space into place. Good storytelling opens new spaces that invite us to explore, to roam free and discover what lies beyond—even as it offers refuge, places to rest and recharge a weary soul. What's more, the stories we tell ourselves, like the ones we hear or read, can be counted on to strike a balance between the two states of being; we trust them all to find the sweet spot that gives us a familiar place to pause and reflect on the past and a strange space in which to wander and imagine the future.

Is this the balance Junior's story is intended to strike? Is this the high-wire act of a seven-year-old boy in the children's picture book *Eight Days* by Edwidge Danticat? What are youngsters nestled safe in their beds meant to take from the story a terrified child tells to reassure himself during the eight days he and his friend Oscar are trapped in the rubble of a Haitian home ruptured by the 2010 earthquake? Or is the story aimed at us, the sleepless adults who fail again and again in our responsibilities to keep the children of the world safe?

Perhaps it is we, the parents reading the story to our children, who are made to feel better, who are set free as Junior transforms the nightmare into a dream we will believe. Skillfully, he embellishes the story that lifts us from the dark, twisted remains of a place once familiar, now strange, and catapults us into the light of an airy space even more familiar where we soar with a boy flying the highest kite, playing the biggest game of marbles, and singing the best solo in the choir. We will cheer as Junior and Oscar play the best soccer game ever—the one leaving Oscar so tired that he goes to sleep never to awake again. How much better we feel imagining Junior at play and Oscar asleep. There is no traumatizing past, no uncertain future, only this celestial moment that is surely meant to restore our faith. For now, at least, we can believe "the kids are all right."

Stories have found our sweet spot for centuries, the one that celebrates "the now," which in the face of so much calamity and chaos, is all we can ever count on—maybe all we really have, even when order is restored and our faith renewed. Like the young nobles of Bocaccio's *Decameron*, who told their ten stories each night for ten nights during the worst rampages of the Black Plague, we too tell ourselves the stories that free us to play—encourage us to revel in the earthly delights of the here and now rather than wait for heavenly rewards in an uncertain hereafter.

We too seek to escape and will retreat further into our own hilltop villas high above the terrifying scourges below. Like our fourteenth-century predecessors, we will romp in the hedonistic stories that praise the sins of the flesh. This is hardly the moment for pious tales about the sanctity of the spirit. How could it ever be? The body is more believable; its sensuality more reassuring and much more faithful to us. Hedonism prevails yet again, and frivolity continues to anchor "the now" that shapes the stories we tell ourselves about a world still out of control.

Sometimes, we prefer stories that play with us, tease us about our frailties—poke fun at our delusions. Such are the stories that dance with illusory mirrors and spin us 'round and 'round with their trick questions about what is real and what is not. Life is absurd, they josh, only too pleased to prove it with a parody that leaves us giddy, a satire that makes us snicker, a farce that reduces us to snorts. We are ever so delighted by the cleverest of them, especially the ones that let us believe we have detected their trickery and grasped their irony. These are the tales we tell ourselves in order to play in their play.

"What a spoof," we chuckle when encountering the play of Diderot's set of moral stories, the first titled *Ceci N'est Pas un Conte* (*This Is Not a Story*) and the next titled *Seconde Conte* (*Second Story*). "How droll," we say with a grin, this eighteenth-century French philosopher is toying with our perceptions of reality and appearance, truth and falsity. Has he played us like so many others in generations past? "Oh, the outrage of it," we feign. Where is the morality in his trick? Or the truth in a pair of stories related by falsity, one denying its very being, the other declaring it so? Which, if either, tells of reality, and which merely appears to speak of such a thing? And now, here we are, right back to Magritte's *Ceci N'est Pas une Pipe* (*This Is Not a Pipe*), and Banksy's *This Is a Pipe*. "Such a hoot."

Oh yes, we expect the play to keep us going for a good long while. No wonder it still tickles us that DreamWorks's feature animation *Shrek* takes what we thought we knew about a once-upon-a-time fairytale world and turns it upside down just to poke us—and scramble our moral compass. Appearances are deceiving, the cartoon's wisdom warns, and we must not be fooled by the handsome Prince Charming aboard his noble steed or by the title character himself, an indolent green ogre soaking up life in the putrid swamp. The truth will out, and we will come to see the good in the medieval monster who defeats the dimwitted prince to break the evil curse trapping the princess between two realities. But Fiona is no damsel in distress, and we are thrown into a tizzy watching her decide her own fate. Who could have guessed the feisty, part-time beauty would choose to live with Shrek in the swamp as a matronly, full-time ogre? A tricky story to tell ourselves indeed, this happily ever after satire.

Then there is the play of video games, adrenaline-infused and unencumbered by perceptions of morality—Diderot's, DreamWorks's, or anyone else's. Reciprocity wins the day, and it seems only fair that if we agree to play long and hard—first-person shooters and role-play games alike—then they must agree to let us bask in the splendid truths of their alternate realities, no questions asked. They are the storytellers, we are the story-players. They set the rules; we play the roles. If they should violate the terms of play, we will move swiftly to shut them down. Should we violate the agreement—dare to tell ourselves the rules do not apply because we are the mightiest heroes in the stories we play—the video games will exact a terrible revenge. There we'll be, the ones made to die over and over and over.

So, it is that we come to live in the year 2160, in a future reality made clear and credible by *Mass Effect*. Or perhaps it is life in a darker past we prefer, and we find ourselves roaming the mean streets of 1947 Los Angeles in *L.A. Noire*. We are just as easily lured by puzzle side-scroller games such as *Valiant Hearts*, which drops us into the trenches of World War I, and *Never Alone*, which immerses us in the folklore of Alaskan Inuits. And now, play is based on authenticated primary-source artifacts that flood our fantasies with history and bring culture to life.

Perhaps we are among the millions caught up in the alternate realities of the hugely popular *League of Legends* or the long-running *World of Warcraft*. These we recognize as global phenomena, truly "mega" massively multiplayer online games filled with strategic and tactical challenges taken on voraciously by our characters, heroic or otherwise, all salivating, hell-bent on destroying the enemy. Like them, we too are rabid competitors and will work tirelessly to make certain the champions and warriors always have what they need to win. This is the story we tell and the mission we serve.

Play is still unencumbered—free of moral concerns about good and evil, that is. Triumph is all that matters, our call to banish vulnerability and weakness from the realm. We play out the story of power and strength, the one that blends perceptions of fantasy and reality. Neither will be distinguished from the other; both look into a world turning on the splendid if inelegant truth that "might makes right." More than an aphorism, this is the ironclad rule we have agreed to follow, the exacting role we have agreed to play.

We are still learning to play, children who tell stories in order to dream. Mostly though, we tell them to imagine ourselves as if we could be stronger, smarter, better looking, more powerful, facile, and willing to believe anything, maybe even *everything*, is possible. So, we resonate with the shy Wisconsin boy who is captivated by a bold Arthurian legend and imagines himself as the knight strong enough to pull the sword from the stone, the would-be king heroic enough to win the heart of the most popular girl in the class.

We understand what drives him to believe that if he could just accomplish these feats—slay his own dragons—then he would know his destiny and everything, even life itself, would fall into place. But he is the young man who winds up in California without his Excalibur or his Guinevere. Now, he dreams only of finding another destiny, another role to play.

We know the story of the boy growing up in Missouri with his cartoon drawings who was destined for fame and fortune in California—the mythical realm where he built his "house" of dreams, including the animation studios, theme parks, and other entities of the Disney Corporation. Disneyland itself is a walk through Walt's imagination, the story he told himself, and multitudes of us since, about a world organized around four "lands" where there would always be a place for fantasy and adventure and room for exploring frontiers and the edges of tomorrow. It was not orange groves that Sir Walter saw through the mists of old Anaheim, but a Magic Kingdom—what soon became his legendary Fantasyland and Adventureland, Frontierland and Tomorrowland. Sixty years on, these are still the dreams that organize a storytelling world around the vagaries of human nature.

Such are the dreams and destinies we understand and want desperately to believe. But there is another story, the narrow one Ramona, a student and prospective elementary teacher, tells herself that limits the options, and in the end, says only one thing is possible. Fantasy and adventure are stripped away, leaving her—all of us—on the edge of a soul-crushing tomorrow we do not want to face. Ramona has no room to dream.

Still, she is made to see her destiny, a nightmare brought into sharp focus by the three allegorical figures in Tiepolo's large ceiling painting *The Triumph of Virtue and Nobility over Ignorance* (1740-50). Two of the figures are so lofty and bright; they must be Virtue and Nobility, the glorious pair in command of the rococo painting's luminous space. In Ramona's story, they are angels representing her sisters—a doctor and an attorney— who shine in the light of their mother's love. Ramona, the future teacher, imagines herself as Ignorance, the dark figure falling into a hellish oblivion, a lonely underworld dominated by bats.

A fourth figure, invisible to viewers but fully present to Ramona, represents her mother and the triumph of bitterness and spite over innocence. For some twenty years, Ramona has been "ignorant" of the "circumstances" of her birth—and of the reason for her mother's duplicitous behavior, praise for her sisters' accomplishments, scorn for hers. When at last she learns she is the product of a rape, Ramona sees the destiny that, according to her mother, awaits them all. In death, as in life, her sisters will be victorious; their virtuous and noble souls "carried into heaven," while the ignorant Ramona continues to fall and is "vanquished" forever.

What now? What story can we tell ourselves to make sense of such a thing? Or at least to feel better about the "circumstances"?

Will we plead with Ramona to distort, or better yet, omit the facts—forget that the parish priest turns out to be her biological father—to make life more bearable for us, if not for herself? We are in a hurry to revive the stories of play and dreams, ready to return to a borderland that is more myth than reality. Ramona is welcome to come along (how we hope she will) as we search for the story that lets us breathe again.

Oh yes, we will find the best stories and reorder the world, especially when it seems most corrupt and incomprehensible. And we will inhabit—become—the stories we tell. This is our destiny, what has always been an existential reveille that gets us up every day to fill in the gaps we cannot understand or will not accept. Happily, we haul out the buckets and paint over the cracks with the brightest top-of-the-luminosity-scale colors until the borderland becomes the playland, the theme park we prefer. Only then are we free to romp and dance with stories this functional, this vital. Yes, Joan Didion, "We tell ourselves stories in order to live."

What's more, we will loop around and around in these stories, dizzied by the thrill for as long as we can—that is, until we feel the pace slowing, the pulse weakening, and it becomes clear that no amount of begging can keep the rollercoaster going forever. Still loyal, though, these stories will carry us to the end of the ride. One last time, they will be tuned up, their wheels greased and readied for the plunge into that darkest of tunnels. We must work quickly now to finish the polishing, make any last-minute adjustments, wholesale changes, if we are to tell them on our own terms—and in the nick of time.

In a grand gesture, our most vivid stories will take us for the final spin, provided we promise not to cling to the lap bar. We must let the pretty colors in and agree now to tell these stories in order to die.

"Ready," we say without hesitation, for they have prepared us well.

We will let go, throw our hands in the air, and with our last giddy breaths, scream with these exhilarating stories, knowing that it is a "good" death we die. Isn't this as it should be? Stories ought to be as comforting in death as they were in life. They must deliver the end-of-life care we demand, ease the suffering heard in Keats's lament, in Panic's cry still echoing across the ages: *I have fears that I will cease to be/Before my pen has glean'd my teeming brain.*

"Have faith," we urge. "A pen is not requir'd, for the brain, which is to say the soul, shall give freely of its stories before it bursts with all they contain." Surely, the best stories will carry out our wishes, secure our legacies, and dutifully fulfill the promises we made to ourselves during the up-and-down ride.

"Take heart," we say. There is still more comfort they will offer, greater solace we will take. Like the jewelry box gems and talismans rubbed smooth, our rollercoaster stories will outlive us to become someone else's keepsakes. They are the gifts we gave ourselves as the tunnel's blackness approached, the same ones we trust others to receive in the light on the other side.

This, we believe, makes stories the instruments of culture, mementos to be passed from one generation to the next like torches burning with the customs and values, hopes and desires that must live on. After all, the stories we tell ourselves are rooted in tradition and laden with the strongest, most enduring values meant to endow a culture with a sense of security, identity, and ease with itself. How tried and true they are, these instruments—and so versatile too, working as they do on behalf of human nature as well.

We will be true to our roots and take care to pass along only the stories that are deeply, viscerally understood in every culture. Such influence they exert, reinforcing the shared beliefs, inculcating the core values. Harmony and happiness are to be treasured, for instance; wisdom and learning too, and, of course, cleanliness and continuity will always be cherished. So, it is that our final stories will accentuate the positive and package up the rosiest memories, the happiest moments, in order to bring peace to the dying and harmony to the living. Hopes for serenity fulfilled, desires for fantasy satisfied, these stories belong to the culture and take care of everyone. This is what the hospice workers can confirm.

There is wisdom to be offered—the kind imparted by cautionary tales that the dying tell to instruct the living, especially the pupils whose lives are in danger of running off the rails.

"Don't make the same mistakes we made," the wise call out, sometimes as an order, but most often in a plea. "Otherwise, you will spend your days overcoming the error of your ways," they warn.

"Learn the lesson but ignore the hypocrisy," they mutter almost inaudibly, their imploring eyes beginning to close. "Do as we say, not as we did," come the parting words.

"Rest easy, Old Man," say the foolhardy. "You have done all you can."

"Sleep well, Old Woman. It's no longer up to you," say the inexperienced. *When was it ever?* they wonder.

Silence settles upon them, stretches across the divide, and tells the living and the dying to go off now to find their own ways.

Themes of regret and remorse stand out like dark, brooding threads in a third story woven into the cultural fabric. Anxious to be relieved of their guilty burdens and secret troubles, the dying will confess everything, apologize for it all.

"Please forgive me," so many of them beg, the ones who will not rest until absolution is granted and they are cleansed of their sins, real and imagined.

In death, the slate must be blemish free to match what was given at birth—scrubbed clean to turn the great wheel in the sky, so the story goes. Peace will descend upon us, spread throughout the culture only if the cycle of life remains unbroken and balance in the universe is maintained. Around we go, practicing the customs that tell us we are connected by ritualistic comings and goings—naming ceremonies and funerary rites—if by nothing else. Spin we must, trusting the natural forces to return us to the stardust from whence we came. *To everything, there is a season . . . a time to be born, a time to die . . . a time for peace . . . it's not too late.*

Perhaps our stars would shine brighter if in the turning, we of the coming and going, were to agree on what matters most in this world. Or if we could grasp what it means to live a "good" life—better yet, if we of the living and dying defined a life "well-lived." If only such things could be reduced to their lowest terms, we whine. Perhaps it is a matter of finding the most profound words and universally understood phrases to tell each other the simplest story that, according to Empathy, is about gratitude, compassion, and redemption.

"Thank you," we the stargazers must tell each other—say the words softly, loudly, and with every beat of the heart. "We love you," must be carried on every breath, and "forgive us" and "we forgive you" must ring out from the rooftops. Such a story this would be—so convincing that it would surely catch Empathy's ear, maybe even reach the stars. Are we humble enough, simple specks of dust living, dying, struggling to understand the magnificence of it all? How intense must we be, mere pinpricks of light, to see each other across vast distances?

How would we hear each other's words from so far away? Or claim the stories not our own, but given by Empathy? How has it come to be that the other creatures of the animal kingdom—Crow and Weasel and Badger, especially Badger—can see further into the deep and understand the stories we tell ourselves? Badger knows there is "one thing" to remember, yet this wisdom is not reductive. It reveals our simple story and why we tell it:

> The stories people tell have a way of taking care of them. If stories come to you, care for them. And learn to give them away where they are needed. Sometimes a person needs a story more than food to stay alive. That is why we put these stories in each other's memories. This is how people care for themselves.

—Barry Lopez's *Crow and Weasel*

Here we are, still the storytelling creatures huddled around the fire, still the subjects of the stories we tell. Badger's "people" who need them in order to take care of ourselves. Stories work on our behalf, to be sure, and must always bring order to the deluge of events and experiences that would otherwise wash us further and further downstream. We employ stories and expect them to point out patterns in the rush of sensations and emotions conspiring to drown us in their clamorous demands for attention. As one of my students said, stories "contain a purpose," and they have rescued us many, many times.

Stories are instrumental as well, multipurpose flotation devices we use to skim across the choppy waters and calm the events and experiences still roiling around us. Such lifelines they toss our way, these stories that navigate the treachery of the sensory and the visceral churned up from deep below the surface. And how we depend on our stories to stabilize the murky memories building up in the silt and sediment yet eroding with every new deposit.

We heap responsibilities on stories, task them with guiding our search for patterns in the emotional currents and eddies formed by the flood of news events and family events that drenches us day by day, year by year. Stories come through for us and will pull us out of the wet and cold, save us from the exhausting blur. At least some events, and our experiences of them, can remain clear and distinctive, and we will remember more than a few of the relentless birthday parties and political campaigns, championship playoffs and turkey dinners, scandals and storms.

We have our islands in the stream now, what we think of as characters in the larger story we/they are telling. The stream becomes more navigable because even the smallest anecdote, worst pickup line, or most saccharine sentiment associated with an event, can light up its story. Whether random or scripted, the event is made vivid and thus more memorable, meaningful, even pivotal—from a champagne toast to a walk in the rain.

Common wisdom tells us that some events are experienced directly, others indirectly. Either way, we make them durable, recording and then recalling them in mental pictures, in body maps that re/present their story. Sometimes a single scene is retrieved, a narrative image frozen, surreal, but made alluring by its astonishing saturation and detail or by its equally haunting, if faded, fragment, a question to be answered. Sometimes rivers of footage are running through our consciousness, and we find an action video playing in the head, rewinding in the marrow.

We reach into this storybook, our internal catalog, often

prompted by the photos archived in family albums and digital frames—the smiling faces with and without braces and the whirling, giddy fun of Disneyland's teacups, the glistening trophy fish and the glowing brides. We pull up what is triggered by the historical footage of cardinal events that reappear each year, further reinforcing our stories—the attacks on Pearl Harbor and the Twin Towers, the assassinations of JFK, MLK, and RFK, Diana's funeral, Harry and Meghan's wedding. Our catalog, our memories, and sensory maps are always lighting up, and we feel as if we are *directly* experiencing and reexperiencing these events again and again.

Meanwhile, the archived images—what the scrapbooks and television news give to us—are always inserting themselves, curating our interior lives, and, thus, determining what the events are and how our stories can describe them. One archive replaces the other, the internal with the external—and vice versa. Indeed, the sensory images and stories of our internal world will always supplant what the external world displays, just as its outdoor galleries will always frame what hangs inside on corporeal walls.

Our experiences, our memories are changed by this looping effect, and we can no longer be sure that a story's purpose is to "describe" or "interpret" an event—perhaps we never could. As my students were right to point out, a story "tells" an event, and like the story itself, this event may be(come) "fictional." The question of what is real and what is not is certainly moot. Now, our own purpose can only be to tell stories about storytelling itself. We are gamers, all right, still playing the childhood game of telephone, passing stories around the circle, garbling guaranteed.

With this, event becomes experience, experience event, and storytelling speaks clearly of both. It is most eloquent, though, when using a *visual* mode, when storytelling serves as the imagistic channel through which event experiences are transformed into attention-grabbing pictures. What's more, storytelling lives to embrace its most vibrant role as the mediator finessing our interpretations of Sontag's image-world and Viola's intermediate zone. It coaxes us to be like Cezanne, filling in the gaps between what we see and what we know, between what we *tell* and believe to be true.

Quilts comfort us with a vivid metaphor of their own, what takes us from event experience to a hand-stitched story meant to fill in the gaps for us and piece together whole lives, cultures, and histories. A quilt begins as an event experience that has much to say about its maker and becomes a storyteller that has more to reveal about us. We loop around and around with the maker, holding on to the scraps of calico fabric, keeping warm under the intricate pattern of triangles and squares that covers us in a shared "we-centric" space made cozy by what we believe to be true.

We are not amazed that a quilt can resonate beyond its patches, but stunned that it can become a story of freedom, the one told by Civil War-era quilts hung on clotheslines to mark the northward route of the Underground Railroad. Stunned that a quilt can become a story of dignity, now traveling beyond the hamlet of Gee's Bend, Alabama, where it began with the six generations of rural quiltmakers who gave meaning and color to lives otherwise impoverished by hardship and isolation. And we are also stunned that a quilt can become a story of remembrance patched together with skill and care as in the massive AIDS quilt that honors the lives struck down by yet another of history's human plagues.

Such storytelling, though, is neither the organizer nor an arbiter of truth and morality. Instead, its purpose is to remind us to use imagination and the "deep feelings we have as human beings" to negotiate the event experiences always occurring in the breathless space between our internal and external worlds. This is the stunning terrain that compels us now to modify Sontag's description of an outside image-world. Our trust lies in what we already have intuited: stories and the event experiences they describe can only be interpreted through the "reports given" by the flash of images both inside *and* outside ourselves. Though they are meant to represent our own reality, we understand that such images are packed with stories *mis*representing what we see but never what we value.

Yes, we covet stories, pledge our allegiance to their images, not as Sontag's "substitutes" for firsthand experiences but as the generators of bodily sensations and impressions we find to be rich, vivid, and directly experienced. We are bewitched indeed, their magic telling us how to package the world inside and out—

and how to be a storyteller blending both domains.

Storytelling lies at the heart of what interests us most. It is our very being, the restless pulse of humanity taking us on the rollercoaster's magical journey of event experiences. We lurch around corners and scream through tunnels, bolt to the top, and, dazzled, plunge once more into our favorite fantasyland somewhere between image and story. But through it all, we have followed its track and managed to stay on course in spite of or because of its adrenaline-greased rails.

Indeed, this is the steel thread holding all of us together, and we are thrilled to find others, especially the storytelling characters of popular books and movies accompanying us on this, the ride of our lives. There in the next car, we spot the grandpa from *The Princess Bride*, the grandma from *Edward Scissorhands*, Jiminy Cricket in another, and a gaggle of characters from *The Canterbury Tales* stuffed in the one behind.

Scheherazade is there too, always near the front, where, in Salman Rushdie's view, she leads the way as one of the greatest storytellers of all time—her spellbinding tales having stopped the slaughter of countless virgin brides. Time and again, she takes us deep into an ancient Arabian world where we share her own ride—the one on which her very life depends—and we are coursing through a thousand and one nights of clever storytelling, each night more bewitching than the last. We find her to be well-read and well-mannered and watch breathlessly as she uses her knowledge of other cultures and other rulers to spin the stories that eventually civilize the savage sultan and put him on track with the rest of humanity at last.

Storytelling can have profound effects, indeed. For Rushdie, the process of creating storytelling characters for his children's books—gifts to his sons—was both liberating and restorative. The first of these, *Haroun and the Sea of Stories*, breathed new life into Rushdie following the publication of *The Satanic Verses*.

Writing the second, *Luka and the Fire of Life*, proved to be just as liberating and enjoyable. In this story, Rashid, the legendary storyteller and father of the young boy Luka, was inspired by Rushdie's own father, who told "elaborate and wonderful" stories about Ali Baba, Aladdin, and Sinbad the Sailor. In Luka's tale,

Rushdie's own storytelling draws upon the great narrative traditions—Chinese, Greek, Aztec, Nordic, Native American—to describe a young boy's quest for fire, which must be stolen from the mountaintop to save his father, who has fallen unconscious. Through Luka, we encounter a cavalcade of characters, human and animal, who, much like Prometheus, understand fire as the flame of life and rally around the quest, accompanying the young boy on a rollercoaster ride back to the dawn of time.

Along the way, Luka is tested by a series of adventures and riddles and comes to believe he is trapped in the virtual world of video games—a complex and novelistic world he knows well. But time is of the essence, and Luka must quickly master a new world—the world of his father's imagination—to discover the thing within it that will save his life. Frustrated, impatient, Luka becomes angry, demanding to know why his travel companions would ever allow his father to die when it is Rashid's stories that have kept them alive—when it is through his father's stories that Luka even knows these characters. In the end, Luka grows wiser, more mature, and recognizes the power of story and what he alone must do to use it well.

Writers and artists are on their own quest to harness this power; journalists and historians too. They are among the many who dedicate themselves to the business of telling stories about storytelling. Like Rushdie, many heard "elaborate and wonderful" stories while growing up. Margaret Mitchell, for example, is said to have recalled the endless summer nights of storytelling, her aunts and uncles gathered on the porch sharing tales of the Old South in the thick, cool air. Their storytelling inspired Scarlett's, and *Gone With the Wind* came to life, recounting a Southern (his)story, a philosophy made vivid, memorable, and enduring.

For Faith Ringgold, it was the evening gatherings on the apartment building rooftop—her tar beach—where, high above New York's city lights, stories about the African-American experience filled the young artist with possibilities. Forged under a vast ebony sky, her storytelling memories still shine bright in the story quilt paintings that have become her storytellers—that carry on the vision, the possibilities of the Civil Rights Movement.

Save for the student cramming for exams, the contestant

preparing for *Jeopardy*, we do not care to collect facts and figures. No, Joe Friday, we must have more than "just the facts, ma'am" if we are to understand, to remember, the Civil War or Martin Luther King's dream—or even the hardboiled police work of 1960s Los Angeles. No, it is stories that we collect, the ones framing current and historical events and turning them into experiences that resonate with our "me" and "we" stories.

The late Don Hewitt, creator of the long-running *60 Minutes*, understood the collector in all of us, and, from the first, knew full well that the success of a news magazine format was tied to the power of storytelling. His reporters' assignments would not involve the mere coverage of news events or the delivery of facts and figures. Focusing on the nature of human experience and the characters shaping it, he famously sent his TV journalists out with one clear directive in mind. "Tell me a story," he said, and so they did, and still do, telling him, telling huge audiences on many a Sunday night something resonant—and something more about our times, more about ourselves.

We rely on storytelling historians, the likes of Doris Kearns Goodwin and David McCullough, and Ken Burns, as well, to give us portraits fully rendered of life in earlier times. We need them, the honest historians, to make our histories bright and dynamic, compelling and relevant. By accommodating our needs—what is hardwired in each of us—their work also responds forthrightly to Rudyard Kipling's musings: "If history was taught in the form of stories, it would not be forgotten."

And so, their (his)stories teach, and we learn the value of this form and why we collect it. We do not forget the well-crafted. Today's elected leaders will even read and pay attention to what the stories reveal about yesterday's political rivals and international diplomats; a husband and wife will stop bickering and be moved to reassess their own relationship in light of the documentary presentation of a letter shared between a couple long dead—a Union officer writing to his wife on the eve of the Battle of Bull Run in anticipation of his death.

Among those most dedicated to the storytelling business are the professionals who work in experience design. These are the writers and architects, the graphic designers and lighting designers, the filmmakers and model-makers, fabricators and master planners of the themed entertainment industry—what the Disney Corporation calls "Imagineers"—who design and build themed attractions and compelling places for us, their "guests," to experience.

We find their work in Amsterdam at the Heineken Experience and Abu Dhabi at Ferrari World, in Atlanta at the Georgia Aquarium and Chicago at the Field Museum, at the London Eye and Ski Dubai and, of course, in all of the theme parks around the world. Whether it is to tell Mickey's story or Harry Potter's, or the story of an old brewery or a red-hot race car, these professionals remain laser-focused on the "storytelling objective," which in the words of master planner Barry Upson is "to create a multi-sensory entertainment experience that [is] easily grasped, fully engaging and emotionally compelling."

The project of storytelling unifies the industry and designers throughout work not as competitors—though they are—but as collaborators reaching across the various companies and entities to create and to maximize connections between story, experience, and emotion. Theirs is a "we business" in which storytelling is "the way to turn attractions into more, into *experience*," says architect and master planner, Michel Linet-Frion. As he explains, "We create emotions in fact, by creating stories that our guest identifies with and uses . . . to recreate his own story."

Like the designer, the guest must call upon the creative imagination to flesh out this story. And what the guest (re) creates is an essential part of the larger story about storytelling that, ultimately, designer and guest create together. Industry designers enjoy this collaboration most, and are happiest, says master planner Jack Rouse, when they "put a smile on the guest's face." Indeed, they love what they do, and like the rest of us, love a good story. It is what connects them, they say, to people, places, and things—to each other, and most importantly, to the guest. Where it is connective and collaborative, storytelling is also found to be a "medium of exchange," says writer Larry Tuch. In this analogy, emotion is the currency and empathy one of the denominations.

At root, this is a serious business, one requiring rigor and discipline as well as a passion for the work. As Disney himself put it, "Before there can be magic, there must be work." To master planner Jack Rouse, this means that the power of story must be carefully investigated, its structures and defining features thoroughly analyzed. And story, he says, must be distinguished from narrative. In his view, "A narrative is a well-written description of an idea, whereas a story focuses on unlocking the inherent drama of that idea."

Moreover, "Stories demand empathy (and serious suspension of disbelief)," says Rouse, "whereas narratives do not."

The industry's challenge then, is to identify the key, what opens up the drama that will release the guests' empathy and emotions. There are no guarantees, no formulas to follow, and with each new project, these storytellers must work to rediscover the magic—decipher how the power of story might be used to win over the guests. Again and again, they work to achieve verisimilitude, a quality of "life likeness," but find themselves deep in the paradox of creating what guests will identify with and *believe in* while at the same time convincing these same guests to let go, to step outside their personal realities. As always, their task is to analyze the experience, to understand how guests can be caught up, swept away, even as their very experience depends on the story's credibility and authenticity.

Sharing such analyses at conferences and in industry publications, these storytelling professionals have come to agree that how a story is told—how its drama is released—is as important as what its drama tells about. This "how" and "what" must be balanced, they know, if an emotional connection is to be made with the guest. Making strong connections is critical to the experience. Storytellers know that these are the connections— good or bad—the guest remembers. Only the mediocre is forgotten, and mediocrity is not acceptable, not up to professional standards.

Industry wisdom also holds that a story can only occur in a "logically correct sequence." Indeed, designers pay attention to the importance of what master planner Bob Rogers calls "thought-ordering."

"The story beats must go in order," he says, "to maximize the guest's emotional connection." And thought-ordered storytelling, according to the industry's architects, can only occur in an actual space. "Locate the story," says Ray Hole, "and work to create a synergy between the architectural space and the story." This, he says, will maximize the authenticity of the guests' experience.

But master planner and architect alike recognize that storytelling is quintessentially a project of listening. They must listen to the story, they agree, if its beats are to be heard, if the space is to reverberate with these rhythms. Listen, and they will understand how to maximize the resonance. When it all comes together, they hope the guest will find the story compelling and the experience authentic.

Above all else, the story must make sense. Whether telling a "nature" story or a story anchored in a cultural-historical site, or one anchored by a cast of characters, designers know that the guests' experience depends on the story's integrity and logic, its clarity and resonance—and always, on the sense it makes. This is true, even in the case of a "nature" story that tells of mysterious, if legendary, animals and habitats. SeaWorld's story, for example, is about "water creatures," that, as one of my students put it, "Share a world we don't really know about, a world of mystery." Yet, to her and millions of other visitors, its story and the mystery it celebrates make sense.

Sense-making is the standard to be met even in the case of a story that appears to be self-evident, straightforward, as, for example, one told by a cultural/historical event or location. Such stories still challenge designers to bring out the inherent drama and to do so in ways that make sense. Professionals must bring their creative imagination, their passion and listening skills, to bear on the task at hand, which, according to Linet-Frion, is to emphasize the uniqueness of the site—to heighten the significance of a story that "cannot be told anywhere else."

Built on reverence, on awe, these stories stir deep emotions and inspire guests to make visceral and very personal connections to a shared piece of human history. Such are the connections made, for example, in Dublin at the Glasnevin Cemetery Museum, or in Jerusalem at the Chain of Generations Center. The latter, located in the underground spaces adjacent to the Western Wall, uses a variety of materials and works of art to tell a moving story about generational connections and encourages visitors to continue the story by finding their own links in the chain.

Glasnevin's guests are taken on an immersive journey through Ireland's past, a journey honoring the million and a half who laid the foundations for modern life and now lie at rest in the Irish National Cemetery. The story, brought to life by the site itself and by the likes of Daniel O'Connell, a historical figure and liberator who serves as the narrator, tells how the cemetery was opened early in the nineteenth century to bury people of all religions.

Many of the industry's stories are character driven, and when they are, designers know that the characters themselves must make sense, along with any dialogue or narration. Disney's Mickey and Goofy are not gratuitous costumed figures roving throughout Fantasyland; they and the princesses make sense to us as well-developed characters integral to the fairytales and cartoon stories that shape and reflect our childhood memories of Uncle Walt's storytelling. Tomorrowland relies on Luke Skywalker, Darth Vader, and the other *Star Wars* characters currently animating its Star Tours attraction to tell an ever-changing story of intergalactic adventure. We step into the simulator and anticipate the many possibilities, just as we anticipate what the future may hold—and how our own stories will unfold.

Such are the characters who, traveling across time and far beyond Disney's "lands," come to rest within the stories shared by so many of us—the guests who have become their hosts. When the characters and attractions make sense, indeed, visitors everywhere pick up the story and make it their own even as it rings out across swaths of the cultural landscape. Guests at Parc Astérix near Paris, for example, have come to host a comic book hero whose story springs from the page to win their hearts and minds and to remind them of the very real battle for France fought long ago. Astérix, they know, is an ancient Gaul warrior fighting against Roman invaders, and guests are thrilled to accompany him on his various adventures—each one intended to reiterate a larger story about French origins and national pride.

Sometimes it makes sense to create a character, a narrator, say, who tells the story that we, the guests, identify with and are willing to believe and to embody. In Normandy at the Grand Aquarium de St. Malo, for example, such a narrator was created to lead visitors on a series of underwater adventures around the world. As Linet-Frion explains, the design team based this character on Jean Kermalo, a local environmental activist whose passion for marine life was used to shape a story that would inspire the guests and convince them to become his fellow crusaders. His is a compelling story about what is vital; a story raising awareness about the importance of saving ocean environments before it is too late. "All aquariums have the same objective," notes Linet-Frion, "but this one is different because you can believe its story belongs to a person, someone like you and me."

If they are to create stories that captivate, that are "fully engaging and emotionally compelling," industry professionals know their designs must have some flair or "personality." Like all storytellers, they strive to develop a relationship with the audience; but as designers who tell stories, they must focus and take up the question, *What is the story of the audience this themed attraction targets?* And then, as designers, they must work to tailor the attraction's "personality" to match the guests'.

As Linet-Frion points out, this means that before they go to their drawing boards, designers must know who the guests are and why they will come visit and spend time in their designs. *What are these visitors looking for?* Because today's guests have "evolved," becoming more and more "used to theming," says Linet-Frion, designers must double down, strive harder to achieve a kind of verisimilitude that will bring out both the drama of the story and the authenticity of the experience. Finally, designers must understand this verisimilitude, this authenticity, and know when guests expect to be tricked into believing and when they do not.

While they know they are not creating works of art, designers also know their work must resonate; what they offer must feel like a one-of-a-kind experience to the guest whose expectations, whose standards, are always on the rise. They cannot cheat this or any guest. Nor can they cut any corners or shortcut the design process in any way—a process that is itself evolving and often idiosyncratic.

Guided by but a few principles, this is the process shoving industry professionals up against a paradoxical reality of their own making, one stipulated by the world of themed entertainment that lays the split, even schizophrenic foundation on which the industry is built. Indeed, designers are destined to struggle with their dedication to storytelling and authenticity, which, as Linet-Frion puts it, are "two very opposed notions." It is as if these professionals must hurl themselves into the fray between (authentic) fantasy and (storytelling) reality, driven to convert one to the other. Designers know they are ever teetering, their work in danger of falling short, of failing the guest who demands more and more of the fray.

The project of balancing the storytelling/authenticity duality is never an easy one—and *resolving* their opposition would appear impossible. But it is always the project defining the design process that is the industry's signature and the truth of its being. As Linet-Frion sees it, both process and project turn on trust; the existential challenge is best confronted by developing a relationship with the guest that is resonant, based on integrity, and on the honesty of passion and imagination. Storytelling becomes authentic in its truth-telling, as it were.

To illustrate this point, he offers an example drawn from his work at L'Aqua Mundo, a water park resort in France's Moselle Valley that features a tropical rainforest. Storytelling in this and other themed resorts is challenging, he explains, because the guests are looking for an escape, a conveniently located place where they can disconnect from their urban lives and reconnect with each other in another, more transcendent world. A quick getaway, they have no time to waste on easing themselves into the experience.

"It needs to be immediate," says Linet-Frion, who adds, "We do this by immersing them in a nature story," which means in "something authentic." As he points out, this also means that, "I cannot invent a story that says 'I'll take you to a hot springs in Costa Rica for you to enjoy our water park experience.'" Well aware that they are in Northern Europe, both guest and designer know this would be absurd. But if the project is trustworthy and focused on establishing an honest relationship with the guest, Linet-Frion says the storytelling shifts slightly and tracks along a different line.

As he sees it, the story he tells needs to say, "I've got passion for tropical environments, and look at how good we've become at reproducing them here in Europe for your pleasure." If the environment is done well, *the guests will resonate with the designer's passion* and make an emotionally satisfying connection with this, the more credible story. In the end, the guests can disconnect and allow themselves to believe they are in the tropics. Each guest "reestablishes authenticity," says Linet-Frion, because "we didn't trick him."

The story of the designer's passion for the design rings true. It is well told, an authentic story that is also well-located, even as it unfolds in an inauthentic space. Yet, it makes sense—and does so at a deep, resonant, and neurological level. The story does not occupy an architectural space but rather locates itself in the "we-centric" space that Gallese has described—an existential space shared between designer and guest in which imaginations of the creative *and* the neurological kind flourish. The story makes sense to the guests who "understand some kind of harmony" between the designer and the design, much in the way Iacoboni described the American participants in the study who understood this harmony between the Nicaraguan actor and the Nicaraguan hand gestures he performed.

The story of this harmony is logical, neurologically sound, and if it is "thought-ordered," it must also be *body*-ordered, based on the logic of embodied simulations that allow guests to resonate with the designer's authentic passion, just as Iacoboni's participants resonated with the actor's cultural authenticity. Indeed, the roots of this and every story lie in the body where authenticity is born.

Sometimes, we want to be tricked; sometimes we do not; but we are ever the dreamers, who, like the designers, are looking for something more. We crave the flair and need to find some small sparkle in our stories—and to feel its dance within our cells. So, we flock to the theme park—to that "large-scale, corporate-owned destination park," with its rides and attractions and "fictional themes"—where we expect to find the shiny magic that will unlock our ordinary lives.

The theme park may be a most inauthentic place—a controlled environment telling us what to expect—but we gladly accept its terms, believing we are free to explore our most authentic experiences, the ones that still delight us and focus our own fantasies. Busch Gardens, Knott's Berry Farm, Legoland, Universal Studios-Singapore, -Japan, -Orlando, and -Hollywood, along with the eleven Disney parks, are not just theme parks, they are "story places," says Bob Rogers. They are the places that make sense to us as rhizomic networks of exuberance, of stories furiously referring to more and more stories, all flickering like summertime fireflies, all working to create their bright bursts of adrenaline and a sense of other worldliness that root us in the spectacular familiarity of our beloved borderland.

Theme parks offer up their tricks and truths, singing all the while in a visceral and synchronizing harmony we understand—a Siren's song that creates the sense of one-heartedness beating throughout our collective soul. We will always succumb to the lure; so, we rush through the gates again and again, in good times and bad, knowing we will understand the dynamics inside, the harmony of what belongs to us, to the designers, to societies of the twenty-first century. This is our shared, always cacophonous microcosm—the place meeting our terms because it "demands empathy and a serious suspension of disbelief."

Theme parks are highly visible sites and signs of what we might identify as a global culture becoming so recognizable that it deeply penetrates our consciousness. Some may resent such intrusion and worry about the consequences. Critic Jean Baudrillard, for instance, argues that theme parks work to create a "sense of placelessness," and that Disneyland-Paris is nothing more than "cultural Chernobyl." Others welcome theme parks around the world as happy places that help to destroy feelings of loss, loneliness, and ill will—and to these fans, the granddaddy of them all, Disneyland-Anaheim is, as Walt proclaimed, "the happiest place on earth."

In both cases, such hyperbole, if not comical, is at least intriguing. Perhaps we recognize some truths in these extremes. Neither is accurate, yet each offers something to be believed. Perhaps we are fascinated by all that theme parks smash together and all that they blow apart. They are the paradox of choice; whimsical places we visit when we are serious about our play, places whose rides promise two minutes of sheer exhilaration only after we have invested two soul-killing hours waiting in line.

We come by the millions, from every time zone and every heritage, to spend our time and money together—Muslims and Jews, blacks and whites, liberals and conservatives—all converging to write a story uncluttered by language and stripped clean of partisan or cultural issues. We recognize ourselves among the school groups and Girl Scout troops, the honeymooners and vacationers. We are the families with the babies who will become overstimulated and difficult to console, the hyperactive children who will go missing, and the parents who will become ever more exasperated, the grandparents too weary and winded to help with the search.

Master planners like Bob Rogers have played their part, have played with "cultural dynamite" to explode old notions about human experience, especially the dualistic ones specifying how and where it occurs. The theme park becomes our cultural vortex, the place spinning us between experiences once said to occur in either public or private realms. We trust this vortex, its dizzying energy creating experiences of mythic realities that are neither subjective nor objective. Its volatility is ours and so, we come in earnest to this place of leisure to find the intimate, yet vast spaces that establish us as Selves and Other Selves. We are the human lemmings who come when the temperature soars and the humidity billows, when the wind slices and rain pelts, some pushing strollers, others wheelchairs, all of us chasing the thrills our credit cards can buy. Together, we jump into the churn to find the "more" of experience thriving in newer, nondualistic realms and realities—the more that tells us about our identity, our synchrony, our empathy.

We arrive early, just as the turnstiles begin their hum, and stay late, dazzled to the end by the park's pyrotechnics, leaving only to catch the last tram for the lonely parking lots. In between, we move throughout the grounds with our shared expectations, infected by de Waal's "convergence of moods," aware of the "unifying effect" of marching along together, "all in synch" and in the "same spirit."

We are constantly on the move, taking in the sights and sounds, but always on the lookout for the shortest lines, the closest restrooms, and where we might get a cold drink or a hot pretzel. With this "group cohesion," we experience the park's synchrony, its design for movement coordinating our activities within its protective boundaries.

We are confident, hubristic even, when venturing into exposition-style exhibits and playing the midway's carnivalesque games. We run laughing through gauntlets of dancing fountains and scream in unison with every swoop and swirl of the careening rides. We pose for photos in front of bright, flower-filled gardens and then stroll along winding pathways leading us still deeper into our dreamscape. As we go, we are creating Damasio's body maps—our bodies mapping themselves onto the bodies of our Other Selves even as theirs are mapping themselves onto ours. And the park buzzes with our collective resonance.

Theme parks are the products of the designers' efforts, to be sure. But they become our products, those that we, the guest/ hosts, negotiate together. They are the vortex of our shared, if unconscious, processes, and the "medium of exchange," the "condensed, entertainment-driven medium" through which we create a we-centric playground and an existential "sense of us" at play. We are performers, playing ourselves and becoming the characters in each other's stories. Our script speaks of hedonism, and overacting is none of our concern. We do not apologize for our self-indulgent ways nor do we judge each other's excesses.

No, we feel for one another, the highs and lows of playing so hard. We understand why the thrill-seekers let go of the bar as the coaster blasts them "over the drop" to thrill us in the darkness below, just as we understand why some will need to sit down afterward, pale and desperate for the nausea to pass. We know how the sunburn smarts after too many hours in the sun, how the feet ache after pounding through too many "lands." We recognize the look of exhaustion marking so many faces and feel the same in our bones. We know why the babies cry.

Such are the tales of hedonism vibrating within and across our millions, the very ones oxygenating humanity's soul. They are what we share with generations past, what binds us to our forebears, who were also looking to indulge themselves and expecting to play out their own fantasies in the story places of their day. As we might turn to the theme park, they escaped into the grand pleasure gardens of Europe, finding those of sixteenth-century Italy and eighteenth-century France to be especially captivating. These were idyllic worlds, Gardens of Eden transporting them to a paradise on earth that floated somewhere between cultural and natural spheres. Visitors delighted in the magic of skyward-spurting fountains performing a Renaissance dance choreographed by clever hydraulic engineers.

Years later, visitors were overwhelmed by the rococo splendor of patterned gardens, losing themselves among the precision boxwoods that outlined the intricate geometry and accented every scallop, every twirl of the botanical filigree. These were their images of perfection, made even more glorious by the bright floral palettes filling in the designs.

In the nineteenth century, another generation immersed itself in great city parks, reveling especially in New York's newly designed Central Park. There, visitors knew they were to experience the park, not as spectators admiring the ornamental, but as social creatures engaging in serene conversation. Taking advantage of the new pedestrian-only pathways, they relished their promenades and strolled carefree in a world defined by an outer berm that set it apart from the city's hubbub and grit.

Still others were attracted by traveling circuses and carnivals that also thrust them into other worlds. But it was the great world's fairs and international expositions of the early twentieth century that enticed the millions who would become part of an emerging tourist class seeking something more, something beyond what they already knew. Like pilgrims, they were looking to be inspired and enlightened.

They sought to understand the mysteries of the future—

what Chicago's "Century of Progress" and New York's "World of Tomorrow" promised to reveal. They expected to find surprises, wondrous displays of new-fangled products and demonstrations of the latest technologies. But these sojourners also came to play, to be entertained by the pleasures of the past. They knew where to find the midway, its familiar amusement strip hawking their favorite rides and games, along with the prizes and memorabilia they would take home. They were voracious, these travelers, consuming the novel and the nostalgic like so many hot dogs and Cracker Jacks.

In today's theme parks, we are immersed in these histories, what our playful predecessors have bequeathed to us. Their legacy is left in the exuberant fountains and Edenic gardens, in the serpentine pathways and comforting berm, in the rides and souvenirs, the novel and nostalgic. We have inherited much, but especially our forbears' metabolism, a hungry appetite, indeed; and like them, we are ever the consumers of pleasure. Like them, we believe that nature is our feast, its lusciousness to be served up in ways that delight and entertain, feed our every whim. We too must have an earthly paradise with its climate of eternal spring; a world complete unto itself that completes us and that fills us with all manner of confections sweet and sensory.

We are like our predecessors, thrilling to the story place that controls all risks, yet offers extra helpings of surprise and unpredictability. We too crave what state-of-the-art technologies and trusted traditions promise to deliver and feel quite satisfied to be among the disciplined crowds in a perfectly controlled environment, one that encourages us to look forward and backward at the same time. We too must make our pilgrimage to what is a public place sanctifying our private impulses and canonizing hedonism's virtue. We must go to the theme park as regularly as others went to the pleasure gardens, the city parks, the world's fairs. And we too will share a utopian vision of who we are as a visiting troupe of players, hubristic and hungry, playing roles for each other and creating stories that are private and public. For generations and generations, we have gone where we can find ourselves taking all we can from the story of pleasure.

Who could blame any of us? As the humanist geographer Yi-

Fu Tuan points out, we have all dreamed of life in the "good place," a kind of story place inspiring us to imagine a world better than the one we knew. Such a place, he says, opens a space that tempts "the mind to wander and the spirit to soar." It must be well ordered, says Tuan, and defined by a boundary—a berm—that secures it and separates its preciousness from the flaws of the larger world.

Yet, this boundary must allow us to move easily between perfect and imperfect worlds. The good place is always dynamic, always drawing us in, making us feel more alive and human than we feel outside its bounds. Of course, we would seek it out, the paradise we find sunny and inviting, colorful and stimulating, with good lines of sight and helpful landmarks or signposts guiding us deeper and deeper into our fantasies. Here, we drift between our sense of security and sense of freedom.

We believe we are free to imagine, to open new spaces that transform one mythic reality into another, even as we enjoy a respite, a refuge in this known if otherworldly place. Here, we can breathe, inhaling the vapors of an exalted past while dreaming of a future still fizzing with possibilities. This is our theme park, the good place that lifts us off the ground and welcomes us into illusion—into the pleasures of myth-making and role-play. It is our theater, and we fill its seats and dance on its stage, giving our best performance of life between earth and sky, between place and space.

But place and space might also be imagined as "two sorts of stories," says Michel de Certeau—stories that tell us how meaning is made. To the French philosopher, place is fixed, objective, and connected to a historical event, whereas space is more subjective, mythological, and open to free-flowing social interactions. The relationship between place and space is a process, says de Certeau, whereby the stories told are constantly at work transforming places into spaces or spaces into places.

What might this process mean inside the theme park's berm? What do we take from its stories about negotiating the twisting and turning of grounded space and airy place? Our response is quick and always the same: We collect experiences of the theme park's rapid-fire transformations that flip space and place faster than a fry cook's burgers. We have discovered that the theme park lies in the blur between them; it is neither but of both. It tells an elastic story about a place-space that is grounded in the air and filled with mythological events and historical interactions and peopled by guest/hosts who are Selves and Other Selves. Theme parks keep us stretching between an objective somewhere and a subjective nowhere where we are lost and found in uncharted territories. There, we enter a storyland of meanings about permeable boundaries and collapsed dualities all telling of our search and our deepest hopes for something more.

But the theme park that creates and transforms place and space also comes fully loaded with other stories—its "fictional themes"—that create places and spaces of their own. These stories and where they might take us are the theme park's *raison d'etre*, and what distinguishes it from the carnival's midway. Designers are zealous, believing that everything must flow from the story—the park's design, its attractions, and our experiences. We are persuaded and find this park aptly named; a story place dimensionalized by heroic warriors, fairytale princesses, and a cast of characters leaping from cartoons, comic books, and movies to roam the grounds with us. As we travel along, they share their tales of adventure and intrigue and explain their forays into fantasy and immortality.

Once, what we knew of their stories floated in the zeitgeist's cloud, in the scudding memories it formed. But here, these memories are reborn, not as wispy mare's tails but as something more robust, more colorful, and credible. We give meaning to what the characters make present, and their stories give us clues about the meaning of memory, of human experience. They teach us about illusion and role-play, and how to live in one mythic reality and imagine another. We learn about contradiction and ambiguity, about relative distances between good and evil and the intricacies of place-space that are neither.

Stories keep us safe between dualities so that we might wander into the unknown and soar over familiar landscapes, always in search of an identity, a morality, a destiny. We are ever so grateful to the theme park that traps us in its loop, the one where we find place and space creating stories and stories creating place and space.

Loops can occur anywhere and are especially prevalent in nature. Indeed, they appear to be universal. At the theme park, the loop is a phenomenon, to be sure, one that rockets us around and around a lightning track. We do not let go of its bar. This is the electric loop that is never redundant, and we trust it to jolt us into a different sphere where the air crackles and we feel most alive. Here the particles glow, and we triumph in the here and now, with no thought of a hereafter. This is our moment, our "bubble of eternity." We loop around again, anticipating nothing but the stardust of immortality. Our deepest fear is denied, and we have heaved it away together, a hundred million strong. In the controlled environment, fear itself is controlled not only by a few moments of hedonistic exhilaration, but also by the constellations of stories glittering inside us since the beginning of time. These are the stories casting light on the ones we tell ourselves in order to live. We will always be the stories we tell.

We loop around and around, reinventing ourselves as we go and retelling stories about destiny's call. We will always be conflicted, on the one hand searching for the story that sets forth a plan for us—what will assure us of something more in life. But on the other hand, we will stomp as hard as we can on destiny's story of the long march along its one-way track to oblivion. We have only the loop, and we will ride it as long as we can—you with your stories, and I with mine, on the verge of what must be called our empathy. We clutch at our tall tales and fairytales, at horror stories and bedtime stories, and see ourselves entangled among the creation myths. Facts are of no interest to us, and we are not held to account, not even by destructive tales of the end. Catching our reflections in the eternal loop, we discover our humanity in a snapshot that gives us a story fully rendered. We hold on tight to this, the story that tells us what we want to hear.

Chapter V

Borers in the Rhizome

Sometimes we collapse, crash out of the loop, and find ourselves waking up bruised, dazed, and facedown in the crabgrass of an old metaphor. Unexpected and most unwelcome, the plunge lands us in an eerie nowhere that is everywhere prickly, thick with cynicism and blanketed by irony. Adrenaline and endorphins drain away along with any expectations for certainty or empathy, and now hollowness pinches the air and silence thrums in our ears. Where have the storytellers gone, fled with the master planners and designers from this post-apocalyptic paradise? What has blotted out the color, blurred the images? Is there nothing left of art but its "system of cruel optimism"? Oh, what could have happened to the disco ball and the audiologist's whistle—to Heidegger's promise of self-renewal in the "wintry field"?

Perhaps it is a sickly spring that explains the wasteland; why when we look around, rub our eyes to make certain, and look again, again, there is only an iris bed still dormant, still bleak with the clutter of winter's debris. It seems forlorn, untended—or worse yet, could it be true that the rhizomic garden has fallen out of a loop and is left helpless to cycle with the seasons from birth to death to rebirth? But what if we were to clear away the decay and stink of the debris? Perhaps its lethal layer is what smothers the new shoots and thwarts their and our impulse to reach for the April sun.

Perhaps, but no. The cause is identified when we dig into the soil and expose the work of underground monsters, thirsty borers that need no light to suck the life out of our rhizomes. Its network of roots and shoots appears withered, the cross-connections broken, and the iris bed, ransacked and ruined, is bereft of potential. There will be no purple petals any time soon. No bloom of what? Compassion? Humanity?

What is to be done about the wriggling larvae in our midst? About the scourge of *Macronoctua onusta* that promises to leave us stranded in the slimiest of all possible worlds? Can nothing be done, other than to shrink from such a vile prospect? Indeed, we are paralyzed and refuse even to assess the damage done by the insidious infestation now festering in our core. We cannot stand it but will not stop the hideous beasts working their way through our biology and psychology, our culture and technology. Nor will we look too closely at the political and economic systems corrupted in their wake.

Driven from the shriveled metaphor, we plod through time and space one empty step after another. What will become of us in deep December when we should be sleeping peacefully under the blanket of storybook snow? Will we find ourselves taken over once again by the requisite consumerism of another holiday season? Are we window-shopping in the glow, perhaps the glare, of festive lights, perhaps hearing a carol or two? Will we find ourselves strolling across the public square when a stranger calls out "happy holidays" and stops us in our tracks with a cheery, warm-hearted hug? How caught up in the spirit are we when we reciprocate, only to discover that the well-wisher, a "hugger-mugger," has picked our pocket?

What do we say when the borers darken yet another season, when they multiply and eat into our most venerable, perhaps vulnerable, institutions? What can we do when they penetrate a historic church on a Wednesday evening during Bible study? What is there to be said about the horrific betrayal, when after an hour of sitting together face-to-face, bodies resonating, Judas's gunfire cracks the contemplative air and leaves nine dead? Can it be true then that the mirror neuron system is so effortlessly overpowered and our hardwiring so easily frayed? Are grief and sorrow all we have to show for ourselves? What the borers would have us share?

How we long for the bliss of a theme-park summer. Bring it back, we beg, oh, yes please, all of it—rollercoasters and ice cream, story and synchrony, and yes, especially authenticity's tricky thrills, hedonism's visceral adventures—all that a safe, secure, and well-controlled world delivers. What then do we say to those who find their sunny bliss not at Walt Disney World or Universal Orlando, but at Machine Gun America nearby? What authentic, adrenaline-charged story do such "guests" hear echoing inside its berm? What do they tell themselves when trading ninety-nine of their hard-earned dollars for an opportunity to fire automatic weapons and their children to shoot real bullets? Such delight a family can take in hitting its fantasy targets—delight and fantasy not unlike our own—so, who are we to judge? We must leave that to Empathy.

What could we possibly say about Vladimir Putin and his lust for life in the "good place," what he and millions of others expect to enjoy in a sunny theme park outside of Moscow that tells the story of military might? Spending the day at his new Patriot Park, visitors will surely thrill with the battles that reenact Soviet military victories, and Russian children will delight in learning to use grenade launchers properly. Putin's park is open for business all right and designed for the serious play and playful work that America's machine-gunners (or maybe all theme park "guests") recognize and understand. Just imagine the shared connections reaching across continents.

Is cynicism also extending its reach, irony at work as well— what the borers have twisted into our biology to intensify the sharpest feelings of anger and fear, spurt the darkest bile of hate and disgust? Or was our corporeal world already tainted but always sanitized by our beloved theme parks? What do we even know about such fundamental feelings, banished as they are from the happiest places on earth? Or about the irony of a berm that limits the flow of cynicism inside its boundaries and encourages it outside such walls? Why is one theme park hateful or disgusting to some, exhilarating, even rejuvenating to others?

There are times when we are of one mind and one body, and such feelings flow freely around the globe without irony or apology. Take disgust, for instance. The sight of a filthy toilet and stench of rotting fruit reach across borders evenhandedly to disgust us all. Such filth and rot are nonnegotiable, indisputably stomach turning. Why these and not other sensations of disgust? Are they part of the hardwiring still intact, an evolutionary design still prevailing throughout the millennia? If that is the case, then would it be too far-fetched, too cynical to believe that the spectacle of pernicious crabgrass taking over a lawn once manicured and the stink of trampled irises once fluttering like flags in the breeze are just as disgusting? The slime of the borers even more stomach wrenching, especially once it fouls our habitat and corrodes the culture?

The toilet and fruit, though, are universally agreed-upon triggers of disgust, and oh so important to researchers investigating links between feelings of disgust and modes of behavior—maybe even more important to those of us who never dreamed that what turns our stomach could affect how we behave toward each other. Evidence shows that research participants no different than ourselves behave unethically as cheats and liars after staring at the image of a nasty toilet and inhaling the odor of putrid fruit. Is this part of the grand and grim design as well? Or what the borers have always envisioned for us?

We cannot be surprised to learn that disgusting sights and smells trigger disgusting behaviors—slime begets slime. The linkage is all too clear, what we have already seen in the images surfacing from a muddy underground. We may deny them, push away the starkest filth and rot, but they are still the signs of above-ground neglect and carelessness, of coldhearted indifference and a selfish disregard for others and the environment we share. Feelings of disgust prompt us to think less of each other and less of ourselves. Why bother to take care, keep clean, and follow a moral compass, we rationalize, when others have failed to do their part? Why care at all when the adolescent in all of us will not step up to do what is needed? What would be the point of it anyway when we have Irony and Cynicism to show us how the world works?

What then can we say about the story of disgust grinding away in the rhizomic network of hot, crowded subway trains where the borers are quite at home and we are known to misbehave? It is rude in the tunnels, people pushing, shoving, picking their noses—and on the N train from Brooklyn to Manhattan, there is a boyfriend and girlfriend popping each other's pimples, a self-entitled man already taking up three seats about to crowd a diminutive woman out of a fourth. How do we feel about Pete, a self-appointed Mr. Manners, who is so enraged by his fellow passengers that he launches a one-man crusade to shame the brutes into changing their behaviors? Will we say anything about his tactics, which require a camera phone and anonymous Twitter and Instagram accounts to post the worst of the worst online? Is Irony setting a trap for our crusader?

When the gotcha guy becomes addicted to the supportive and validating comments posted in response to his rants, what do we say then? What kind of intervention is needed when the angry Pete is only too happy to post more and more pictures with harsher and harsher captions just to get his validation fix? What happens when or if the shameless addict realizes that the subway behavior he detests can never change as long as it feeds his habit? How hard will he fall, yet another one of us victimized by what psychologists call the "online disinhibition effect" that is always associated with the anonymity of our cruelest, most dehumanizing texts, tweets, and emails?

Oh, the slime we are free to spread, the vitriol we will vent when no one, not even Empathy—especially not Empathy—knows our name. Such a shame, what reaches across the rhizomic Internet to shame us all, yet leaves our behavior unchanged. What if we were to crawl out of the pit, perchance to stand in the light with the psychologists who would remind us once again that dark feelings betray us and are guilty of spewing their toxicity on ourselves as well as on others? Just look at the Twitterverse, the shrinks would tell us. Angry tweets will get attention, to be sure—much more limelight than what joyful tweets can provide. Angry tweets are much more likely to be retweeted than the others, but in the end, they will be the ones to renege and promise only to leave us raging, angrier than we were before. Hostility begets . . . wait, is this our intent, our preferred state of being? What the borers have predetermined and the psychologists are powerless to change?

When will we stand on our own, stare into the face of Anonymity and acknowledge that its insidious power can turn any one of us travelers on the information superhighway into another troll skulking in the shadows along the way? Or more to the point, when will there be . . . no, what if there were a better understanding of what they, what we, are trolling for? Yes, what if, indeed, and if such insight should point to their and our need for power and control, for validation and attention, all born of the same fear and insecurity that has dominated the species from the beginning—then what will this mean? What is bequeathed to humanity?

Still, travelers and trolls alike understand plenty and know full well that viciousness waits to be unleashed, inflicted without warning upon even the most unlikely of targets, along with the misogynistic lashings that no woman deserves. They also know that vengeful counterstrikes are to be expected and that hardened hearts and reptilian brains will too often prevail. Soon enough, everyone will add to the bulletproof evidence already indicating that disgusting feelings trigger disgusting behaviors. But no one will have even a whispered hint of what to do about it, nor how to keep Hypocrisy's hot breath off our backs.

Are we on our own to figure it out, travelers and trolls connected only by a shared sense of outrage that also putrefies our silicon rhizome? Is there no strategic approach to be taken, no concerted effort made to bleach away the slime? Would it be so hypocritical to ignore the trolls, those hateful, infuriating lowlifes, and strip them of the power they wield? Or starve them, those slithering, bottom-feeding larvae, of the attention they crave? Do we become hypocrites if instead we call them out, those poor, misunderstood bullies, and persuade them to atone, mend their evil ways? Or sit them down, those sad, pitiful creatures, and help them summon the courage to confront the most terrifying of their fears and insecurities? Would there be enough courage to go around for all of us?

How do the perpetrators of identity theft get what they need? Or the victims duped by the fake identities of such scheming predators? How do women gamers handle the constant and notoriously cruel barrages aimed at their play? At their anatomy, their character? Or the feminist bloggers whose thick skins are not always thick enough to withstand the endless whippings they must take?

What do Hypocrisy and Cynicism have to say about a grieving Lindy West, feminist and comedy writer, who ignored her usual trolls and called out the one that crossed a line by impersonating her late father only recently buried? What could Anonymity or Irony even begin to say when courage was hers, just enough to fend off the voice from the grave that screamed out, "You were the worst daughter a father could have!" She hunted down the troll, confronted him to extract an apology and a pledge that he would own his disgusting feelings and reform his disgusting behavior. Do you hear that, Empathy?

Trolls or not, we must have our technology. Indeed, we will insist, regardless of what Empathy or Irony have to say about it. They had better get out of the way as we flit from platform to platform, anxious to count our Facebook "Likes," Twitter followers, and LinkedIn connections. So many passwords and wireless codes to sort out, but never mind—we are desperate to boot up, log on, check in whenever we want, and will overlook the minor inconveniences. Just let us chat, post, and stream wherever we are. We don't care about the snarl of copper wires and fiber-optic cables about to strangle us. We cannot see the satellite transmissions and radio waves trapping us in a digital world where our fundamental need for the human touch will never be satisfied and FaceTime can never substitute for "living in the facial expression of the other." But there we sit, more and more wired, less and less connected. Oh well, we say, not to worry. Siri and Alexa will take care of everything.

What's new, we want to know, and a nanosecond later, what's next? How exciting to hear about the coolest technology, the sleekest devices—what motivates us to upgrade again and again. We must be among the early adapters looking for still more power or portability, more speed or compatibility, maybe a bigger screen, a smaller one, but always ready for more bells and whistles. Expectations are high and getting higher, the software and hardware must perform. But why is that we expect more and more of our machines, and less and less of ourselves and each other?

Bragging rights matter, all right, much more than privacy rights. So, we will not really question the latest face-recognition technologies nor quibble with Facebook about how it became the curator of the largest face-print gallery in the world. Why should we when such a collection will solve the problem of Anonymity for us? We are confident that the devices strapped to our wrists tracking heart rate, number of steps taken, and hours slept will not feed the data-mining habits of large insurance companies. Of course, these trackers will disclose only the information we need to verify the body's authenticity and nothing more—not even a mention of Empathy's bodily birthplace. We trust our technology and Siri too.

And when Alexa cannot understand our whims and commands, where does that leave us but stuttering in the crabgrass, naked and penned in by the electric prods of Irony and Cynicism, Hypocrisy and Anonymity. Wild-eyed, we veer left and right, but it is clear that their walls block Empathy's bridges. How could Empathy leave us with no escape? Abandon us yet again when we are still so baffled, still blind to all of it—the filth and rot, the rhizomic infestation and fraying metaphors? How are we to explain any of it, especially our own antagonistic needs and dualistic nature? Surely, we cannot be expected to understand why the ancient tension between the individual and collective persists or how the twin drives to compete and to cooperate could ever be reconciled. This is well above our pay grade—how or why a cooperative, even compassionate group of us could turn into an angry, lawless mob accountable to no one.

We will struggle to explain the group around the fire, one-hearted, all in sync, and caught up in the power of communal storytelling that fractures into individuals, coldhearted and cunning—the lone wolves on the prowl, clawing for power of another kind. They will trample the collaborators, so driven are the competitors to gain control of bridges and walls—and the dreams of land, water, oil, and gold that lie beyond. But there it is, "we" becomes "me," and survival is a story about owning more, not of sharing more. Does anyone think it odd that power can be distributed equally throughout the group but is most often concentrated in the hands of an individual? Tell us again—what is the difference between "sharing power with" and "holding power over"?

What has happened to the mirror neurons, to their biological wiring and evolutionary design intended to connect us collaborators and competitors alike? Are they powerful enough to override our antagonistic drives and fend off the cultural values these urges spawn? And if not, well then, we will not always mirror each other but act on the self-preservation instinct instead and reflect the pernicious beliefs and practices of cultures corrupted by greed. Friends become "frenemies" and are quickly unfriended; selfishness becomes a virtue, and victims are left further and further behind. The meek shall not inherit this earth.

We must remind ourselves that Empathy was given its English name at the beginning of the twentieth century, the very one that turned out to be the bloodiest in human history. While the irony cannot be lost, we might also ask ourselves if the twenty-first century is on track to seize this distinction for itself. Evidence is mounting, and already we must add Syria to the examples of bloodletting emblazoning our recent history. Such violent strife, such brutal subjugation, echo what happened in Rwanda and Srebrenica, Sarajevo and Belfast. We have already heard these stories and the many, many others, some with details about mustard gas and muddy trenches or napalm and rice paddies. Battles have been fought, some of them iconic, but none glorious. They are all horrific, those at Pork Chop Hill and Hamburger Hill, Guadalcanal and Midway, Fallujah and Benghazi; and those in Kosovo, Chechnya, Helmand Province, and now back to Anbar province.

We are ever the tribe defending territories, wall builders keeping other tribes out. Once it was the Romans and Chinese who built such wonders, and now it is the Israelis and Americans.

Lines have also been drawn, separating warring factions at the 38th parallel and the 17th, while other lines divide Greeks and Turks, who must share an island, or Hindus and Muslims, who share a subcontinent. We have seen images terrifying and poignant of Dachau and Auschwitz, Nagasaki and Hiroshima. And the carnage on the beaches of Normandy and in the killing fields of Cambodia is still vivid, as is the footage that came in from the Afghan mountains and Iraqi desert. Through it all, a simple question is left hanging in the smoke, the late Rodney King's lament, "Can we all just get along?" We cannot answer; we dare not, not now, maybe not ever.

How could Empathy ever persist—survive—in the face of such atrocities? Or how could we be expected to discover it, let alone bring it back to life? No, Empathy will remain lost in an unmarked space between human biology and human culture, we are told— what must be an eerie place for sure—where it is attacked by both. Of course, we are uneasy, especially when learning that Empathy wobbles in a no-man's-land—a demilitarized zone— between shaky and always contested lines.

Even we realize, and rather quickly, that our biology and culture are not enemies but conspirators, each plotting what to launch upon us. At any moment, biology could hit us with confusing, conflicting feelings—the pain of our own "personal distress," for instance, caused by the pain of another—what hurts inside us then hardens and turns us cold as we turn away. Culture's cunning unleashes a narcissism that will spread throughout post-industrialized societies, what we Westerners find aggrandizing, a call to show off and publicly confront others with our imagined gifts of greatness.

We find Empathy's terrain weary, sagging under the weight of such threats. When it gives way, an "uncanny valley" opens up, dropping us into limbo, where we encounter humanoid creatures of all kinds. Wandering in the depths, we stare at the faces, delighting in the beauty of some and approving of others that simply state their humanness. But there are those that feel like a punch in the gut, so violently repulsed are we by their disfiguring birth defects or severe scars—what we take as proof they are not fully human, not like us at all. Our face-to-face encounters are not always based on reciprocity, after all, and we do not live in the facial expressions of others and we will not feel them living in ours. The land of empathy may have its shining peak, one capped by Merleau-Ponty's existentialism, but it also falls into a deep valley that is filled with uncertainties about what humanizes us and certainties about being dehumanized.

Empathy lies fallow, neglected, its place made more unstable still by the tunneling borers our biology and culture have also released. The borers' charge is to disturb the ground on which Empathy stands, thus shifting boundaries and leaving us unable to distinguish between compassion and compassion *fatigue* or between self-*esteem* and self-admiration. Where does one leave off and the other begin? Relationships are undermined as well, leaving us confused about ourselves and others—who might be a "Thou," an "It," and how are we to recognize our own "I"?

The borers pursue their mission with zeal, working to hollow out a space for perversion to take hold—part of the plan to affect everything we do and everything Empathy has to offer. Our virtues and talents, our abilities to learn, to communicate, and connect are planted in this taint, and as Phil Zimbardo reminds us, will always carry the potential to bloom as their opposite, something quite perverse indeed. Heroes could be villains, saints, sinners, victims, abusers, travelers, or trolls. And the line between good and evil is carried off like dust in the wind. Our own biology and culture have seen fit to act as corrosive forces that can transform us—the ordinary, good people—into perpetrators of evil.

Lost, we look around for the signposts, the landmarks that might guide us through this sunless place where we are made to feel less human and less alive. Perhaps we could use the images that clutter this space like the billboards blighting our rural highways and urban landscapes. What we see around us—the messages, the "reports given" about Empathy's reality—seem clear enough. We cannot help but notice the loudest, the images of war that scream out and trigger our most visceral emotions. There, writ large, is the little Vietnamese girl running straight at us, her naked body terrifying us for forty-odd years now, confronting us still with napalm's—our—brutality. No less terrifying are the old images of coffin after coffin arriving in

Dover, ready for their Arlington burial and welcomed back by a culture still uncomfortable with its Southeast Asian foray. In more recent photos, we see the naked prisoners of Abu Ghraib, hooded and chained behind the walls, their smiling guards standing over them as dogs strain at the leash; the dusty, dazed five-year-old boy in the back of an Aleppo ambulance who reaches to feel his bleeding head.

Empathy's image-world cannot find a focus and reminds us only of struggle. We are blurry ourselves, unable to appreciate Empathy's effort to push us higher up the mountain, beyond the impulse to conquer and control. But gravity wins the day, and like Sisyphus, we are doomed to slog once more uphill among the placards advertising our battle zones. We are unprepared to decipher the accompanying images of the enemy that loom overhead like enormous balloons. They are insidious, we sense, and hideously bright, their Kool-Aid colors commanding attention and provoking a perverse curiosity.

We can see that they give the enemy a face, showing him as the evildoing barbarian, the snake in the grass, the scary Other. They hover, and we are uneasy, unwilling to pull them down for closer inspection. We do not challenge their message or identify its origin. Staring up at them, we have not noticed what is missing on the ground, the images left out—the ones creating gaps in our cultural awareness, even as their absence fills us with the most grotesque propaganda of all. We forget about the missing, the coffins we did not see returning from the battlefields of Iraq or the wounded arriving in Germany. But we are well aware of the cynicism and the fear taking over the land—what tears at Empathy's roots, leaves the billboards blank or blurred, and the balloons unpopped. And the fearmongers have done their best to redraw the line between good and evil.

Yet, we are at home in this image-world, so familiar is its mountainside, its boulder—the up-and-down that biology's tactics and culture's strategies have set in motion. They are what we know and would not think to question. We do not ask what the images represent, or misrepresent, even though we are not always sure of the story they tell and who is telling it. Without a context, we are not likely to challenge what we are fed, what we should value or believe to be true. Such are the images that have much to teach. But mostly, their lessons are about power, where it is concentrated and where it is not.

We must pay attention and learn how the powerful use their techniques to show the powerless, those who are made to take passive roles and are unlikely to question the rules. The rule-makers know that the helpless, the hapless will believe these images and adopt them as their own. Indeed, those in power control the megaphone and have much to say about how the game is played on their tilted turf. When they overreach and the oppression becomes too much to bear, will the oppressed rise up to level the field and replant Empathy in healthier soil? Or is the oppressor to be demonized and a new line drawn between good and evil? Will we find ourselves shivering still, hunkered down in the mud and wondering about an image-world that teaches everything and nothing at all?

Where do we tribalists turn for comfort, but to our clan, our family that shares a heredity and a heritage. Biology is the bond, the blood types and eye color we share, the genetic predispositions for diabetes or arthritis, cardiovascular disease or high blood pressure. Photo albums frame the image-worlds enshrined within our family fortresses. Some members are restless within these walls, but most are validated by the identity and security they enforce. If your family is like mine, there is at least one member who resonates viscerally with such solidarity—the one insisting a little too vehemently that everyone is thriving inside the stronghold and nestled blissfully in the family's nurturing bosom.

Despite evidence to the contrary, this relative fiercely believes all is well: The sons and daughters are deeply caring, mutually supportive, and the cousins close-knit, every one of them doted upon equally by generous aunts and uncles. Of course, the grandparents are well loved and respected as the wise matriarch and patriarch. What's more, the weddings have all been just lovely, the marriages perfectly sound, every in-law a welcome addition, and every birth a blessed event. Young people are all on track, living up to their responsibilities, doing what the family expects of them. Without question, they will emulate their successful uncle or older sister who went to the right school and launched a career that is both professionally and financially rewarding. Everyone lives in a nice home, stays fit and healthy, finds life fulfilling, and is delighted to attend the frequent family gatherings. In the photo albums, there are ever so many frozen smiles to prove it.

This is the relative who sees only a quilt, a valued heirloom spread over the family to keep everyone warm and happy. It is also the quilt smothering any issues or anxieties that threaten this sepia-toned image. In this zealot's eyes, the squares and triangles are nothing but bright and cheerful, like the family members they represent, and beautifully stitched together to form a sunburst pattern irradiated with harmony. There can be no rips in the fabric, no stains, and any ripples, any ugly disappointments below the surface are conveniently hidden from view. The quilt covers them all—the hurt feelings and rivalries, the testiness and attention-getting stunts. Even the overheated discussions that have been known to rear up—arguments about birth control or gun control, immigration or health care—can be made to disappear.

Choosing myopia over reality, this relative stays on red alert, ready to spot the first sign of trouble and more importantly, to beat it back with a swift and certain counterattack of merciless diplomacy. Distraction and diversion are other tactics deployed, and the question "Who wants pie?" is understood by everyone as a warning to stop any unpleasantness during the Thanksgiving dinner and start enjoying a stress-free meal. No one is to be worried about family pressures to perform; there simply is no room at the table for failing grades or bad investments, unemployment or foreclosure. Concerns about a broken government, an increasing rancor, a failed economy—or worse, a failed family member—are not to be aired. No, the ferociously happy family member knows how to suffocate us all with that cherished quilt.

Chances are, the relative who works with militant might to preserve the appearance of family harmony is a troubled soul looking to crush the noisy dissonance within. But this inner world is secret, hidden away where no one can know its distress or see it teetering on the edge of darkness and terrifying imperfection. Seeking comfort, this internal life is wrapped in the quilt that denies the possibility of flaws, not only in the family itself but also in this most frightened of its members. The cozy quilt warms away the cold, negative feelings churned up by the relative's worst fears of one day having to face these perceived flaws.

Until then, this person is obsessed by a family portrait of perfection and will chant over and over, "Happy, happy, joy, joy—*or I'll kill you!*" What might have been a mantra is a battle cry instead, one intended to rally the internal forces and focus the mission at hand. This is the family member who likely suffers from what has been described as "militant humanism," and who represses the personal flaws—feelings of self-doubt and inadequacy—that threaten a sense of equilibrium. Living in fear of being found out, this person uses the family as a diversionary tactic when, in fact, it is always a self-orientation that leads the charge to capture harmony's happy territory.

Such an individual may also suffer from "personal distress" and will work tirelessly to deflect the pain of others because it might stir up too many issues, too much hurt inside the precarious self. In this case, it is words of outrage inspiring the chant "How dare you hurt me—how dare you make me feel bad about what hurts you!" And behind the outrage is Empathy looming like a stormy threat, so dangerously provocative that it must be knocked back with a preemptive strike. What are we to make of it when, for instance, one friend comes to visit another known for her exercise and good eating habits who unexpectedly requires hospital care. "What did you do?" demands the "well-wisher," as if to protest a grave injustice. "How dare you scare me like this with what is ravaging you—you with the healthy lifestyle that is now making me confront end-of-life issues!" Oh, the risks Empathy expects us to take, the concern we must show, the moral sympathy we must develop, just to take on another orientation!

The visitor is not alone. Like so many others similarly affected, the price of caring is simply too high, the loss of self-protection too great a risk. Even among those who *are* altruistic—much more willing and able to care—there are costs to be borne. In a peculiar twist, those who are drawn to work on behalf of others also risk losing themselves to the hurt. Their empathic concern, their altruism, cannot protect them after all. We have our biology to blame—what makes it possible for us to feel too much or feel too little, and sometimes, not at all. Biology is the culprit lurking in the shadows of our psychopathology.

Human biology is also guilty of triggering compassion fatigue. But in this case, human culture rejoins its coconspirator, and together the two work to wear us down—gradually lessening our compassion. Too often, we find our deepest empathic impulses boxed in by cultural rhythms and routines, the demanding roles we play day in and day out. Those in caregiver roles who have no time to care for themselves—the ones working alone, giving all they have to a deeply depressed spouse, a child with severe autism, a parent suffering from Alzheimer's, a diabetic sister on dialysis—are especially vulnerable to compassion fatigue's exhausting ways.

Those who regularly attend to the needs of others—who must routinely show concern for their well-being—are sometimes left feeling isolated and apathetic, their emotions suppressed and in dire need of release. These are also the nurses, doctors, and social workers, the paramedics, first responders, and disaster workers, who may be struggling with substance abuse or suffering from what is known as secondary traumatic stress disorder. Their survival often depends on their ability to distance themselves, detach from the concern they are called to show. The support, the care *they* need—what society owes them—may or may not be forthcoming.

Compassion and compassion fatigue are twisted together in a dysfunctional relationship that affects us all, whether we work as caregivers or not. The media appears to be complicit, what enables their perverse codependency. Piercing the routines of everyday life, the media prompts us to show we care for those ravaged by tragedy and is largely responsible for shaping a culture of charitable giving. Again and again, we are bombarded by distressing images meant to raise awareness of human suffering wherever it is found on this disaster-prone planet. We stare at the blinking, bewildered faces, the bedraggled children wandering among the ruins, and feel the pull on our heartstrings and our wallets. We come together, one-hearted, to accept some responsibility for those the media has put in front of us.

Too often, the media fails us—reneging on its responsibility to provide a context for the disaster currently grabbing the headlines. We are given no explanation of the causes, no analysis of the unique circumstances. Nor do we ask about the implications of yet another flood in India or China, another famine in Ethiopia, or fire in the American West. The Indonesian earthquake, the typhoons capsizing Filipino ferries have blurred together. Tell us again, which horror is this? What does it mean to the region's economy? Or to the world's political stability? Where are the social and cultural fabrics torn, and what will it take to make them whole? What might such ruptures portend for the fabrics we are weaving?

Sensationalized images are too often mind-numbing and decontextualized. They desensitize us and leave us flagging, our caring on the wane. We are tapped out, emotionally and financially. Frustration builds as we are asked to donate yet again, often sparking a cynical resistance to giving anything more. Hearts harden, and a self-orientation reappears. Caught by compassion fatigue's pernicious claws, some of us will also become skeptical, doubting that donated dollars would ever be well spent.

The culture of charitable giving is reshaped as a culture of not-so-charitable investing. Years after Haiti's massive earthquake, donors demand an accounting of the funds raised and spent in the Western Hemisphere's poorest nation. They want to see some return on what they invested—something tangible—preferably in the form of infrastructure. How many new schools and medical clinics have been built? Where are the houses, clean and freshly painted? The bustling markets, the shops and businesses returning to profitability?

Looking for dividends, these investors are impatient and seem to have forgotten the faces, the children, and the stories like Jeanette's about raw anguish and survival. They do not remember the chaos and cholera, the vital, but intangible gifts of food and clean water, medicine and treatment given in the darkest days of unknowable and *immeasurable* suffering. And in the world's wealthiest nation, where hunger is a plague much too widespread, compassion is insufficient to motivate the well-fed. Donations are not charitable but practical. In this country, we feed hungry children not because they are hungry. We feed them so they are better able to learn.

What is already perverse and dysfunctional is made even more tedious by an unforgiving irony. The media images that routinely penetrate our buttoned-up lives—the ones intended to humanize suffering's overwhelming scale and scope by giving it a face—are the very images that dehumanize us all, victims and viewers alike. Everyone is numb to what overwhelms the senses and the spirit. We stare blankly at the devastation and cannot recognize anyone, not even ourselves. How are we to connect?

The possibilities of "I" and "Thou" have faded away, and we are left fumbling together as "Its" sucked dry. Yet, we know the faces on the screen. We have seen them many, many times. They are always the same tragic faces, their hollow eyes like our own, staring into a void that will forever remain incomprehensible. Like the victims, we have nothing to hold on to, no details or distinguishing characteristics, no signs of authenticity. Everyone is made anonymous; no one is unique or special in this empty story. Sharing this unwanted connection, our prospects for empathy are lost, along with our humanity.

But the media is not yet finished with us. It moves quickly to rename us, as if branding us with something we will better understand and find more appetizing. Ever the enabler, it prepares a sumptuous culture of self-absorption for us and then invites us to gorge. The images that once left us feeling tapped out, numb to ourselves and others, are replaced by a feast of entertaining delights—the layered cake of a cultural *tour de force* tapping into our most narcissistic impulses. Where we were starving, the media now fills to overflowing our voracious need to be special and dishes up the special treatment that makes us feel good about ourselves. In the Western world, indeed, the media is entertaining and happily feeds the hunger of its self-focused audiences. Playing a masterful role, it spreads the sweet, sticky syrup of cultural narcissism over us, and we lap it up. How pleased we are to connect with what enables us.

Our gluttony is satisfied only when we stand atop the media's many platforms—the ones celebrities once had to themselves. Devouring the pages of *People* and *Glamour*, *Self* and *GQ*, we inhale the gloss, what we need for improving our self-presentation and making ourselves more like the stars. Their success is mouthwatering and drives us to work harder at the gym and stay longer in the tanning booth. We want the same special treatment, their bags of swag filled with toys and overpriced products promising perfect hair and skin. We will undergo their plastic surgeries and try their special diets, practice the routines that allow us to try on their brand of star power.

We reassure ourselves regularly—sending our tweets and reading theirs, friending them, downloading their content as we upload our own—and admire the celebrities, not so much for their talents but for their self-admiring ways. Talented or not, we know we are entitled to do whatever it takes to grab more than the fifteen minutes of fame Andy Warhol once allotted to us all. Our story is as big as Marilyn Monroe's, and we would be oh so delighted if an artist like Warhol would acknowledge us and make our own iconic image the subject of pricey mass-produced prints seen by millions.

We are all celebrities now, fierce competitors vying for attention on talk shows and reality TV. One strategy is to imitate the kings and queens of pop, giving big performances with bigger voices belting out the lyrics of a pervasive and self-absorbed sensibility. Like Justin Bieber, who believes "this world belongs to [him]," we too know we are "born to be somebody." Of course, we'll "light up the sky like lightning" and there "ain't nothin' ever gonna stop [us]." It's all part of our plan to impress ourselves, along with the judges and screaming audience. We expect to garner the votes of millions and to win contracts worth millions more.

If not singing and dancing, we scheme to win the bachelor's rose or to find the "yes" dress for the intimate wedding we must have televised for all to see. We will also squabble over private family matters with Judge Judy or spill our neurotic guts to Dr.

Phil. Our personal dramas, our meltdowns on remote islands or in glass houses, must have a showcase—what the spotlights of center stage will make even more important. Surely, we are entitled to at least as much attention as Kim Kardashian or Caitlyn Jenner, Snooki or Octomom. Like Lindsay Lohan and Charlie Sheen, we bargain with the media. We will exploit its many platforms and pretend to be incensed when the media exploits our narcissistic brand. The spotlight shines, promoting the brand, and in exchange, the brand brings in the ratings and the advertising dollars.

Just like that, we find ourselves riding another loop. We are back in the eternal bubble, living in the moment, determined to push aside the needling questions about blemishes and wrinkles, scars and mortality. Young people are especially exhilarated and proud to show off their freshly branded faces every time they go around. To the core, they know they are invincible and more than ready to establish themselves in what is always a youth-oriented culture of self-absorption. Like them, we are ever so grateful to the media for trapping us in the loop—the one where we warp the culture to make it even more self-oriented, and the culture warps our identity to make it even more self-admiring.

To be clear, the brand of Western culture is not the narcissism of psychopathology. Most of us will not be professionally assessed and diagnosed with narcissistic personality disorder. Instead, we are symptomatic of an afflicted culture, one trending in a direction that worries some psychologists, if not others. Jean Twenge and Keith Campbell are so concerned that they have rolled up their sleeves to work at measuring the degree of cultural warp. They have turned to the young and invincible, plucking those eighteen-to twenty-four-year-olds from the loop just long enough to ask them how they see themselves and their place in the culture of self-absorption.

Using the Narcissistic Personality Inventory, these research psychologists set about surveying more than sixteen thousand students on thirty-two college campuses between 1979 and 2006. Students sat down to consider the NPI's forty items, deciding whether they agreed with statements such as "If I ruled the world, it would be a better place," and "I can live my life any way

I want to;" also, "I like to be the center of attention" and "I think I am a special person." They were most forthcoming, and the results are clear: Two-thirds of college students in 2006 scored above average on the measure, which, as Twenge and Campbell point out, is about 30 percent higher than students in 1982. They also note that the rate at which the numbers are increasing is on the rise, especially among young women. What emerges, says Twenge, is a picture of young people who are self-centered and attention seeking, who have inflated expectations, are unwilling or unable to take the perspectives of others, and are not very good at relationships. Those who are happy about themselves and their own self-importance, she adds, often end up alienating others. In the long run, feeling special and entitled is not good for this or any other society. What might she say about a reality TV star who rises to claim the highest office in the land?

Why would we be surprised? A new study conducted by Eddie Brummelman confirms that parents believe their children are quite special—and very bright indeed. Theirs are not just Lake Woebegone kids fabled to be "above average." Parents participating in the study attested to this in a survey asking them if their children were familiar with the historic events and figures listed among the items. These parents believed their kids were so smart that they would surely have a strong grasp of what is historically important and recognize everything and everyone on the list —even the bogus names and places mixed in with the *bona fide*. Is this a multigenerational narcissism talking? Cynicism and Irony gloating in the scientific findings?

Taking a different approach, Nathan DeWall turned to the culture itself and studied pop songs as one of the products— "tangible artifacts"—that reflect its trends and shifting values. Rather than rely on students' self-reports, this psychologist parsed the lyrics of songs topping the charts between 1980 and 2007. His analysis reveals an increasing narcissism among pop singers—the very ones whose certitudes about their own self-importance fill our airwaves, our iPods, and CD collections before that—and buzz in our heads. In the last twenty-five years, says DeWall, songs that once crooned of relationships in terms of "we" and "our" have shifted their focus to become monologues about "me" and "mine." Where Michael Jackson, Paul Simon, and so many others once proclaimed, "We are the world," Justin Bieber now owns it, and Kanye West rules his own planet where he stands tall and brags, "Can't tell me nothin'."

Interpreting the results, DeWall is left to conclude that the self-focused lyrics mirror the self-focused culture. But one might also wonder if this is a matter of art imitating life, or life imitating art, or what is most likely some combination of the two. In any case, de Waal is concerned. All that seems to matter, he says, is how we are feeling. Like the pop singers themselves, we encourage our own emotional states and well-being to dominate our lives along with our culture, and we are not interested in much else—certainly not in what others have to say. No, there *are* no others and no need for their uninteresting feedback. Our self-image will not be challenged. We will remain forever young and invincible.

Irony's tense, sour humor reappears, a double agent in the psychological warfare waged by the culture and its media henchmen. But their not-so-secret tactics have become so routine that we stopped paying attention decades ago and no longer feel the grip tightening around us. Now, we are just pleased to have witnessed the cultural frame of reference shift itself from the Other to the Self. While media images occasionally present the sad suffering of the generic Other, they mostly glorify the importance of the special Self.

Have our narcissistic families, pop songs, and media culture saturated the brain? Rewired the temporoparietal junction, reprogrammed its function as an enabler originally intended to help build our capacity for balancing Self and Other? Have our cultural values prompted so much gray matter to build up in the TPJ that we can only recognize the Self? Oh, but this is so much better, we say, than to struggle with too little gray matter like the victims of "mirror touch," a form of synesthesia that renders them Selfless with only the Other to recognize. We would rather not feel in our bodies what others feel in theirs— not be overwhelmed by the physical sensation of their pain. Nor do we wish to sit at a dinner table and feel the forkfuls of others' food in our mouths, the sensations of chewing, swallowing, and sending their meal into our stomachs. The self-obsessed Self we glorify is just fine on its own, thank you.

Such glory does not save us from this ongoing disaster, the gluttonous black hole eating our character and dignity. We are our own victims of the media onslaught that will always desensitize and dehumanize us. In our rhinestone rubble, we are connected only to the brand that fills us with nothing but angst about staying young and vibrant, staying in the limelight and looking good, with no thought of *being* good to others or even to ourselves. Becoming a rich and famous cardboard character is all that matters, Irony tells us. Once again, there is no context provided nor are we interested in understanding the meaning of our entitlement and self-promotion. We will not ask ourselves what is required to mend the social-cultural fabric shredded in recent years. And choking off our empathy, along with our humanity, the media's head games will always intrigue us.

So, we continue to tweet and update our status; stream and binge watch whole series, to stare in TV's mythic realities, narrate our own theme-park stories, and play in a video-game world—and the scientists continue to believe in the truth of our biology. The neuroscientists are still passionate about the brain scans that reveal the wiring of our empathy, and the evolutionary biologists still believe our species survives, no, thrives by our instincts for group cohesion and synchrony. Yet, a pernicious culture overwhelms the Western world, disconnecting us from ourselves and each other; clearly foreclosing on biology's virtues. Can science be wrong? Its methods flawed? Is the scanner that encloses us in its high-tech bubble any more credible than the shiny bubble of Sontag's image-world, the one floating us far beyond a landscape of cells and synapses?

Inside the scanner, images flash at us, what Sontag calls mere "substitutes" for the real-world experiences the scientists expect to study. A digitized face appears on the screen just inches from our own, and we already know how far removed we are from any possibility of interacting with the fullness of humanity it is meant to represent. But it is the *image* we prefer, Sontag reminds us, the thing the face has become. Excited, the brain lights up, yet the scientists will only measure our neurological interactions based on the "reports given" by images that misrepresent our face-to-face encounters in the world of others. Could it be that science is trapped in a bubble of its own, one filled with the magic of electronic images that bewitch us and package the research results?

Our biological drive to move together in synchronous patterns is leading us to arrange ourselves as groups that are ever smaller, more defined, and tribalistic. Such are the in-groups drawing new boundaries that must be defended—the zealous tribes threatening the health of a species still warring over old battle lines. Indeed, we seek the likeminded, those whose brains must surely share the same wiring. Moving closer and closer together, we cloister ourselves in communities that are as clearly labeled as they are self-focused—those that are gated or gay, ethnic or online, religious or political. Some of us take comfort, others pride in living among the Orange County housewives of Coto de Caza or with Florida's "friendliest" seniors at The Villages. Perhaps it is Fire Island or the Castro, Little Tokyo or Harlem that defines our tribal headquarters.

Some of us are devoted to our Facebook friends or the church's swaying congregation; others to Fox News or MSNBC. We are in sync with what is homogeneous—the partisan beliefs that drive us to build our castle walls. Though we know there are other beings beyond the moat, we can no longer see them. Or listen to their ideas. Or stand in their shoes. And the sequestered wealthy are not aware of the needs of the poor sequestered elsewhere. The fine leather wallets remain closed, while the poor empty their pockets, giving all they can to help their neighbors. The riches that diversity might bestow upon a sprawling human community are lost to tribalism's urgent cause.

We live in our protracted adolescence, hyperaware of in-groups and out-groups. Making it into the cool kids' club is all that counts—along with avoiding the nerds we judge to be inferior and less human somehow. We put ourselves at risk of stereotyping, and worse, demonizing those outsiders we do not know, the inferiors whose circumstances and perspectives remain a mystery, along with the moral foundations shaping their worldviews. Unraveling nothing, we will believe the stereotypes instead, the narrow images we create to fill the void. If by chance we were to make contact, to discover that some people believe fairness and caring for others are most important in life, while we ourselves believe loyalty and liberty are what matter most, neither we nor they would be prepared to discuss the differences. We would be at a loss too discovering that some of us look upon Michelangelo's *David* and see only magnificence, while others see only a larger-than-life penis. Liberals and conservatives will continue to shout past each other, and those who relish the openness of space will stand across a divide from those who must have the security and predictability of place. What is this instinct that moves us not to synchronize but to self-segregate; this biological wiring that short-circuits our willingness to engage the Other?

Our need to be accepted by the cool group is as strong as our fear of being rejected by its judgmental members. So, we connect with the hipsters, not as brother and sister tribalists sharing a deep bond but as con artists and private investigators working on the sly to uncover what they think of us, how they see us, and what we must do to enhance our image. Acceptance is won, we believe, by making ourselves look better than we are in their eyes and in our own. So, we deploy our considerable skills honed to manipulate our self-presentation, privileging deception over authenticity—and ensuring that our connections will be shallow and ever more mercenary. The very purpose of human connection changes, and we are interested only in confirming what we already believe about ourselves—the lies we want to be true. Rather than getting to know the others in the clan, exchanging ideas or sharing stories and feelings, we bond with what psychologist Jonathan Haidt calls the Confirmation Bias. This bias is on full display, he says, when we use Google, not to search for information that furthers our lines of inquiry or satisfies our curiosity and creative urges, but as a weapon to gather evidence supporting the argument we are always making in the name of self- or group promotion. We are cheerleaders all, our singsong squads chanting more and more loudly about how great we are—and proving synchrony's big lie.

Such are the arguments becoming shriller and less nuanced. Harangue replaces debate, and the great dialectic is outmuscled by ideological diatribe. We seek the likeminded, not the open-minded, and even the relativists who argue for shades of gray are just as insistent as those whose positions are absolutely black or white. To some of us, context is important and enlightening, to others, irrelevant, even detrimental. We can agree that *David* is an important work of art, but bicker, sometimes bitterly, over the meaning of the iconic sculpture. Some of us are convinced that Michelangelo chose to capture the future king in the moments before Goliath is slain, while others see him as the victor in the moments after. Interpretations vary and, too often, divide sharply along different lines. There are the literalists who see a courageous young warrior about to face the evil giant with only a rock and a slingshot. They admire such courage and the stunning realism with which the supremely skilled Michelangelo presents it. But they are also confused by the unreality of David's nudity. Why would this biblical hero make himself even more vulnerable in what is already an unfair fight? Where is his armor? In their view, there is something inappropriate, if not immoral, about the exposed body that threatens David's virtues, his valor, fortitude, and sacred duty to save his people.

There are those who admire the vulnerability and Michelangelo's genius in presenting David as a towering figure—the classic ideal of male perfection rivaling that of a Greek god. Yet, he is a mere mortal, the lowly human being alone with his thoughts, a resolute look on his face as he contemplates what he is about to do or has done. These are the contextualists who will situate the seventeen feet of gleaming white marble within historical and aesthetic canons—and who will interpret the story of the giant-killer as a metaphor. To them, David is not simply the brave underdog who takes on the threatening giant, but he is also an inspiring symbol for the city of Florence once threatened by the massive papal armies of Rome. Some also believe that David is Michelangelo himself, slaying the mighty Medici to free his art from their stifling patronage.

Convictions run deep, to be sure—whether we are arguing about aesthetics or morality. Though we know exactly what our beliefs are—"this is the truth of art, that is not" or "this is good, that is evil"—we cannot explain how or why we came to hold them. We just do. Such are the black-or-white positions we stand on, stand for, and will bitterly defend, sometimes drawing upon factual information and rational thought, sometimes conjuring up personal experiences and primal instincts. Logic and emotion test each other, and in a flash, will resolve the inconsistencies every time. There are no dilemmas of any kind. We stand on solid ground.

Even when presented with a hypothetical situation intended to thrust us into a moral dilemma, we have our answer. No matter how horrifying the scenario, we know what we must do—smother our coughing baby to save ourselves and our fellow villagers from the murderous enemy soldiers hunting for our hideaway. Or hold the baby's life sacred above all else. Sacrifice one to spare many, sanctify all lives to share one death. Where this either/or decision comes from—religious teachings, empathic awareness, practical judgments—is not at all clear.

For their part, scientists roll up their sleeves to explain the mystery behind what is clear to us. Still, Josh Green's brain-imaging technologies can only pinpoint so much. Scans of his research subjects who responded "yes," they would smother the infant, and those who said "no," they would not, revealed the same brain activity—what lit up in emotional *and* rational areas. Primatologist Frans de Waal takes a different direction and argues that morality is not simply a question of wiring but something more complex that develops out of an ability to empathize with others and cooperate as a group. Emotion? Reason? Empathy? What is the mix? How do we learn to blend them into a morality cocktail? We just drink it down, hearts strong and heads clear, even when science is not. We know what is right and who is wrong. Our positions do not change.

Shared by the likeminded, principles of morality become principles of solidarity. Beliefs coalesce then harden, and tribes unify around the values at their core, what they hold sacred. Donning their colors—red or blue—and hoisting flags to match, they forge their identities and root for themselves. Showing such spirited pride, they are more than ready to outcompete their rivals. Tribes are much less interested in connecting with others and much more interested in winning the right to dominate— to control and convert the misguided to their just and moral cause. Sometimes the competition is too raw, the bare-knuckled crusading too intense, a battle between good and evil. One group demonizes the other, provoking a rabid retaliation that requires another and another; the overheated outrage, the righteous indignation intensifying all the while. Both see themselves as a force for good that will vanquish the evil they imagine in the barbarians and scary others they have come to fear. They will use any means possible to achieve their noble ends.

Sometimes, the tribes exhaust themselves and their resources and must step back from the dusty line they have been kicking back and forth. Empty-handed, they trudge through a no-man's-land, searching for the common ground beneath their sacred truths. They at least will agree that certain principles of morality, like certain works of art, are important indeed. Fairness, for example, is recognized as something foundational, the bedrock of a civil society—what keeps it strong and healthy. But even as with *David*, they will argue over its meaning. Once again, the red and blue appear, the tribes unable or unwilling to consider rival interpretations, and the purple flag that flew the promise of civility is desecrated.

One group sees fairness as a principle tied to an ethic of caring—taking care of others—especially those who cannot take care of themselves. Another group believes fairness means taking responsibility for the Self and having the freedom to compete and reach a God-given potential. One group values the collective, the other the individual. One is ready to redistribute the wealth more equitably, and the other to double down, its members each working to build up their own. Selfishness is seen as a virtue or a vice, and wealth redistribution is morally debasing *and* morally uplifting. It is either an intrusive, creativity-killing policy that moves money from "makers to takers," ruins the economy, and leaves us all poor. Or it is a badly needed balancing mechanism for creating a just and cooperative society; a rising tide that lifts *all* boats—not just the yachts.

We recognize the tribal leaders, colorful and charismatic, portraits of the legendary Robin Hood and the Randian John Galt, each filled with their convictions. We have heard their real-life stories narrated more academically by the likes of John Maynard Keynes and Milton Friedman. But there is someone else in the portrait we must acknowledge: a lone figure standing in the breach between tribes. His story is fierce, one of defiance, its chapters written in his angry eyes that stare at us so warily, so intently, and in his clothes that tell of grime and tatter and a life lived on the streets. He is Édouard Manet's *Ragpicker*, who steps out of his one-hundred-fifty-year-old canvas to claim his dignity, with only a stick in his hand, a sack over his shoulder, and a smashed champagne bottle at his feet. He picks through the rags he finds on the streets of Paris—what he will sell to the fine paper manufacturers of the 1860s.

He could be the homeless man we have seen picking up cans and bottles to cash in at the recycling center in our own hometowns or the spidery kids picking through the garbage piles of New Delhi and Rio de Janeiro we have seen on our screens. They are neither makers nor takers, but noble gleaners all— the nonpartisans who, fending for themselves, are undaunted, unafraid of morality's good and evil. They may or may not want to be helped by the caregivers, but most certainly they want the freedom to put a few coins in their pockets. They will belong to neither tribe, feeding off the excesses cast off by the one but not fed enough by the good intentions of the other. Nor are they a part of society, the one weakened and sickened by the tribal warfare they ignore.

We do not ask them what they have gleaned, what they have to teach about the meaning of fairness or the color purple.

Unlike the gleaners, we are always vulnerable to the tribal tensions, the strife fomented by a gargantuan political-economic system that wraps around the globe—its coils tightening against the skyscrapers of London and Tokyo, New York and Hong Kong, but also sucking the air out of the grass huts bordering Uganda's Mgahinga Gorilla National Park and the aboriginal villages dotting Australia's Outback. We are the unwitting pawns left gasping by such a system—what is a loud capitalist culture that quietly, yet methodically, victimizes us all and thrusts us into all manner of untenable situations—those of us living in the homeless shelter or jetting between well-appointed winter and summer homes alike.

Revered and reviled, capitalism captures us, entangling us, whether we lust after the monetary wealth it promises or push back hard against the crass materialism it delivers. It is the system that infiltrates our dreams and determines how we work, play, and define success. It is etched as deeply into the playwright and poet as into the hedge fund manager and bond trader. No one escapes, not the preschooler, the video gamer, or health care provider; and in recent years, capitalism has left its distinctive marks upon the Ugandan Forest People, who tour paying customers through their former homeland, and upon the Aborigines, who sell reproductions of their sacred rock art online.

No, we are not gleaners and cannot pick among capitalism's deeply held convictions, the premiums it places on accumulation and private ownership, profits and competitive markets. We cannot separate what we do and do not value in its massive structures, those extolling the virtues of efficiency and the laws of supply and demand or preaching the morality of its winner-take-all dynamic. Nor can we fend for ourselves in the face of its supercharged forces always working to maximize profits, minimize costs, and perfect the bottom-line mentality—the forces always unleashing the pathologies of consumerism upon our social and spiritual lives. Instead, we must live by the rules and procedures it establishes—the very ones that influence how we see ourselves and understand time and space—and that, ultimately, ensure its continued world dominance. Vesting itself with authority, the capitalist system installs its captains as champions, its titans as leaders, and lavishly rewards the robber barons who enforce the rules, especially those that sustain the market economy on which they know the whole of humanity now depends.

Sometimes, the system's size and scope are checked by governments, by public institutions looking to impose a different set of rules. In some cases, these agencies are motivated by their own greed. Looking for a hefty slice of capitalism's pie, they work to form what they call "public-private partnerships," cronies delighting in the collaborative deliciousness that satisfies the needs and interests of both entities. In other cases, though, public agencies do not see a tasty pie but a garden wildly overgrown—what is capitalism's jungle habitat, choked by its slithering greed and by the weeds of corruption and predatory practice—the dank, airless place in dire need of pruning. These institutions swing their machetes in the name of justice and morality, equity and civility. They are among the very few willing to go up against capitalist might, the Davids who step into the fray armed only with a vision of new regulations that, if enacted, would lay the rose-colored foundation for a shared prosperity and a clean fantasy life lived in the public square. More typically, governments must step in to prop up a faltering Goliath that is too big to fail—and "too big to jail." In the grip of the system's "political capture," they must dip into the public pie and rescue a capitalism beaten down by the weight of its own recklessness.

In every case, fairness is up for grabs. Who will decide which tax policies are fair? Or which labor laws, wage and benefits packages, and safety regulations? What about health care and public education? Trade policies and property rights? How much is too much? When is the air clean enough or the water? Where is the balance between workers' rights, owner profits, and shareholder expectations? Or between consumer protections and product sales? What is the distance between competition and cooperation? Or between private ownership and the public good? Between integrity and corruption, ethics and predatory practices? In the space between—the purple territory of gleaning—is there a place for the color of empathy?

But capitalism does not wait for answers. It powers on, rippling along its sleek, linear track, even as we still squabble in our public hearings, even as the compromises we reach and the ungainly policies that would enshrine them are left on the table. Silent, but focused, and unencumbered by the artifacts, the dust of public discourse, the capitalist system stays true to itself, an arrow pointing straight at its goals—the very ones that soon enough will become our own.

With an integrity of its own, capitalism works to reframe our questions and reset our priorities. It is geared up, mass producing the spectacular images of prosperity guaranteed to dazzle and inspire the affirming vignettes we mass consume and metabolize as our aspirations. This is the imperial power that colonizes our fear of death and exploits our need for story and play, for invincibility and self-admiration. And co-opting the mass media, telling us how to use our social media, it then sucker punches us into believing we are the winners, the shrewd investors who will double and triple our shares of the system, who will earn its most scrumptious dividends.

Of course, we are deserving of a portion of its massive wealth—the bigger, the better. Lit up by these shiny images, we know we are more than worthy, which is to say, entitled to what counts as capitalist success. We are entitled—and yes, we too will be reckless, maxing out our credit cards, jumping into subprime mortgages, gambling our retirement on high-yield, high-risk stocks. And we too will sacrifice the soul of humanity in the process.

To be successful, we must act like the winners we believe we are. Acting on this, our own deeply held conviction—the internalized capitalist principle—we know we must be focused, aggressive, self-promoting, and willing to do whatever it takes to get ahead. From kindergarten to college, we must get into the right schools, the ones with the right connections, and believe that we are as special as our parents and teachers have always told us. Our narcissism is on full display, preparing us for every competition, every prize, a chainsaw buzzing through the extraneous, the expendable, and clear cutting a path to the plutocracy that animates the mythic reality we have always imagined for ourselves.

Efficient, goal driven, we waste nothing and will show no empathy, no mercy to the anonymous, the Its we step over or step on along the way. We too are Its, but unlike the downtrodden, we are bold, the ones who will enter the plutocrats' world as the polished, exquisitely cut gems we have worked hard to become. Willingly, *willfully*, we have tightly scripted and packaged ourselves in the luster. Standing tall on the auction block—and bringing the highest price at the market—we sell ourselves into capitalism's slavery. How pleased we are to be among its sparkling commodities, caught up in that most precious business of producing and consuming ourselves—and everything and everyone around us.

We resonate along with the objects and the Its commodified by capitalism's commercial enterprises. Our canonical mirror neurons are on fire, and we are experts in knowing how to grasp and manipulate the objects bought and sold in the grand marketplace. This is the enterprise, the world we understand— the comfort zone that is the analog of the stories we tell ourselves in order to live—as well as the impetus for telling them. We cannot step outside the zone nor advocate for an authentic social life we know nothing about. We are not worried about what Guy Debord sees as the decline of being into having and the decline of having into appearing. Dazzled by our expertise, by our own appearance, we are blind to the French philosopher's "society of the spectacle," what he says is a system characterized by the fusion of advanced capitalism, allied governments, and mass media. We do not question its stealth or how this mightiest of systems inverts images of society such that "relations between commodities have supplanted relations between people" and "passive identification with the spectacle supplants genuine activity."

Our lives are mediated by what is upside down, and we are unaware and unconcerned.

On the contrary, we expect to be entertained by the spectacle of movies and TV shows that flip our social values and shape our stories. They are the very media projecting the images that, according to writer David Sirota, stay with us for decades. "Greed is right . . . greed is good," we heard Michael Douglas's Gordon Gekko tell us in the 1987 film *Wall Street*, a proclamation that rang out across the land and still reverberates to this day. We remember Alex P. Keaton, the Michael J. Fox character in the '80s sitcom *Family Ties* who told us the peace-and-love kumbaya of commune-living hippie liberals was laughable, out of step with the real world, advocating instead the hard-edged, market-driven province of conservatism.

Guided by what we find most vivid, most tilted, our Debordian decline continues, and we are delighted that our own stories—even the idea of story—have been co-opted and commercialized; so delighted that we are willing to pay more for their spectacular packaging. We smile when our Starbucks scones and holiday gingerbread are handed to us in little bags declaring that "Stories are gifts—share. Good food is like stories." It is as if the coffee corporation has given us an extra treat. Those of us in Southern California are rewarded—seduced—by the Hollywood Bowl's tagline promising "there's a story in every seat," even as the venue's commercial interest lies in selling us as many tickets as it possibly can. We all remember Oprah and marvel at the massive and profitable empire she built by listening to our stories in exchange for telling her own. Stories of the spectacle stand us on our heads—and make us feel good and feel the sugary rush that flushes us with the appearance of success.

The society of the spectacle is the only story reflected in our kaleidoscopic realities. It treats the mirrors and glassy colors we love as commodities and puts us in a world that is even more mythical—and materialistic—than ever before. In these spectacular realities, the boundaries between work and play have collapsed. Our own stories are written merely as captions below the images of an inverted—a collapsed—society—a few lines about the virtues of serious play and playful work. We know we are authoring an ethical story always guided by the principle of competition and the heroism of winning. Ours are the thin but fully developed stories describing a contemporary work ethic that finds us shopping online and Facebooking in the workplace—but not using all of the vacation days we have accrued. Meanwhile, we are not at all confused about the seriousness of our play, what we take to be a precious commodity that must be handled with extra care. Some may argue that we have always taken our play seriously, but now, fully ensconced in a spectacular society, we are hyperaware of it—and laser-focused on its worth. This is especially true in the world of video games and theme parks.

We work hard at the *World of Warcraft*, a story that can only be told as a capitalist fairytale—a shiny, market-driven fantasy/reality. The characters we play—our alter egos—must work at accumulating, or "farming," gold to purchase needed potions, special ingredients, and supplies at the all-important auction houses and shops. Hunters must have enough to buy food for their dogs, wolves, or lions that accompany them on their quests. Leather workers who require tanning supplies or thread must spend some of their gold at one shop in anticipation of earning it back—and then some—when selling the finished goods at another. There are the gold farmers, thousands and thousands of them, whose real-life job is to amass capital, the gleaming bullion they will sell legitimately inside the game—and illicitly on questionable websites outside its bounds. They know there is demand for what they can supply to paying customers looking to boost their characters' wealth and power. Whatever it takes, we will dedicate ourselves to the game of life, a highly commercialized one that can only be played seriously. Like the gold farmers and our own free-marketeering characters, we are cutthroats who are out to win.

Theme park stories thrill us, not because they provide an escape but because they plunge us into yet another market-driven fantasy/reality. Though we arrive at the gate not as characters but as the capitalist creatures we are, the story we will write inside is still about our work ethic and the calculus of serious play. Indeed, the park's berm separates nothing, and the spectacular world outside molds the space inside—life in the good place is thoroughly commodified. True to our characters, we expect to conquer the territory and outcompete the system that sells it to us. Before we spend our hard-earned cash or swipe the card, we work to get the best deal—whatever we can squeeze out of Disney and the other industry giants. Perhaps we will conclude, just as Disney hopes, that a three-day pass is a better value dollar for dollar than the price of a single day's admission. And there are the park-hopper specials to consider—tickets that cost more but give us access to more than one park—the side-by-side Magic Kingdom and Disney's California Adventure in Anaheim, for instance.

How about a trip to Orlando, where there are even more options and package deals to factor in? We might visit Universal Studios Orlando and Islands of Adventure and then take in Disney's Typhoon Lagoon, Animal Kingdom, and EPCOT Center, all for a spectacularly calculated deal. We are very serious about our flash passes, what will give us appointed times to jump the line and get into the attractions ahead of everyone else. This, another victory, gives us a rush, and we are upside down—dizzy with exhilaration—before we even get on the ride. We are the winners who revel in the ecstasy of this hedonistic capitalism— what centers us in the society of the spectacle where we work hard to feel good.

We are much less clever when it comes to calculating the cost of compassion—the price of the priceless comfort and care we need when feeling bad (not at all our spectacular selves). Sometimes our bodies succumb, and we are left to struggle with all manner of losing propositions—the disease that ravages, the injury that devastates, the death that awaits. Now, we are confused by what capitalism commodifies, an ethic of care that shapes and reflects an industrial complex built by insurance and pharmaceutical giants.

We need help, not stories about the expense of developing and patenting new drugs, or tales of treatments deemed too experimental to be covered by any plan. We do not want to hear about small private hospitals turned into big profit centers by aggressive, dividend-earning administrators. Nor are we interested in the plutocratic cardiologists and orthopedic surgeons or the primary care providers with their fancy concierge practices. These industrialists do not soothe but remind us again and again that they are the winners, who, for a price, will meet the minimum standard of care, nothing more, nothing less. Such images are neither dazzling nor affirming. What we cannot escape is clear—the commodity they depict and the human relations they supplant.

Walking into a doctor's office, for instance, we recognize the market forces at work. They plant us in the crowded waiting room, where we will spend far too much time flipping through old magazines, playing Candy Crush or Angry Birds, checking email again and again (how we might wish for a flash pass now). But no, best to use this time—what will typically be more than twice the amount spent with any practitioner—to search for the right words, the right way to tell the story of our symptoms within the fifteen minutes the market allots to us. We already know that even this bare-bones version may not be heard, as the provider who enters the exam room at long last will be focused on the computer screen—and very pressed to update the electronic medical record meant to keep costs down.

The precious time must be used to check boxes, to check off the sixty-five quality measures, not to listen to stories. What would be the point anyway? The EMR template makes no provision for the doctor's comments, no summary of what we have tried to share. Efficiency is the only story to be written, one in which we appear not as patients, not even as health care consumers, but as insurance codes only. Tests may be ordered, procedures scheduled, and medications prescribed, but there is no time for healing what ails us all.

We see it everywhere, the bright banner reminding us that *time is money*. That phrase, capitalism's mantra, penetrates us deeply, working itself into our bones and emblazoning the sampler we hang above the hearth—the one whose embroidered letters painstakingly spelled out *Home Sweet Home* in an earlier era. We have long since lost our sense of a more natural time originally ingrained in us—the cyclical time on which a pre-industrial world turned. Now, we cannot imagine time as a gentle pendulum swinging to and fro, patiently inscribing a circle in keeping with the rhythms of the earth—day following night, moons waxing and waning, and seasons turning from planting to harvesting to replanting. We see only an arrow pointing to the future and the hard-charging goals we must achieve, the deadlines we must meet, and projects we must complete.

Time pierces everyone and everything. Keep moving, it says, quick marching ahead. The cycle is broken, and we are made restless and cannot afford to inhabit the moment. No, we will not be one with the environment or ourselves. Rushing from one obligation to another, we have forgotten the spiritual world, Empathy's world, the world of others. Even divinity students are pressed and hurrying off to deliver a sermon on the Good Samaritan and will not stop along the way to help a stranger clearly in need. There is no time to practice what they preach.

The world of the dusty past is also worthless to us—something brittle to be jettisoned altogether. What wisdom the old Bible stories may have had to impart has already withered away, and we have lost our connection to the ancestors, forgotten the ways of the elders. Time is not fluid, not a continuous flow of natural and ceremonial events, or a river to go a fishin' in, as Thoreau described. Rather, it is something linear, something directional and incremental to be objectified and measured more and more precisely. Though we work diligently and systematically to deny it, the fact is that time is still the one commodity we cannot control and never have enough of.

In the face of such failure, time will show us no mercy, marching us forward at a faster and faster pace instead. It is always in control, always accurate, predicting our decisions, our destiny, and setting the ultimate deadline—the precise moment when the very last of its relentless grains slip through our cold, crooked fingers. Time's a wasting, we insist, still focused on efficiency, productivity, and the drive to maximize our pointless profits. Wound up tight, we must lead frenetic, finite lives that minimize our being—and wither a human spirit already out of balance with the cycling and recycling of continuous time.

The arrow points, and time moves us closer to what we fear most. How desperate we are to climb back into the loop, our eternal bubble where there is no end in sight—where we are one with the sticky hedonism of Debord's spectacle but never with what is left of the natural world's nectar. It is capitalism's demand for linear time and our demand for capitalism that foment a perverse psychology, one shoving us deep inside the classic approach-avoidance conflict that rides around and around and gnaws at our soul. We are on edge, neurotic about our life's project of jumping ahead, competing for wealth and status—all the while beating back the fearsome truth that delivers us directly to the fangs of decline and dysfunction at life's end.

Fear is what capitalism emphasizes and its advertising agents exploit. Preying upon our susceptibilities, the ad men use the strategies that trick us into believing we can avoid the inevitable. They are the experts who know the psychology, what gratifies our need to be invincible, and thus, inauthentic. We know their work; the ads that dangle shiny colors and neon promises in front of us and jingle their way into our reptilian brains. But we do not seem to recognize the shell game they play, mixing up our needs and wants. Nor can we see their sleight of hand, the magic they perform creating wants and instantly transforming these wants into our newest needs. Now, we must have—*need*—the magical products that will make us look and feel better. We *need* to appear younger, thinner, hipper, happier, healthier, stronger, sexier, more attractive, and more alive than we are.

We see the inverted images—the slickest ones planting their seeds of doubt and confirming that we do not measure up. Clearly, we do not look like the fashion models, the commercial actors and celebrities who pop up on our screens persuading us that we should not put up with our pedestrian selves one second longer. Our breath is much too bad and our teeth too yellow, they chide; our skin is too blemished or wrinkled, our hair too limp, too dull, too gray. Nor do we live well enough. We have too much heartburn, too much joint pain, and not enough sexual satisfaction. Our kitchens, bathrooms, and clothes are not clean enough. But with the right brand-name products, the expensive supplements and drugs—and then, the next new-and-improved versions—we can overcome it all—our inadequacies and disappointments, our angst and mortality. We *need* to believe that fifty is the new thirty, sixty the new forty if we are to have more time to push away our fate.

The doubts persist, and we are afraid we will never be good enough—never strong enough to fight for a place in our Debordian delusion. We will be destined to wander in the fresh fields of crabgrass searching for a painted plastic self sleek enough to get us into the splendor.

As the heartburn returns, we wonder and worry: What if we are the Ragpicker? Or worse, imposters unfit for society's artificial lifestyle? Misfits too weak to compete—to win—in capitalism's spectacular world?

What are we to do but rush out to buy more. We *need* the mall, real or virtual, to romp on the Astroturf of this, our most therapeutic playground where we are all winners. What we take from the boutiques and big-box stores and order online are the trophies that boost the self-image we show off on Facebook. Such are the conquests suppressing our fear and the story of the forlorn soul. We congratulate ourselves, knowing we are good consumers who are doing what is good for the economy. Indeed, shopping is more than a temporary stress reliever—a quick fix for what ails us. It reflects our patriotism or so we were told after the towers fell. So, we pledge allegiance to the gargantuan system wrapping up our world—its gift to us.

But we have not stopped the spectacular terrorism. The crabgrass, tangled and rugged as ever, still thrives. The underground borers still dance among our rhizomic roots. Content in the sun, the worldwide snake still lurks in the grass. What is it then that we might dream of?

Chapter VI

The Way Between

D o we dare to dream? Should we trouble ourselves with the project of wonder? Adhere to the philosophy that would have us imagining ourselves as if we could be otherwise? Why would we undertake such things—*how could we*—when human nature remains immutable, geopolitical situations intractable, and our own elusive Empathy seems unable or unwilling to blunt any of it? Hope for Homo empathicus to finally emerge from the swamp is too cruel. We would be better advised to remember Empathy as it was before our questions began to fly, better off picturing Empathy when it was still rumored to be warm, caring, devoted—the Good Samaritan glimpsed now and again as a nomadic figure clad simply in a faded purple robe and worn-out sandals that appears reliably in our time of need and wraps us in a tear-stained quilt stitched by its own hand.

But it is too late for the metaphors of old. The questions, still unanswered, have been loosed with the fury of a dialectical swarm that stings the sky and sends idyllic notions of Empathy as one of our better angels clattering to the ground. Empathy, we now know, has not lighted upon our shoulder, never claimed to

191

be a savior or promised a moment of grace. It has always posed as the lonely fugitive destined to wander throughout our conflicted nature and get lost in our stifling situations—only to exasperate us with its fierce expectations and embittered demands that we improve upon our condition. Oh, Empathy, "why didst thou create these harmful beasts, which but exasperate our thorny life?" (OED attribution, 1591 Sylvester Du Bartas)

The story is long and unbroken, writ large upon the multitudes; writ small here in an absurd piece of nonfiction set in ancient thickets that tell of Compassion's pitiful tears, Entanglement's frustrated oar, Connection's bridge to nowhere. How long has Empathy stood by, waiting for us to find our way through the brambles? How long can Empathy be expected to stand in the breach, watching us lurch left and right and stumble between comforting places and airy spaces? How long must Empathy hold its breath, aghast that we would still mistake shoots for roots and sky for earth?

How long before we navigate the nodal connections between kindness and cruelty, myth and reality, self and other? When will we understand our drives, control our impulses, and take care to balance the needs of our inner and outer worlds? When will we leap from the rollercoaster to put on our work shoes and begin the long march forward? What if we resolved to meet Empathy along the way, and no matter how treacherous, agreed to take the middle road between all things natural and cultural, linear and cyclical, spiritual and material, moral and commercial?

When will we know what Empathy knows, what would have been imparted by now had we ever listened? Or is it that we have heard, but feign ignorance, of its inconvenient canons? Or perhaps we resist altogether and have never read the tomes and treatises distilling the essence of who and what Empathy says we are. Too headstrong to rethink the position, we refuse to resolve the difficulties of our capricious, perhaps duplicitous, nature. Too heartsick to cope with the consequences, we surrender to the difficulties of our untenable and muddy situations. Where is our resilience? Our diligence? Our remorse? How are we to comfort ourselves? Find the escape—transcendence—we need? Hone the skills required to balance it all?

Explain it again, Empathy, the nature of our harmful beast. Why, for instance, the insightful Heidegger would stare into the "dark opening" of the peasant woman's work shoes and praise the "ripening grain"—and stare into the bright face of a dedicated SS officer and praise the Third Reich? Tell us how Robespierre could go from his guillotine's unwavering blade in the public square to his private quarters, where the dog's wagging tail offered the comfort he needed. Or how Emerson could transcend his reality and preach sermon after sermon from his New England pulpit, knowing that he liked Mankind, but not men—especially not the ones coughing or drowsing in the pews. Oh, the needs that must be met, the balance that must be struck.

Empathy, are you there? We must know now. Remind us again. What skills were honed when one homeowner offered to charge the cell phones of superstorm Sandy survivors for free and another required five dollars to provide the same service? What and whose needs were met when family members sick with grief gathered around the Charleston church and reached out to the blasphemous shooter with their healing forgiveness? What explains it, the angry man on the N train made angrier by his shaming tactics who came to see the light, who recentered himself and found some inner peace? Or the feminist comedy writer and vicious troll who spent considerable time on the phone together, listening to each other's stories and drying each other's tears? What about the fleeing Vietnamese girl captured by the AP photographer—why did Phan Thi Kim Phúc and Nick Ut find each other again, and stay closely, lovingly connected over the forty years since napalm burned out of control?

What's that you say? "Ya can't always get what you want?" Listen to Mick Jagger, you say? He got it right . . . *But if you try sometime, you just might find you get what you need.* We must try sometime, we must try real hard, is that it? This has always been true—look to the Paleolithic people of seventeen thousand years ago, you say? Study the hardworking cave dwellers who knew even then that they needed more than food, clothing, shelter, and sex to survive? They got it, you say, the comfort and transcendence vital to any tribe, because of their grit and their efforts to stay alert and attuned to each other and tell stories that stretched their imaginations and extended their vision. They had heart, you point out, and the skills and finesse to balance them all. This is what centered them and kept them going?

We could be—should be—more like them, you're claiming now? If we were to try real hard, we could become accomplished hunter-gatherers who take the middle path and know precisely where to forage for what stabilizes a needy population and promotes at least a modicum of well-being? Like elders and trusted shamans, we would know exactly how to transcend the disappointments of daily life and imagine something different, possibly better—the "something more" we crave. What's that? Speak up. We would also know how to comfort each other and find some solace in an otherwise terrifying world. Most important to our budding humanity, you're insisting now, we would know how to find a balance between tipping points, identify the common axis around which our lives spin, and stay centered between myth and reality, self and other, earth and sky.

Like the Stone Age ancestors, we would search for the perfect cave. It must be like the one at Lascaux and serve both as a comforting place and a boundless space, a sacred shrine and a movie palace—the still point from which the wonders of movement across the vastness of space and time can be pondered. Lascaux is the prototype for what we need—have always needed— its hybrid chambers intended to make any visitor ancient or modern feel whole and more alive. We must try real hard to reclaim our heritage.

The Lascaux artists who were the temple priests and movie magicians did everything they could to launch Humankind and even now bequeath to us the legendary galleries that still present much more than a pictorial record of the horses and big cats, bison and bulls once found in the Dordogne region of France. We are still bewitched by the magic of images that seem to ripple with the energy of pounding hooves and stealthy paws, still awed and humbled by what they represent—the speed, power, and strength that are not humanly possible, yet make us more human. Oh yes, Lascaux is for us, and we must have the flickering light of its juniper wicks in reindeer fat to recreate the special effects that blend reverence and magic with the dreams of eternity.

Oh, Empathy, how you mumble so. Did you say something about the Middle Ages? About a twelfth-century leprosarium? The walled compound of Saint-Lazare located . . . where? On the outskirts of Beauvais in the Picardy region of France not far from Paris, is that right? Come again? You're telling us to go stand at the gate? We must get a feel for it—and picture the leper who waits to be taken in? He is yet another one like the many others already inside whose cure of bathing in animal blood has failed, you say, and now there is no other place for him, for any of them to live—or die. Saint-Lazare promises no cure, you say, but offers a moment of relief, a whiff of dignity. Neither a still point nor an endpoint, you say this *maladrerie* must be thought of as a journey encircling both—the busy path the new arrival will follow with the old hands, all laboring together to claim a synchrony of their own. How frail is the flesh of one, you ask? How strong the spirit of many?

This is too hard for us, Empathy; too ghastly. Try harder? Is that all you have to say? No? There's more? We must also imagine the nuns about to take in the pariah, another soul ravaged by shame, the body already declared dead, already wrapped in a shroud, and given last rites by a village priest. Imagine now the family members and neighbors who must heave spadesful of dirt upon the leper's back to carry out a symbolic burial before sending the breathing corpse inside the walls, never to be seen or heard from again. If the nuns are to raise this Lazarus from the dead, he must shoulder his burden, enter now, and join the community of the afflicted to even out the load.

But why, Empathy? Why speak of a leprosarium long ago abandoned? It must be reinhabited, you say? Look at ourselves, you say? Who among us is not afflicted? Go, you say; the gate stands open today—open to anyone's curse, everyone's cure. Get beyond the old stone walls, walk the grounds. Take it all in—what you say we have forgotten, but still wails in the nuns' dormitories and Gothic chapel, still sighs in the massive barn and animal pen, still sings in the pastureland and vegetable gardens. Find the path, you say.

We must try real hard to catch the echoes of Dignity's conversations, you say, and resonate with the songs of grunting and sweating, sowing and reaping, living and dying—the strains you say that lifted a self-contained community entirely absent from the larger whole, yet completely present unto itself. Listen, and be present, you say? If we try hard enough, you say we will follow along with the walking dead who trod the path that still spirals around cruelty and kindness, casting out and gathering in.

If we do not blink, we might even imagine the piece *Red Bowl* installed in the courtyard pond by the landscape artists Xavier Perrot and Andy Cao that gathered visitors in, at least for a few months in 2012. Perhaps we can still see the concave configuration, its slender steel rods topped by beads of blood red glass rising from the water in a pattern of concentric circles, the shorter rods forming the inner rings, the taller the outer. There it is, the whole creating a vessel to hold the story of Saint-Lazare and bring it back to life.

But hang on, you say now? Oh, Empathy, give us a minute . . . No time, you say? There is yet another story about the one and the many to be told. We must balance the two with care, you warn, if in the throes of a thousand-year affliction, we expect to survive this most bitterly contested world made more unstable now by a dearth of natural resources, more cacophonous by an abundance of cultural differences. Listen closely, you advise.

We are members of the "precariat," you remind us; the needy and duplicitous who must live up to what the complexity and contradiction of a global environment demand of us. So it is, you say, that we must step in now and tiptoe between the tipping points of Nature and Culture to save ourselves and our terrestrial home. Our imperative, you stress, is to balance the one-and-the-many stories written into the shakiness, the first insisting that the one join the many, and the second crying for the many to speak as one.

It is true, we cannot hide away in the unrestored dormitories of Saint-Lazare, or sleep in the grand barn, no matter how high it soars above the ruin about to shame a jittery planet. Nor can we hole up in a magical cave, not even in a replica of the replica at Lascaux. Perhaps we should do as Empathy bids, as the artist Charles Sandison invites, and walk with the many who become one in a river of light like the one projected on the floor of the long entrance ramp of Paris's Quai Branly Museum in 2011. Sandison's piece *The River* can still show us the way of flow— what we see in the tributaries and torrents and eddies that feed the mainstream and hydrate a world in drought. In the flow, the names of sixteen thousand cultures appear to swirl and dance and rush downstream, oxygenating the river that runs through us. We must remember the droplets of water, each on its way to an ocean rising quickly with the truths of tomorrow, still foaming with the desperation of today.

Look now, you say? Where? Over there is the environmental artist Andy Goldsworthy, who works with rivers and tides to find a way into time. He is not interested in old metaphors *per se*, you argue, but in a new storytelling about time as experienced in a space between the fluid motion of the river and the up-and-down actions of the sea. Watch, you command, as he works all day in the sweet spot found at the confluence of the river and the ocean, the sculptor staying in the flow at the river's end, an existentialist stacking stone upon stone to build—balance—his "cone" sculpture on the seaside beach.

The hours tick by, and he is working against the clock, you observe. The tide turns, and he is weary. Yet, there is a timeless harmony, a timely authenticity inhabiting this work. Notice his satisfaction, his serenity and balance as he finishes just in time for the waves to come up and carry his energy back to the sea.

Where will we find our sweet spot, you ask? When will we, the office workers and burger flippers, the appointment-makers and calendar-keepers, rebalance ourselves and find a way between the relentless demands of linear and cyclical time? Will we try harder to write the story of harmony or dignity? Try hard enough to walk steadily, forthrightly between the needs of nature and culture? Will we ever follow an upward spiral leading one to become many to become one? How willing are we to change our nature? Change our situation?

How shall we respond? What is there to say, but that we are what we are: visceral, cerebral; competitive, cooperative; caged, free; connected, alone. Prisoners all—the apples thrown into psychologist Phil Zimbardo's "rotten barrel." Sometimes we will scream, "Hell no," other times mutter a more qualified, "Yes, if . . ." And in the best of conditions, "Yes, and . . ." may ring out like peals of laughter in a community of the healed.

Oh, how we have searched for the way between. We have already had our time on the Appian Way and the Great White Way; already followed the Silk Road to the Yellow Brick Road and still walk our own trail of tears. But Empathy's path is not well marked, and we have yet to find what can only turn out to be the rugged road less traveled, the one more demanding that will require . . . what? Special gear? Detailed maps? Extra provisions? Paleolithic perseverance? If it is to be attempted at all. Surely, Empathy is sensitive to our plight, aware of our struggle to find what, for us, will be a new way, ostensibly a better, more stable one, if not more altruistic, or morally true, wherever it may lead.

Surely, Empathy knows what we know—understands that we are the exasperated ones who have tried to make life less thorny; tried our best to tame the harmful beast. We still hope to tell a compelling and credible story about accomplishing both one day soon. Until then, these are the truths we claim for ourselves, even if Empathy finds the arguments unpersuasive and our efforts wanting.

In fact, we have taken steps and tried to follow the way of the scientists whose direction is clear, method systematic, and focus intense. They have the beast in their sights and believe they are closing in, about to pin it down. How we look forward to the latest research, to the moment when their brain scans will identify the neural correlate of consciousness, and we will know at last or at least *where* this beast comes into being, if not *how* or *why*. Meanwhile, we eagerly await news of the super mirror neurons that will clarify their status and declare them to be the *bona fide* overseers of our hand actions—arbiters of the gestures we would otherwise make without any conscious awareness at all. Such progress to be made in the world of objects, such insight to be gained into the world of others—such conclusions to be drawn about the wiring of our beast.

Surely, imaging technologies will point the way, and scientists will count on their precision to pin down Empathy's being as well. Elusive and fleeting as ever, perhaps Empathy has met its match and such technologies will capture its bolts of synaptic lightning, its waves of violet-ultraviolet energy otherwise unseen by the human eye, unknown to the human heart. Or better still, scientists will fine-tune their methods and come up with a measurement of the distance between the self and other in the temporoparietal junction.

To be sure, we are impatient, anxious even, but will wait a little longer for further evidence of Empathy's sensory pathways, especially those carrying messages that tell of pain—the kind experienced when we ache with our own and when we imagine the ache of others. There are whole stories yet to be told about the pain we share—what the insula, anterior cingulate cortex, and thalamus must be made to give up to the saner sooner, rather than later. Only then will we find neurology's way between the nature of Empathy and the beast of ours.

We have also tried to follow the way of the artists and trusted their images to probe the harmful beast much more deeply, if a little less precisely, perchance to reveal its soul that may yet redeem this thorny life. Painters and sculptors across the globe have mounted a massive exhibition that, in a "single perceptual act," can be taken in as one powerful and poignant portrait—our beast captured not so much in paint or clay, but in irises, many purple, one white, all reaching out of the frame, and in apples carefully studied and imparting what they know to the master, apprentice, and seekers beyond. We see its anguish in the saintly eyes that implore, in mallow fibers that "run deep," and in two angelic figures that float in the light, a third "vanquished," falling into the darkness below. We have seen such things, the mirrors shattered, the bumpers bright, the Buddha broken, the tree blown by the winds of chaos—and they all make sense, the parts and the whole that illustrate the difficulties of our nature and our situation.

Such are the images giving us "visual codes," the keys to unlocking an image-world that shape and reflect conditions in the lived world. Images deliver themselves as metaphors and discover truths about who we are, how we feel, and what we believe is still possible, even as their treachery reveals all that is not or never was. Susan Sontag, your images still bewitch, still (mis)represent, still drive us to covet, and collect them as the "things" we ingest whole. We must have them, use them as the "substitutes" for "direct experiences" of a world still hungering for its soul.

It is incumbent upon us to search for our own, and to find the middle way in spite of or because of our ever-expanding collection that would have us lurch between the latest footage of shootings and beheadings and favorite videos of kittens and puppies. We can do better, steer straight, and trust the iconic photo of the little Syrian boy lying dead on a Turkish beach to show us how to walk the line with Empathy.

The philosophers have also permitted us to accompany them on their path, and we have tried to keep pace with them. But the path soon split, and we found ourselves stranded somewhere between the way of Descartes and the way of Deleuze without a new proposition or mantra to rescue us from this limbo. We cannot proceed with Empathy's plan by chanting, "I think, therefore I am," and celebrating the triumph of the enlightened individual. Nor can we always sing of life in the communal chaos championed by the hubristic claims, "We are, therefore we dance," and "We resonate, therefore we are." Perhaps we will look beyond the philosophers and discover the wisdom and way of a South African proverb. "I am because we are," it would have us hum, hiking along the middle path.

The way of the word has also beckoned us, and guided by the Oxford English Dictionary, we have tried to follow the etymological lines no matter how twisted, hoping to discover the one rooted most deeply in Empathy's being—the one not yet taken hold in ours. In the snarl, we have traced the Greek roots that inform the *pathos* of "empathy" even as they failed to distinguish it from the *pathos* of "sympathy"—and refuse to clarify the mission of either. We have sorted through roots buried in Latin and Old French, in English Old and Middle that hint of the common bonds between "connection" and "compassion," "concern" and "understanding." Yet the intertwined roots say little about a shared meaning and nothing about expediting our mission to find the way between them all—the path that will finally lead us to whatever lies at Empathy's mysterious core.

It would appear that we need a different dictionary and new words uncomplicated by knotted roots leading nowhere. We might try "sonder," for instance, defined by the *Dictionary of Obscure Sorrows* to mean the "realization that every random passerby has a life as vivid and complex as [our] own." Everyone has a tale to tell, it seems to say, and we are all connected by these stories—all part of an "epic story," according to sonder. Rooted in rhizomic storytelling, this newly invented word seems to overlap with "empathy," once newly invented itself. Is there room for both? Will the pair rise or fall together, still trying to convince us, still justifying their or our existence?

Perhaps we should consider an old, established word instead, one more venerable and true to its roots. We shall rescue "werifesteria" from its obscure sorrow and appreciate its derivation from the Old English for "wander" and "forest." We will take its definition, "to wander longingly through the forest in search of a mystery" to heart. Is this it? Is this the wandering way between the search for Empathy and the discovery of ourselves?

We are ready to take stock of the situation now and eager to recognize and commend the ones among us who no longer wander—the activists already on the path, busy designing projects and launching programs intended to improve conditions and make lives more whole. Such are the projects bringing authenticity into test-ridden classrooms, the programs drying the tears of forgotten communities. What if we were to scale them up, extend their reach? Perhaps Empathy would exhale at last and escort crowd upon crowd—whole populations of us—into the clearing, where we might hear the first whispers of cooperation and self-sacrifice in a world shouting of competition and self-preservation.

We shall begin a list of what works, make note of where it is still possible to rebalance priorities, rebuild imaginations, reestablish connections. Our task, it turns out, will be complicated by an abundance of candidates, so many gems unnoticed, projects underfunded, programs shouted down—so many worth a look. How about including the "Portrait Project" on the list—the one undertaken by an American art teacher who took photos of village children during a summer trip to Central America? These were the faces to be carefully studied by his high school students in the fall and winter, every detail to be captured in paint, every smile to be preserved on canvas, and untold connections to be built in the portraits they would complete by spring—paintings their teacher would present to the village families, along with photos of the student artists during his return trip in the summer.

How about considering the after-school program Life Pieces to Masterpieces? Yes, it must be listed, this jewel tucked away in Washington, DC's Ward Seven that glimmers with the energy and creativity of young African-American men and boys learning to work collaboratively and brainstorm ideas for the pieces of art and poetry they produce as individual "apprentices" and share as a community fully fledged. These are the pieces that burn with the tough truths about lives in pieces and speak powerfully of dreams about to expire in a neighborhood struggling to breathe. Yet, there are masterpieces to emerge, young men graduating from high school, going on to college and trade schools, but not to jail (NPR, *All Things Considered*, April,18, 2013).

We notice too the list-worthy approaches meant to ease our pain when illness stalks us down or injury leaves us flat. New, more humanistic medical education programs, for instance, that will prepare the next generation of doctors—some with bachelor's degrees in philosophy, history, or literature—to pay close attention to their patients' life stories, even as the latest chapters on healing and recovery are unfolding. Along with diagnostic skills, med students studying narrative medicine will also develop listening skills. These they will depend on, the skills fine-tuned for getting the details of the patient's backstory and establishing a context in which to understand the storyteller's pain.

And when a devastating diagnosis leaves us without words— patient, friends, and family alike—empathy cards are available now to bridge the gaps, a set of six to choose from and more to come, all with just the right thing to say. Surely the message, "I promise not to refer to your illness as a journey unless someone gives you a cruise," will reassure the sender and recipient both. Or perhaps they would prefer a sharp battle cry, "This really sucks . . ." or "Fuck cancer" to fire them up and unite the two as soldiers ready for combat on the frontlines. Perhaps the disarming honesty of "I'm sorry I haven't been in touch. I didn't know what to say" can fill the awkward space opened by shock and the pain of it all, and the well-wisher's "personal distress" will be managed, along with the patient's symptoms.

More and more examples can be added to the list, new projects and directions in media and technology, for instance, that question the *status quo* and aim to change the calculus. Social activism inspires the mission, and we are particularly interested in the *Huffington Post's* decision to publish news of "what works"—to give coverage to solutions, not just to problems. Though it is too soon to know the impact of the online news aggregator's policy shift, we can say that the *Huff Post* is bold enough to break with the old journalistic tradition, "If it bleeds, it leads," and to experiment with a different and more optimistic slant—what could establish a new frame of reference for interpreting the world and its successes or failures.

Meanwhile, there are "Empathy Maps" to help IT workers help us. The geeks at the help desk, on the sales floor, or in the repair shop now have a tool especially designed to help them develop some insight and a better understanding of us, the users—these trusty maps billed as "complete guides for crawling into the customer's head." What's more, IT experts can volunteer to work on projects through "Code for America." They might develop apps, say, for cash-strapped city governments that need help tracking and maintaining infrastructure. In Boston, for example, volunteers were able to identify the location of every fire hydrant in the city, along with the citizens who would adopt one in their neighborhood and keep it clear of snow. It was tsunami sirens in Honolulu that Code for America programmers mapped and matched with residents who promised to check on their adopted siren and to see that it stays in good working order.

Video games too must be noted; that is, the ones immersing us in situations both edgy and nuanced that require us to pay attention to others and make consequential decisions about their needs in light of our own. To play these games is to face and resolve one moral dilemma after another. Games such as *If*, for instance, present kids with several options to choose from when deciding what is fair and how best to restore balance to life in Greenberry, a land of mythical forests and mushrooms and animals where unforeseen situations arise. A seven- or eight-year-old might click "I will help," "I'm not sure if I will help," "I'll help if I get paid," or "It's not my problem," yet some choose the "good" option, "I will help," over the other "bad" ones, no matter what the consequences.

Adult games, on the other hand, put players in disturbing life-and-death situations that force them to consider a rat's nest of issues and concerns when weighing their options—and trying to balance the risks to themselves with the risks to others. In *This War of Mine*, players are caught up in the Bosnian War, struggling to survive the siege of Sarajevo. Again and again, they must decide if they will rob a pharmacy or steal from a priest; grab groceries for themselves or share them with hungry neighbors, kill an armed soldier threatening a stranger when a shovel is the only weapon available. How willing are they to sacrifice their own life to save another's? The options are few, none "good," some "less bad."

When it comes to the world's theme parks, one franchise in particular calls our attention. KidZania, with parks in cities such as Seoul, Tokyo, Dubai, Santiago, and Mexico City, offers us—our children and grandchildren—a different kind of "mythic reality," one that dignifies dreams of work and validates visions of making a living in a "good" and well-ordered place. Kids ages four to twelve venture into scale-model cities too small for adults and spend the day working as bankers and taxi drivers, doctors and shopkeepers, firefighters and entertainers, judges and police—all the while earning "KidZos," the currency they deposit in their savings accounts and withdraw from the ATM machines. How purposeful they feel, these junior capitalists, and how delighted as they dance in the shoes of their elders.

And what is the story of full-scale global capitalism, in particular the newer models that piqued our interest earlier on? We had such hopes for hybrid approaches to strike a balance between competition's ruthless self-preservation and cooperation's self-sacrificing synchrony. Once, we had even dared to believe that the innovative "sharing economy" of "peer-to-peer sharing" would showcase a more "people-based," less profit-driven approach. But the two best known examples, Uber and Airbnb, are gargantuan industries now, the former valued at fifty billion dollars, the latter at ten billion. Both have provided greatly appreciated services to millions of satisfied customers, to be sure—but not without consequence.

Uber has upset its drivers, who argue through their attorneys that they are not contractors, as the company insists, but employees—and as such, are entitled to more benefits and compensation. Now, workers' rights and labor laws hang in the balance. Airbnb stands accused of destabilizing neighborhoods in cities such as Los Angeles, where greedy landlords are looking to cash in on Airbnb's popularity by converting whole apartment buildings to no-lease, short-term rentals—cheap hotel rooms—thus, significantly reducing the available housing already in short supply, and at the same time, depriving city coffers of badly needed tax revenues collected from traditional hotels that stand half-empty.

Capitalism's political-economic system is still worrisome. Empathy has convinced us of this much and persuaded us that there must be other forms of wealth to be accumulated and other ways to be productive. Perhaps we should look to the Bhutanese government and learn how it came to establish an index for tracking the country's "gross national happiness." We should ask the Estonians about the "Bank of Happiness" set up to take people's offers and deposits of goods and services meant for others to withdraw and use as needed. Is this just their way? What is ours?

Were we to dare—summon up the courage—what is it that we would dream of? The question seems more compelling now that we have a list, crisp and new, if incomplete. Its glimmers, though faint, will give us strength and make us believe that at least some change is possible and some conditions could improve. Perhaps we will even be brave enough to retrieve an old, abandoned wish list made difficult to decipher by its tatters and tear stains. Yet it is easy to see that the new and the old read the same, two versions of one simple truth: We can be better, it holds, and should do more to make the beast less harmful and life less thorny. We can, we should, because we must.

Together, the lists will surely rekindle our interest in the project of wonder. "What if . . .?" will dangle before us anew, no longer the jeer that mocked our sorrow, but a promise to rebuild a collective imagination and deepen a worldwide resolve. Yes, we will pledge to reenvision the mystery of Empathy—and yes, we should revisit what was captured once by the proclamation mounted on a rustic bench at Moonstone Beach. Perhaps the inexplicable impulse is still there, the bond still resonant—the dream still alive—and we will discover why we too have always loved a purple iris.

So, it is that we return to the Central Coast, this time to balance ourselves on the edge of a craggy continent where Empathy drinks in the salt air, even as it hurls itself upon our rocky shores—and we are driven to find a way between the possible and the impossible. The skies may be bright, they may be overcast, the beach socked in by a morning marine layer—the soupy "June gloom" of coastal California that occurs nearly year-round these days. We will be prepared for either now, adjust our expectations, and trust that our fogginess burns off to make way for an afternoon sun.

We may see the harbor seals sunning on the rocks near the observation point or catch the humpback whales spouting in the swells at the distant horizon, but we may not. Perhaps we will hear an otter pounding an abalone shell against the rock cradled on its abdomen or listen to the westerly winds for the cries of the gulls and calls of the crows. Perhaps not. There may be wet-suited surfers or energetic kayakers to catch our eye, clouds of silent sailboats to stir the imagination as they drift north in the morning, south in the evening. Maybe, maybe not.

Like ribbons of sparkling sapphire or creases of pewter gray, the waves will rise and with a rhythm of their own, break on the beach, sometimes dropping driftwood with their regular deposits of broken shells and lanky kelp, sometimes not. But they will always be capped by frothy foam, lacey white and bright in any circumstance. We can count on this, just as we will count on the wooden walkway to protect the delicate ecosystem above the high waterline—even as its creaky planks carry us into the heart of it.

Here we are, you and I, strolling with the vacationers and dog walkers, admiring the wildflowers and their bursts of buttery yellow and deep purple, their dots of white and lavender sprinkled throughout. Here we are, all of us, promenading with the squirrels that stop only to pose for a picture or beg for a bite before darting under the boards just as we pass. We are delighted to spot rabbits in the bush and lizards on the railings; delighted to greet the human visitors who, like us, belong to this place, at least for a little while. Have we found our sweet spot, our still point, the way between?

The bench is in sight now, and our pace quickens as we approach the old touchstone looking even more worn and weather-beaten than before. Vegetation has grown up in front of it, and we wonder if anyone would step off the walkway to sit among the splinters and gaze upon a sunset from the fading glory of this vantage point. Then again, the bench belongs more to a timeless mystery than to the dying sun—its small plaque still fastened securely to the lower left corner of the backrest. Yes, the unknown iris is still beloved, still sharing its quiet love story with the dozens of little hearts carved into the wood around it.

But there is something loud that we can no longer ignore— there, confronting us, the long, horizontal sign centered across the top of the backrest that will not be denied. This new placard is bold and appears to label the bench as property belonging to its owners, "Neil and Denise," who declare that they "heart" each other. What they dream of or imagine for themselves we cannot say, nor are we meant to, but how they tell their story is clear. No one should dare take a seat on the once humble bench that is now their proud domain. Where is the wonder in this, our spot made bittersweet?

Still, theirs is a wondrous story, another grain of sand or bit of shell like the countless others carried on the restless tides— another tale to be retold at the edge and carried by the restless wanderers crisscrossing on the path above. Our morning has gone, the skies are clearing, and we see beyond the bench now, a scene wide enough to take in Sonder's epic tale and its promise to explain Empathy's purple mystery. We are beachcombers, the story goes, who gather all we can while walking across the sands of time—desperate to leave our mark. But we are also random passersby who would do well to remember that each of our lives is already vivid and complex.

We must be resolute now, continue on the path to the observation point—continue on to points beyond. We will agree to explore this middle way and keep an eye out for other placards, new signs of the impossible journey we share. Yet, we will always be the werifesterians who wander longingly through forests and deserts and marine environments, through drought and monsoon, cosmopolitan cities and historic villages in search of Empathy's mystery. Perhaps we will arrive in Arles, a mid-sized city in France, once the capital of Provence, and notice the sign written on a small chalkboard in a local cafe. Who has placed the pots of young lavender on either side and scrawled the message to carry us through the soupy gloom? *"J'aime celui qui rêve l'impossible,"* it reads. I love the one who dreams the impossible.

O, Empathy, why hast thou tested us so? Why didst thou don the cloak of mystery which but lured us in, even as it wouldst keep us out?

It was you, Empathy, you who hid yourself in the bamboo forest, you who eluded the scientists' scanners and twitched in the artists' brushes. You were the one to refuse our wizards' strongest potions, deny our detectives' best theories, and the one to goad us into taking the road less traveled without permission of any kind. It was always you, the ethereal witness who saw our halting gait and ignored our pinched toes and blistered heels, you, Empathy, who watched us falter every step of the way.

Why, Empathy? Why did you heap so much upon our narrow shoulders? Why would you trust us to carry on in spite of the scars?

Yes, it was you who kept the faith—the one who pulled us from the looping rollercoaster and rattled our sanctuary windows with your disgruntled winds; you, the one who ordered us below deck when we were sick on the stormy seas and hijacked our flight when we sought refuge in the cloudy skies. Why, Empathy? Why would you fling the images of treachery at us and frighten us with the ghosts of history? Why make us put on shoes too tight and walk with Certainty and Uncertainty on the long march, then strip us naked and turn your face away from the shock of Cynicism and Irony's dehumanizing pens?

The story is long and unbroken, indeed, but we have come through it just as you have always believed. We have seen a bit of Authenticity and Dignity along the way—even glimpsed the lavender of your worn-out robe about to betray the secrets of that heavy cloak. Survival is ours now, maybe little more, but surely nothing less. We are willing to try on your sandals and follow your spiraling path. Stumble we will, yet we will also get up, one by one, multitude by multitude, and perhaps we will dare to dream. *"J'aime celui qui rêve l'impossible."* This, we know now, is the pledge we are meant to share.

Acknowledgments

My deepest appreciation goes to those who suffered through early drafts with such patience and grace: Marji Campbell, Sheri Klein, Linda Huetinck, Leslie Gaudineer, Nancy Richardson, Maureen Harrington, Mary McCorkle, Ann Storc, Barbara Boyer, Penny Semrau. This includes Jeff and Anne Jeffers, my father- and mother-in-law, and my sister-in-law Ingrid Saile, who did not live to see the book published.

Heartfelt thanks to my editor, Courtney Davison, who whipped the final draft into shape.

I wish to acknowledge my students, the generous young people who appear in these pages, gave the gift of their metaphors and led the way into empathy. Their names have been changed, but their experiences remain true, their feelings deep.

CPSIA information can be obtained
at www.ICGtesting.com
Printed in the USA
FSHW01n1644280818
51626FS